Pathways to Utopia

Pathways to Utopia

TIME AND TRANSFORMATION
IN THE LANDLESS WORKERS
MOVEMENT OF BRAZIL

ALEX UNGPRATEEB FLYNN

Indiana University Press

This book is a publication of

Indiana University Press
Office of Scholarly Publishing
Herman B Wells Library 350
1320 East 10th Street
Bloomington, Indiana 47405 USA

iupress.org

First Printing 2025

Cataloging information is available from the Library of Congress.
ISBN 978-0-253-07374-7 (hard cover)
ISBN 978-0-253-07375-4 (paperback)
ISBN 978-0-253-07376-1 (web PDF)
ISBN 978-0-253-07377-8 (ebook)

CONTENTS

ACKNOWLEDGMENTS

I would like to thank the many people who helped and supported me in Brazil. This book would not have come into being if it were not for the many members of the Landless Workers Movement (MST) who welcomed me into their families, spent time with me, and cared for me. Their spirits and voices are deeply present in this book, and for the profound kindness they showed me, I will always be truly grateful. In particular, I would like to express my gratitude to Vera, Clarice, Tais, Lúcia and Thiago, and Gaetano and his family. They invited me to share a different way of life, and I miss them very much.

Throughout this project, I was able to exchange thoughts and ideas with many wonderful scholars and practitioners. Maria Amelia Schmidt Dickie, Bernadete Aued, Elisa Schemes, and Lyvia Rodrigues welcomed me to the academic community of the Federal University of Santa Catarina (UFSC). Dan Baron, Ruy Blanes, John Burdick, Elena Calvo Gonzalez, Melinda Gurr, Jeff Juris, Marianne Maeckelbergh, George Meszaros, Maple Razsa, Vânia Cardoso, and Scott Head all helped me think through questions regarding protest, activism, and aesthetics. These conversations were often joyful and fun and invariably the highlight of whichever event at which we had crossed paths.

Many times, these conversations provoked new material and fresh ideas, and I'm indebted to friends and colleagues who read material associated with this book. Catherine Alexander, Leonardo Araujo, Khadija von Zinnenburg Carroll, Christine Chaves, Eduardo Dullo, Yulia Egorova, Thomas Fillitz, Nayanika Mookherjee, Steve Nugent, Jean-Bernard Ouédraogo, Jonas Tinius, and especially Diána Vonnák offered generous critiques of my writing, putting forward helpful suggestions and pointing to potential departures. The anonymous peer reviewers of the manuscript were equally committed and offered careful and engaged close readings. I'd like to say a particular thank-you to Marcelo Mendes. I learned how to speak Portuguese with Marcelo, and many years later, he translated sections of this book into Portuguese.

A special thanks is due to John Gledhill and Lúcia Sá. As mentors, they were supportive, generous, and insightful, and it was a pleasure to learn from them. I also gratefully acknowledge the assistance of the Economic and Social Research Council (ESRC). Without this financial support, it would not have been possible to undertake this project.

Above all, my gratitude goes to my wife, Noara Quintana, whose critical thinking, love, and constant support are at the heart of this book.

Portions of the introduction, scene 1, and scene 2 are revised excerpts of the article "Once upon a Time as Utopia: Bergson, Temporality and the Remaking of Social Movement Futures," published previously in *Social Anthropology*, volume 29, number 1, 156–73. Revised excerpts of "Mística, Myself and I: Beyond Cultural Politics in Brazil's Landless Workers' Movement," published previously in *Critique of Anthropology*, volume 33, number 2, 168–92, appear in the introduction and scene 3, and revised excerpts of "Transformation and 'Human Values' in the Landless Workers' Movement of Brazil," published previously in *Ethnos*, volume 80, number 1, 45–70, appear in scene 2. In some cases, the pseudonyms of MST members differ from previously published work.

August 2023, São Paulo

DRAMATIS PERSONAE

The coastal settlement near Água Branca

Kleber—regional leader of the production sector and de facto leader of the settlement

Marcia—Kleber's wife

Tais—Kleber and Marcia's daughter

Maíra—regional leader of the health sector with an interest in medicinal plants

Maicon—Maíra's husband

Paulo—an ex–trade unionist from the city, an up-and-coming leader of the *frente de massa* sector

Jessica—Paulo's daughter

Douglas—Jessica's partner, a young man from the outskirts of Joinville, the state capital

Seu Humberto—a local landowner

The northern settlement near Bom Jardim

The Fernandes de Castro family

Vera—a principal character

André—Vera's husband, regional leader of the frente de massa sector

Clarice—Vera's daughter, mother of two, earmarked as a leader when young, later sent to the Josué de Castro leadership school

Artur—Clarice's brother

William—Clarice's brother

Lúcia—Vera's sister, community organizer, and mother of two, battling illness

Dona Neusa—the Fernandes de Castro matriarch, living with Lúcia

José—Vera's brother, living with his family on the settlement

Enzo—José's son, the only member of the second generation to devote himself to the land

Rui—an older brother

Rosalete—an older sister living on the settlement with her family

Gaetano—an older man quick to temper

Silvia—Gaetano's wife

Alvise—their son

Marina—their daughter

Davi—originally a member of the settlement's co-op, often greeted me with a caipirinha

Jurema—Davi's wife

Juliana—their daughter, earmarked as a leader from a young age

Guilherme—their son

Randolfo—their younger son

Deise—their younger daughter

The collectivized unit of the settlement

Luizinho—state leader, later national leader of education

Roberto—main leader of the collective

Ana—Roberto's wife

Adenir—a collective member

State leadership

Bianchini—originally from Abelardo Luz, trained as a lawyer, state leader based in Florianópolis

Carolina—member of the MST office in Florianópolis

Grimaldi—state leader of frente de massa, based in São Caetano

Busatto—state leader, de facto leader of Santa Catarina, based in Abelardo Luz

Franciele—state leader of frente de massa, famous for attacking a police officer with a scythe

Osni—state leader of frente de massa

Teresa—former state leader of education replaced by . . .

Mariana—state leader of education

Alcides—Mariana's husband and state leader of culture

Martelinho—Alcides's father and one of the original members of the MST in Santa Catarina

National leadership
João Pedro Stédile—well-known MST leader
João Paulo Rodrigues—MST leader, trained in social sciences
Miguel Stédile—João Pedro Stédile's son

People encamped
Polaco—encamped in both Vitória and Novo Horizonte
Márcio—schoolteacher in the Novo Horizonte camp, expelled by the state leadership
Wanderley—encamped in Novo Horizonte
Marinho—encamped in Novo Horizonte

Map 1 A map of Brazil with the three southern states highlighted

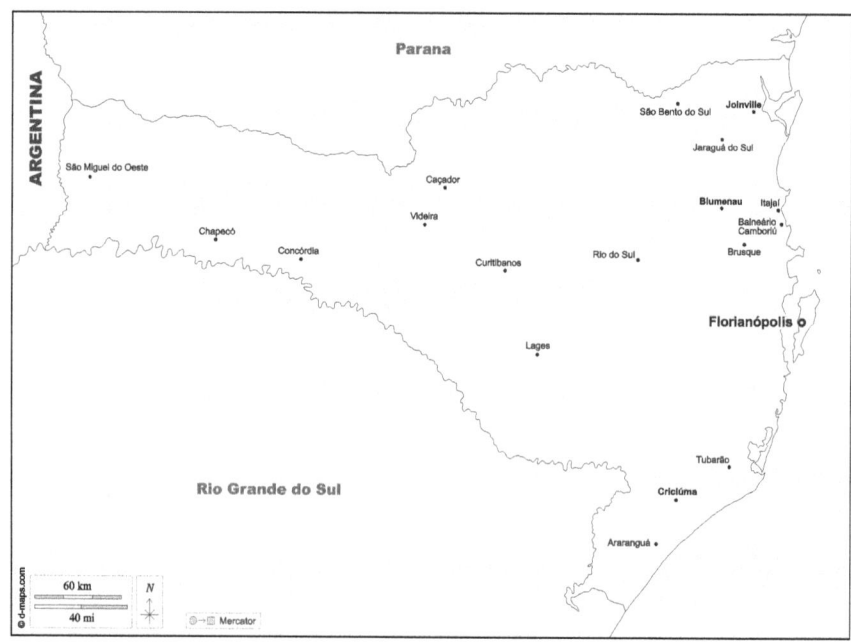

Map 2 A detail of the state of Santa Catarina

Pathways to Utopia

Introduction

Island
your mountains and your valleys
do not feel the passage of time,
they remain in a dream world
—the dreams of your children.

AMÍLCAR CABRAL[1]

Clarice doesn't have much time. She's on an hour-long break from work and has two children waiting for her at home. She asks a friend to film her on a cell phone while she sits on the grass, speaking about the Landless Workers Movement (Movimento dos Trabalhadores Rurais Sem Terra—MST) and the patriarchy of land. Identified at a young age as a potential leader, Clarice was sent to the Technical Institute for Education and Research on Agrarian Reform (Instituto Técnico de Ensino e Pesquisa em Reforma Agrária—ITERRA) school in Veranópolis, in the state of Rio Grande do Sul, where she studied under the overall direction of Miguel Stédile, an education-sector coordinator and the son of longtime MST leader João Pedro Stédile. Now back home in Bom Jardim, a small town in the state of Santa Catarina, and late for her shift, she sends me a series of four clips, which we translate and edit together. Clarice has been invited to contribute to an exhibition and public program entitled "Soil Is in an Inscribed Body: On Sovereignty and Agropoetics," organized by SAVVY Contemporary, an independent art space in Berlin. Scheduled for September 2019, the exhibition examines anti-colonial struggles and anti-extractivism conflicts across the world, with a focus on connections between artistic practice and agroecological strategies. Clarice speaks to the camera, addressing an audience thousands of miles away:

How can we conceive of the patriarchy of the land? Patriarchy is rooted in private property, private ownership of huge tracts of land, in which agrobusiness focuses on the production of commodities on a large scale. The MST, on the other hand, since its beginnings, has concentrated its efforts to fight against this model of agriculture driven by capital: to fight against a model that doesn't value land or its natural resources, and especially seeks to deny access to land. In this sense, the democratization of land is a utopia. The men and women of the MST organize themselves to confront an agricultural model that only contributes to capital. Our struggle is carried out directly and indirectly through the conquest of land, and we work the land in a different way, based on a model which values peasant origins, natural resources, and native seeds. In this way, we negate the patriarchy of land that derives from private interests and the conservative vision of dominant agricultural models.

She's wrapped up warm. Despite the spring sunshine of Southern Brazil, the temperature plummets in this rural region in the north of Santa Catarina, located on a high plateau. The camera moves, lingering on rolling hills dotted with distinctive Araucaria trees. The force of Clarice's words remains. She explains a series of complex concepts in a didactic way: agribusiness, patriarchy, capital, utopia. And there's something in the manner of her speech that communicates a deeply embodied knowledge. Clarice was born in an MST encampment. Moving from place to place and threatened by police evictions and hired gunmen, her family lived for eight years in improvised shacks made of rough branches wrapped tightly by black plastic sheeting, the *lona preta* of the MST. On an earth floor, without electricity or running water, her mother brought her into the world on the very land they occupy to this day. Clarice's words communicate a dignity, a resilience, but also a bloody-mindedness. "This is our struggle," she says, and I understand suddenly that I am privileged to be participating in a creative expression of *mística*, a profoundly subjective understanding of what it means to be *sem terra*, one of the landless.

As I continue to work on Clarice's text, there's a word that keeps coming back. Perhaps there's something about the emphasis. *Utopia*. I cast my mind back a couple of years. We're sitting on the porch of Clarice's mother's house as the sun goes down, talking idly about the movement. There's a stillness you find in the countryside, and the beginning of a breeze makes the cornfields sway. Suddenly our conversation crystallizes to a point, and Clarice, frowning, starts to speak: "Agrarian reform and the MST, all together, is a dream, it's something that drives us forward. There is a certain contradiction, it's a utopian movement. It's impossible but it's a way forward. It's a dream, but it's also the *dispositivo*, the mechanism."

The house is solid brick. Surrounded by the land her family farms, which they won through long years of struggle, I ask her what she means by contradiction.

"You can't think of the movement, with many things and people, as a beautiful and wonderful thing. It's not as if this will change huge things and structures, it's not the case. Huge things? I refer here to the third dimension of the MST's struggle: create a new society. Or even the second, agrarian reform. This isn't something that is solely within our control." Clarice seems torn. There is a pause. "But [agrarian reform] is possible to discuss, but in these small spaces, not the big ones. Because the MST is not totally utopian. I mean, you get land. You achieve agrarian reform in small spaces."

We go inside. On a kitchen counter, there's a basket of recently harvested red beans. They're round and smooth, beautiful really. Clarice's mother, Vera, comes into the kitchen telling me how this year's crop is good. She fries us some eggs on the *fogo a lenha*, a type of wood-fired stove that warms the whole room. Clarice leaves us, headed for the *casinha*, the wooden house out back, to go to sleep. I look again at the counter. There are some neatly folded baby clothes with the design of a little girl dressed in a red MST T-shirt. The lettering says *somos todos MST*—we are all MST. There are jars of pickled cucumbers and a biscuit barrel sitting inside a snug knitted jacket. There is a photo of Vera's three children and a book, *A Convenção dos Ventos*, a collection of poetic short stories about agroecological farming. Next to the table, two large flags are pinned to the wall. The first is the MST flag. Red, with a drawing of Brazil at its center. Worked into this representation and positioned in the south are a white man and woman, close together, the man holding a machete, pointing it skyward. Their expressions are stern, and they look left, into the middle distance. The second flag is purple, representing the Movimento de Mulheres Camponeses (MMC), the Peasant Women's Movement of Brazil. The flag is based around a female sign and three figures: a Black woman, a white woman, and an Indigenous woman. They meet my gaze with a smile, holding a hoe, a baby, and a basket of agricultural produce, respectively.

"Just like the state meeting, right?" Vera says. "Remember 2007?" We laugh about how I met the family at the state meeting in Fraiburgo, in the interior of Santa Catarina. Once a year, the Santa Catarina MST holds its meeting there, in the Parque de Maça, the Apple Park. It almost seems like yesterday, my first institutional interaction with the movement. A huge meeting hall, almost empty. There are hundreds of empty chairs facing a stage raised above ground level. More seating is provided by concrete steps that run down one side of the hall. Above, huge banners have been stretched lengthwise from one end of the hall to the other in a panoply of red, yellow, and green. The stage has been decked with flags. The largest is the movement's flag, instantly recognizable among the others, and next to it the national flag of Brazil. A banner runs from the roof to the stage, with the word *SOCIALISMO* printed in red letters on a white background. At the front of the stage are other flags: the Movimento dos Pequenos Agricultores (MPA, the Movement of Small Farmers) flag, the Via Campesina flag, and the flag of the MMC. All around the hall are reminders of the movement's collective past, including photography by Sebastião Salgado, the renowned Brazilian social documentary photographer. Here, famous images such as "Meeting for the Land's Occupation," "A Massacre, a Wake," and the omnipresent "The Icons of Victory" are displayed, connected by a long piece of cord, each image mounted on a black card. The line of images stretches fifty yards, the entire length of the hall. In the far corner is a display area showcasing the best of MST produce. There are pots of honey, conserves and jams, the greenery of lettuces and salads, and two-liter soda bottles filled with beans.

At some point, a couple of kids see me taking photos. They run off with my camera, and I don't see them again until everyone is having dinner. Mariana, the deputy head of the state education sector, has given me a plate, and I join the queue. I'm worried about serving myself too much, but watching everybody eating heartily, I fill my plate. The dinner consists entirely of MST produce grown in the surrounding settlements. There is *arroz e feijão*, the Brazilian staple of rice and beans; fresh lettuce leaves; and fresh tomatoes. Everything is delicious. Looking for somewhere to sit, I see the two kids, a girl and a boy, and they introduce me to their father, André. The little girl is Clarice, many years back, with her brother Artur. She's around ten years old; Artur is a couple of years older.

The next day, early in the morning, everyone gathers in the main hall, and MST leaders appear on stage. They greet the audience of five hundred people with an amplified *bom dia!* Good morning! The response is halfhearted, so it is repeated twice more until the audience roars "bom dia" back to the stage. We are asked to embrace the person to our left. Clarice and Artur are running around the hall taking photos and generally making mischief. Now the speaker calls the name of the one of the *brigadas*, the units of organizational subdivision into which the MST is divided. I've been invited to join the Alzemiro de Oliveira brigade. *Chimarrão*, the erva maté (tea) that is common in Southern Brazil, Uruguay, and Argentina, is passed to me, and as I drink, I ask what everyone is writing down. A woman called Pretinha tells me it is a *grito* and tells me to memorize it. I recite the lines a couple of times. "You're learning already!" She smiles.

At the back of the hall, a brigade stands up to chant. This is the grito. My new friends in Alzemiro de Oliveira are trying to memorize theirs in time as each brigade, one by one, recites theirs to the hall. It seems our turn is coming closer, and Pretinha starts to complain about how this one is new and how they keep changing it. I notice that when the members of the brigadas chant their grito, each member raises their left fist to every second beat. Our turn comes. We shout out our lines and pump our fists. I'm conscious that we want to make a good impression on the other brigades from the state. There is pride involved in being part of Alzemiro de Oliveira.

Now a leader, Busatto, begins to speak. From the stage, his amplified words echoing in the concrete hall, Busatto refers to Florestan Fernandes, a Brazilian sociologist and Workers' Party (Partido dos Trabalhadores—PT) federal deputy; Karl Marx; Che Guevara; and Antonio Gramsci as inspirations for progress. Outlining the movement's strategy, Busatto breaks down the movement's key objectives into three distinct goals. First, the MST must take land: we must occupy. Second, we must ensure the continuation of the struggle for agrarian reform: the movement's longevity is key. Third, we must create a new society: an alternative society to capitalism must be made real. He continues: "The bourgeoisie must be confronted, and through education we can prevail. The struggle begins through people's examples of character: we must demonstrate sem terra values and behaviors through the way we behave, each and every day." He asks us to memorize a specific phrase. He reads it out, and we repeat it in unison, twice: *O movimento tem que superar o sistema do capitalismo—é possível realizar.* (The movement must overcome the capitalist system—this is possible to achieve.)

The state meeting comes to a close, and it's time to say goodbye. Clarice and Artur wave from the windows of a bus taking them back up to the North. They've had a good time and taken a lot of blurry photos. André shakes hands with me and says, "You have to come and visit." He's headed elsewhere, engaged in movement business. As we go our separate ways, none of us can know what will happen over the next fifteen years. The struggle finds expression through examples of character, we are told—a struggle not only to take land but also to create a new society. What is the nature of this lived and embodied struggle? How will transformation be brought about on such a scale? Unknown to us at the time, Clarice will be selected as a teenager and sent to a residential MST school to be trained as a leader. She will have two children, work desperately to make ends meet, and reflect critically on the MST's utopian politics: the struggle as dream but also as practice. I will lose my mother, lose my sense of self, and spend years trying to put back together things that can never be whole again. André will find his own path characterized by a violence he can't escape, a path that will take him away from the movement. Vera, Clarice's mother, will become a true hero, fighting for what she believes is right. In the worst of times, she will go back to school, triumph in the face of fear, and transform her life and self as she simultaneously demands transformation of the movement to which she has given so much.

But in this moment, we don't see any of those things, even though unceasing time connects and encompasses us. Fragments and traces of all our futures already exist as a series of interpenetrating moments in which the present, drawing on the past, prefigures the future. For us all, this marks the beginning, middle, and end of a resolutely nonlinear story, a story of hope, sacrifice, and struggle, of resolution and redemption in search of a lived social justice. As Clarice questions a utopian dream, talking to the camera, the temporalities of transformation swirl inexorably upon us in the spaces between ideal and material worlds.

* * *

I began to understand the scale of the MST for the first time in an office of the Federal University of Santa Catarina (UFSC). It was March 2007, and I had just arrived in Brazil as a visiting PhD student. The MST's achievements across Brazil are extraordinary: 450,000 families settled through a struggle for social justice; more than half a million people with houses and land; the security of a place to call home; the possibility to access education and health. Growing up in a small island country, it was hard for me to imagine the vast expanse of lands into which people's hopes and dreams were invested. I was in Florianópolis, the state capital of Santa Catarina, with my friend Elisa. A history student, she was part of a *núcleo*, a research group, run by the UFSC sociology professor Bernardete Wrublevski Aued. A collaboration among students and faculty, the group had started out looking at changing understandings of labor but was now focused on the MST. Elisa took me to meet Bernardete, and we spoke about the kind of research I might be able to do. She was interested where in the state I might work and led me to a large map set up on an easel in the corner of the room. The map detailed the state of Santa Catarina, the space to which I had decided to limit my field research. A land mass bigger than Portugal. Bernardete gestured to the map: would it be north, south, east, or west? I remember that there were small red and yellow pins affixed in almost every part of the map, each pin denoting an MST encampment or settlement. According to agrarian reform data from the Instituto Nacional de Colonização e Reforma Agrária (National Institute for Colonization and Agrarian Reform—INCRA), in 2007 there were approximately four thousand families living in forty-nine different MST settlements in the state. Even then, it was hard to reconcile this map and the sheer scale of the MST's activity with what I sensed must be a very intimate struggle for each community involved in the fight for agrarian reform. I knew many MST members in Santa Catarina had been part of the movement since 1985, and I wondered how the MST's stated aims came to be negotiated amid everyday realities over such a long period. What did it mean to be landless? What might be the contradictions of a movement that was so rooted in the practicalities of gaining land but at the same time maintained a utopian commitment to the realization of a new society? What kind of durational transformation might be engendered by a movement to which members made a lifelong commitment?

This book is about that transformation. Through a powerful and embodied experience of social justice, hundreds of thousands of people have won pieces of land, built homes in which to live, and established profound dignity premised on struggle. Against overwhelming odds, people like Vera and Clarice show what it means to make and negotiate an ongoing commitment to transform the world around them and, in doing so, bring about transformation in the movement to which they have given so much. In a world where so much seems inevitable, the actions of MST members show we shouldn't resign ourselves to the notion of the foregone conclusion. Their belief, defiance, and steadfast refusal to bend to the naturalized and the preordained calls into question the sense that all is given and allows us to glimpse a world in which the possible is already the real. Drawing on fifteen years of ethnographic work accompanying the MST, this book traces the lives of the movement's members, focusing on their struggle for land, dignity, and what it means to be sem terra, to be landless. Contextualized by resilience and determination in the face of overwhelming odds, the stories of these people show how members of social movements transform the world around them and, in doing so, demand transformation of the movements to which they belong. Many MST members I became close to, people like Vera and her family, have been part of the movement for twenty years or more, and such commitment allied to such scale is in part what renders the MST so extraordinary.

While the movement is well established in Santa Catarina, the MST is also active in twenty-four of Brazil's twenty-six states, from the Amazonian state of Roraima bordering Venezuela in the far north to the state of Rio

Grande do Sul bordering Uruguay in the extreme south.[2] Today, roughly five thousand families constitute the movement in Santa Catarina (Cristina de Souza and de Oliveira Estevam 2021), and with over a million members in total, the MST is the largest social movement in Latin America. Founded in 1984, the movement coalesced around two basic principles: the struggle for a more just society and the necessity of the means to achieve this: a program of agrarian reform. From its first meeting, attended by a mere eighty representatives, the MST grew rapidly and, through the use of direct-action occupation tactics, succeeded in placing agrarian reform at the heart of Brazil's political agenda. The movement's success to date is remarkable: almost half a million families have been granted land, educational programs have reached over two hundred thousand children, and the movement has invested in agroecological production methods to the extent that it is Brazil's largest producer of organic rice. In the 1980s, one of the movement's first priorities was to build an effective organizational structure and a strong collective identity. Identifying unproductive tracts of land and organizing landless families to occupy them required discipline and a long-term mindset: the MST's objective was to settle land, as opposed to merely occupy it, so that families would have the opportunity to create a sustainable way of life in the following years. But waiting for the federal government to devolve land and settle these *acampados*, the people carrying out the occupation, was painfully slow. In the movement's first phases, occupations often lasted from five to ten years. If a case was successfully made, the occupied land was devolved to the encamped families, and what the MST terms an *assentamento*, a settlement, was established. Registered with INCRA, families were given right of use—not full ownership—of roughly ten hectares (approximately twenty-five acres) each to build a house, plant crops, and work the land. This method of identifying unproductive tracts of land, occupying them, and simultaneously lobbying the federal government to have the land devolved has not changed in the ensuing decades, and occupations continue to this day.

Encamped for months, maybe years, in hope of land means that MST members participate in a particularly lived and durational struggle. And a mode of transformation held in abeyance, into which so many hopes and expectations are invested, generates a very specific spatiotemporal frame that is different from other forms of activism and social justice. Even if MST members are successful in gaining land, to be part of the MST is an ongoing struggle that demands commitment and endurance. The rewards are great, but the process is drawn out, unforgiving, and dangerous. In 2017, Via Campesina, the international organization that focuses on peasants' rights, reported that since 1985, 1,833 peasants and leaders of the struggle for agrarian reform had been assassinated in conflicts over land in Brazil while during the same period the number of estates with over one hundred thousand hectares grew almost fourfold.[3] Such a concentration of landholdings is daunting, and the MST's struggle takes place in one of the few countries worldwide where a substantial program of agrarian reform has never been implemented. Programs of agrarian reform that occurred in Chile in the 1960s and 1970s, in India post-1947, or in Mexico in the 1930s have never taken place in Brazil, the fifth-largest country in terms of arable land area worldwide. This lack of reform means that a tiny number of properties take up almost half of all available land: a huge concentration of land in the hands of very few. Given Brazil's size, the dimensions of this modern-day *latifundia*, the landowning elite, can be difficult to grasp. De Almeida and Sánchez (2000, 29) commented that "it is as if just 35,083 people possessed an area equal to the combined territory of France, Germany, Spain, Switzerland, and Austria." Brazil's largest farm, the Fazenda Nova Piratininga, at 135,000 hectares, is over twenty times the size of Manhattan.

Reform has been on the agenda many times throughout Brazilian history, but it has always been frustrated. The most recent attempt was signaled on March 13, 1964, when the democratically elected president of Brazil, João Goulart, gave a speech outlining a new political program that would bring about a decisive solution to the problem of Brazilian agrarian reform. On April 1, seventeen days later, Goulart was overthrown by a military coup. With vested interests threatened by Goulart's intention to break up centuries-old landholdings, a military column moved on Rio de Janeiro, and with the support of the governments of the United States and the United Kingdom, a military dictatorship was established that ruled until 1985.

Faced by the weight of history and a concentration of the forces of capital, how does the MST articulate its struggle and bring about transformation? Ever since I started working with the movement in 2007, I have been asked this question. In Europe, where I was studying, people with a passing interest would ask about the situation in Brazil and either express their dismay at its inequalities or rather blithely dismiss the MST's efforts as futile in the face of global neoliberalization. Others, perhaps with a greater repertoire of the radical politics of the 2000s—the experiences of the World Social Forum or the violent police response to protests at the G8 meeting at Genoa, for example—wanted to know more about the movement's strategy. Just as today, from the late 1990s onward, the MST was an important actor in a broader coalition of global left-wing politics, and I was often asked about its direct-action tactics, the way it occupied land, and its powerful mobilizations of resistance to landowners in the struggle for agrarian reform.

One of the interesting things about these discussions was the temporal register in which transformation was often framed. Whether speaking about MST occupations or even the establishment of MST encampments, transformation was somehow reduced to a distinct moment and, by extension, a transition from one state to another. This perspective is best symbolized by the notion of *cutting the wire*—the moment when an MST leader symbolically severs the barbed-wire fence of an unproductive tract of land and a column of landless people takes possession. A powerful metaphor, this iconic phrase inspired one of the first and best English-language books on the MST, Sue Branford and Jan Rocha's *Cutting the Wire: The Story of the Landless Movement of Brazil* (2002). On the back cover, the authors write, "Cutting the wire is how the MST describes the act of occupying the land, the cornerstone of their movement. It is the baptism of fire for the militant, an essential part of their identity and it plays a key role in the *mística*, the moment of collective ritual that kicks off all MST events." With endorsements from Eric Hobsbawm and George Monbiot, *Cutting the Wire*'s powerful allusions to transformation as rebirth and its emphasis on a kinetic moment of resistance contributed to the widespread view that posits transformation as a distinct action with a clearly defined before and after. Monbiot, a veteran left-wing columnist based in the United Kingdom, commented, "[This book] will become essential reading for anyone hoping to understand where the new politics came from and how it works." And central to this politics was the idea of seizing history in distinct moments—"activists who have taken their lives into their own hands," as Branford and Rocha framed it.

Trained and practicing as journalists, Branford and Rocha were understandably looking for a moment of metaphorical significance. Such a device, *cutting the wire*, encapsulated the potential of the MST but also served to explain to an English-language readership how the movement had grown to become Latin America's largest social movement. And yet the experience of transformation as embodied and practiced by members of the MST was never about a mere moment. Having coalesced in part from a roadside encampment that came to be known as Encruzilhada Natalino that lasted from December 1980 to September 1983, MST members fully understood the length of time that would be required to bring about change in Brazil's conservative rural areas. The idea of cutting the wire was perhaps the best way to communicate a simplified politics of transformation to the audience of that time: a temporality of protest premised on rupture. In reality, however, both in 2002, when the book was published, and over twenty years later, being a member of the MST is to undergo a lived experience of struggle. It is to dwell, to live, and to plant crops as the seasons change from summer sunshine to winter's frost, year after year, decade upon decade. It is to gain a piece of land, build a house brick by brick with the help of the community, plant and harvest and grow old, then pass on what you have built to your children and grandchildren. For members of the MST, the change they strive for manifests itself through the cycles of the year and the calendars of harvest—a continuous process of transformation. For this book, therefore, the question becomes less about how movements realize change and more about the sense in which we can understand the temporal frame in which this occurs and its latent flow. Having shared so many experiences over the years with members of the MST, I argue that we should take our cue from MST members' lived experiences of striving for change to rethink the temporality of transformation. While much attention has been devoted to the iconic and spectacular with regard to protest, I argue that transformation should rather be understood as located within a durational mode of time. Transformation in this sense occurs from within the contradictory spaces and temporalities that characterize a life lived as struggle. It is sparked by creative gestures that subvert established norms and reorder social relations both within and beyond networks of agents seeking change. Some of the world's largest social movements are driven by a utopian politics that articulates a vision of change premised on linearity. By focusing on how people make and negotiate an ongoing commitment to social justice, this book details how a durational activism is characterized by what I term *counter-utopian* practices, powerful forces that sit in tension with existing movement structures. And it is this very tension—generative and productive—between the utopian and counter-utopian that impels movements in new and unexpected directions.

Such a realization points to questions of scale and fundamentally how we understand transformation to take place. If we understand activism not as one-off intervention but instead as a longitudinal lived experience replete with subjective expression, the smallest of community actions can shape the largest of social movements and, by extension, rework the forms through which such movements seek to change the world. In this sense, it would be a mistake to identify counter-utopian practices as the actions of individuals or to think that to pay attention to the counter-utopian is to somehow construe an individualization of struggle. On the contrary, counter-utopian practices within the MST occur in community contexts and in a relational sense, and this book reveals how such practices acquire their transformational significance in relation to others as they travel, shifting attitudes and accruing greater meaning as they resonate.

In the ethnography that opens this book, Busatto put forward a utopian vision: the construction of a new society, the overthrow of capitalism, a world to be led by new social citizens. And yet, the lived reality of the MST's struggle takes place not in performative rupture but in a period that extends and dilates through the embodied actions of its members and their relationship to the land. Tracing the lives of MST members and their quest for justice, this book speaks to the productive contradictions that arise from within such an elongated period: between complex life worlds and a normative teleological linearity; between the creative gestures of autonomous communities and notions of unity as sameness that can characterize the MST as an institution; between differing ideas of what it means to be sem terra, to be landless, and by extension the direction in which the movement should turn. The year 2024 saw the MST commemorating forty years of struggle. How has the MST managed to endure as other social justice movements have fallen by the wayside? Most explanations emphasize its centralized organizational power and unity of purpose. This is without doubt true, but it is only one part of the story. My ethnographic analysis of duration speaks to how the MST's resilience is fundamentally premised on forces that act on one other, generating an elasticity and tensile strength that ensure the movement's continuing relevance and guarantee its existence. Normalized utopian values are contested by a minoritarian, community-based positionality, and the resulting friction is wholly productive: without the movement's framework, settlements would almost certainly fold; without the pushback of emergent counter-utopian politics that transform the movement from within, the MST would stagnate and become irrelevant. The MST has successfully inhabited the eras of twentieth-century utopian politics and a twenty-first-century political horizon characterized by the prefigurative and horizontal. And it is transformation as located in duration, less visible and ultimately less spectacular, that ensures the MST's resilience as a movement of our today, yesterday, and tomorrow.

Utopia and the Subjunctive

For Raymond Williams, utopia was ultimately a subjunctive mode. In his analysis, utopia was characterized by a mechanism in which the vision of a promised land could define the pathway toward progress, structuring and shaping the journey. Williams (1978, 208) identified what he termed a "willed social transformation" as the defining trait of utopia, describing how positing a distant objective could justify any and all means to get there, enabling those who articulated that vision to determine how the journey would be undertaken, by whom, and under what conditions: "The sweet little world at the end of all this is at once a result and a promise ... the sweet promise which sustains effort and principle and hope through the long years of revolutionary preparation and organization" (209). For Williams, the contradictions that such a utopia inscribed were totalizing: striving for a distant horizon became the motor of any project of willed transformation and the raison d'être for almost all daily activities while the question of whether the new world to be realized really lay within the ambit of possibility or was even entirely desirable could be left to one side, to be confronted "when the time comes." We can think back to Clarice's comment on the MST: her awareness of the impossibility of the movement's stated aim to create a new society and yet her belief in agrarian reform being possible to achieve in small spaces. Clarice speaks to the lived experience of a utopian dream and particularly its temporal dimension, which she described as a mechanism, premised on a linear understanding of time.

Echoing Clarice's critique, recent academic work—for example, Ruy Blanes and Bjørn Enge Bertelsen (2021)—has sought to move beyond the ideals of utopia and toward micropolitical domains, interrogating the strictures of politically conformist notions of the real. So how might a book on a traditional Marxist mass movement like the MST contribute to this discussion? While change as a political project has become increasingly connoted with micropolitical, horizontalized contexts (see Cooper 2014; Blanes et al. 2016; Razsa 2015), less attention has been devoted to how transformation occurs from within the contradictory spaces and temporalities that characterize movements that maintain a political, territorial, and ideological constancy. Engaging with the anthropological framework of generative socialities, I have found it helpful to think with the French philosopher Henri Bergson when considering how utopia as total and large-scale order (Blanes and Bertelsen 2021) can be interrogated: its contradictions understood as productive as opposed to limiting and how its linear direction of travel might be creatively waylaid by unexpected twists and turns.

My conviction here stems from Bergson's theory of difference put forward in *Matter and Memory* (1991), *Time and Free Will* (1910), and *Creative Evolution* (1944). Bergson sought to analyze the seeming contradiction that exists between the continuity of all living beings and the implicit discontinuity and vitality that underlie creation. Life reproduces in a continual sense but always with an evolutionary impulse, meaning that continuity must necessarily be complemented by discontinuity. But from where might such discontinuity emerge? And what prompts it to take form in the first place? Bergson's interest in change and from where it springs was premised on his understanding of time. Questioning a linear temporal ontology, Bergson argued that time should be thought of in two different ways. Everyday understandings conceived of "objective time"—the time of watches and calendars, time as composed of distinct moments that can be separated and measured. Time in this sense is actually an attempt to measure the phenomenon rather than the phenomenon itself, as these measurements merely serve to link time to space—for example, the sundial measuring the movement of the sun around the earth or the sweep of the second hand around a watch. For Bergson, such an understanding was mechanistic. His counterproposal was to conceive of time as lived and experiential, and he termed this as *la durée*, duration, a kind of lived time that expands and contracts in resonance with our inner subjective experience. Duration cannot be measured and, importantly, cannot be divided into past, present, and future. For Bergson, the fact that duration is not linear meant that feelings and memories from the past are active and influential in our present experience, which in turn is shaped by anticipation of the future. Conceived of in this manner, duration is the source of "invention, the creation of forms, the continual elaboration of the absolutely new" (Bergson 1944, 14), and the lived experience of MST members, contextualized by such a temporal framework, suggests critical insights into how we can understand transformation from within sociality characterized by temporal contradiction.

Scholarship on the MST and Alternative Paradigms

Cutting the Wire was published in 2002 and has been complemented by perspectives from political science (Ondetti 2008; Vergara-Camus 2014; Pahnke 2018), social geography (Wright and Wolford 2003; Wolford 2010), and education (Tarlau 2019). Gabriel Ondetti presents a large amount of macro-level data, charting the MST from its formation to 2008, and complements this with meaningful ethnographic accounts, highlighting the nuances and contested spaces of the struggle. Ondetti argues that the movement's success has largely been shaped by making the most of changing political opportunities and suggests that life in the MST is characterized by "strong internal discipline" (2008, xvi) in which movement encampments can become spaces of "collective identity building" (114) for a movement that demands "organizational loyalty" (138). Wendy Wolford (2010) also puts forward a considered and subtle analysis. Writing almost a decade after her first monograph on the MST, she notes that "academics and activists often champion social movements in ways that unintentionally exoticize the very subaltern they hope to support" (10). And she offers a defense of her focus on the internal workings of the MST, arguing that a more granular approach makes possible productive analyses of contestation, tension, and what she terms "subject elision"—the conflation of the individual with the collective for strategic ends (11). In adopting this perspective, Wolford adopts anthropological perspectives of new social movement theory, specifically John Burdick's (whom she cites) notion of decentering social movements—the notion that any productive anthropological analysis of social movements must begin with a view that understands such organizations "as internally heterogeneous and contested fields" (Burdick 1995, 362). From this standpoint, Wolford (2010, 14) issues a challenge to scholars who have sought to uphold a homogenous portrayal of revolutionary movements: "Why not admit that there are all sorts of people in the movement . . . ?" she asks, adding that "[a simplified vision has] certain consequences, as do all representations."[4] Making this move allows Wolford to address how local contexts and moral economies matter and to question whether the size of the MST and its commitment to massification—the expansion of a unified struggle to all parts of Brazil—is really its most important aspect. Rather, she suggests, it may be that the MST has provided a discourse and vocabulary for resistance more broadly and a means of imagining the world in a different way.

Attention to detail in a movement as big as the MST matters. As Lygia Sigaud (2000, 83) has observed, being sem terra, being landless, does not necessarily correspond to an identification with the MST, and the manner in which the utopian goal of creating a new society is diversely interpreted speaks powerfully to questions of identity and the struggle. In challenging conventional assumptions that numerical strength translates to greater power or that internal diversity weakens collective unity, I accompanied the lives and trajectories of MST members as they navigated normative expectations of productivity, gendered labor, and creative expression and as they strove to bridge the immediate demands of the here and now with a transformative vision promised for the future. Much of the richest and most complex scholarship on the MST has been conducted by Brazilian or Brazil-based scholars such as Christine Chaves (2000, 2021, 2022); Nashieli Rangel Loera (2006, 2010, 2014); Janaina dos Santos Moscal (2017); and Lygia Sigaud (2000, 2005); in a similar vein, works by Rebecca Tarlau (2019), Ashley Lebner (2019), and Melinda Gurr (2017, 2019) articulate powerful ethnographic depth. Living with MST members as they occupied land and, in doing so, disaggregated linear understandings of time in relation to space, I came to appreciate how the European conceptualization of new social movement theory might enter into dialogue with the highly specific histories of Latin America.

One thinker who was important in this sense was Arturo Escobar, whose work examined the emergence of movements without centralized leadership—a form of organization demonstrated at the World Social Forum, first held in 2001 in Porto Alegre, southern Brazil, under the slogan "Another world is possible." This emphasis on loosely affiliated collectives, horizontal structures, and identities that went beyond that of the worker was far from universally embraced. But despite some resistance, such work on social movements in Latin America opened pathways to notions of affect, materiality, and autonomy and moved away from alignment, teleology, and unified goals. A key element of this shift was the rejection of utopian visions of the future. In her analysis of the intersection between Marxist and feminist movements, Norma Stoltz Chinchilla (1991, 305) called attention "to the need for a holistic view of change . . . a vision of the future in a context decidedly lacking in alternative Utopias." And in "Beyond the Third World" (2004), Escobar suggested more in-depth work was needed on collectives that left behind utopian imaginaries to work with practices of social, economic, and ecological difference—a necessity, he argued, in a world where modernity could no longer provide tangible solutions to the very problems it had created.

Creative Gesture: Another World Is Possible

If power was being challenged by new types of collectives and through innovative uses of media and networking in Latin America, it was a rallying call for activists and scholars writing for an anglophone audience in the early 2000s. Marta Harnecker's *Rebuilding the Left* (2007), Tariq Ali's *Pirates of the Caribbean: Axis of Hope* (2006), Niels Barmeyer's *Developing Zapatista Autonomy* (2009), and Richard Gott's *Hugo Chávez and the Bolivarian Revolution* (2011) spoke of the Latin American struggle against a US-led neoliberal hegemony, making connections to the alter-globalization movement, a broader coalition that had come about in the period between the 1999 Seattle WTO protests and the 2001 World Social Forum in Brazil, coalescing amid resistance to the structural adjustment policies of the Washington Consensus. Its logic was not based in a paradigmatic program to wrest power from the state or create a new society with new social citizens. Rather, it pointed to the political, social, and ecological consequences of neoliberal globalization and demanded human rights and justice from within scales of globality. As Geoffrey Pleyers (2013) has argued, the alter-globalization movement was not a unitary entity but rather an approach to bringing about social change underpinned by autonomous nodes working in networked solidarity.

It was an exciting time to work with questions of social justice. Prefigurative politics, defined by Carl Boggs (1977, 100) as "the embodiment, within the ongoing political practice of a movement, of those forms of social relations, decision-making, culture, and human experience that are the ultimate goal," was gaining ever greater traction (see Swain 2017; Srnicek and Williams 2015; Van de Sande 2013). Such an approach to social movement politics was characterized by a shift toward the antiauthoritarian, horizontal, and participatory and became widely read in part due to David Graeber's (2002, 2009) unique writing that espoused a commitment to direct action in everyday life in which the means became the ends. On a theoretical level, prefigurative politics also offered a partial exit from visions of change premised on linearity. As Van de Sande identified (2013, 230), the actualization of an idealized society in the here and now implied a collapse between discrete elements of present and future and in this manner offered a challenge to utopian temporalities. While scholars and practitioners of prefigurative politics were thus raising questions of the relationship between time and change (see Maeckelbergh 2009, 66; Lazar 2014), a more detailed exploration of the implications of such a collapse was not being put forward. Rather, the focus of Jeff Juris's (2008) and Marianne Maeckelbergh's (2009) detailed work on the alter-globalization movement was to demonstrate how decentralized movements could bring about societal transformation.

Juris's emphasis on a "cultural logic of networking" and Maeckelbergh's notion of the "process" inherent to activist work centered the discussion on horizontal and networked organizational logics and the constitutive importance of the elaboration of activist subjectivities. Maple Razsa's subsequent account of political activism in postsocialist Yugoslavia sharpened this analysis with his elaboration of the "subjective turn"—the struggle on the part of activists "to develop individual and collective subjects who are antagonistic to dominant social relations and yearn for radical change" (2015, 27). The emphasis on affect was particularly strong: one arena in which subjects were formed was violent street confrontations with state actors, where Razsa identified activists as "feeling the state on your own skin" (99). In working over a period of years in the Balkans, Razsa connected work on the alter-globalization movement in Zagreb to instances of Occupy in Slovenia and made explicit—not least through the title of his book, *Bastards of Utopia*—the divorce of such politics from the traditional Marxist left. In doing so, Razsa echoed a position that Maeckelbergh identified as characteristic of alter-globalization activists: the abandoning of the dream of revolution and the creation of other worlds in the here and now (Maeckelbergh 2009, 224). Juris's "cultural logic of networking" was an important step in understanding how this process might occur and built on Graeber's theorization of movements where a decentralized model of organization was their unique strength, a means of "creating and enacting horizontal networks instead of top-down structures like states, parties, or corporations" (2002, 70).

A particularly exciting aspect of such scholarship was its detailed ethnographic accounts of an activism characterized by playfulness and performance. In working with the Occupy movement, Juris (2012, 2015) highlighted scenes like a group of young men at Occupy Boston wearing nothing but red Speedos and holding placards saying "Speedos Now!'" and "1% of this Speedo is covering 99% of my ass!" By focusing on the performative dimensions of protest, Juris highlighted the importance of the body, aesthetics, and gesture in how activists engaged in creative practice. Despite the laugh-out-loud moments, Juris's intentions were entirely serious: his analysis brought to the fore the transformative capacity of embodiment and affect at both macro and micro levels as protesters performed carnivalesque inversions on the street, an approach he suggested could shape activists' identity and bridge the mind-body dualism that he saw as characteristic of work on social movements (2015, 98). Yet such aesthetic interventions—like the speedo-wearing Occupy Boston protesters or the Clandestine Insurgent Rebel Clown Army, discussed in Maeckelbergh's *Will of the Many*—were often dismissed as trivial by traditional revolutionary frameworks. Maeckelbergh acknowledges this skepticism in her playful aside, "I start with the Clown Army, not because they are the most important or the largest section of the alterglobalization movement, but because they are hilarious" (2009, 41), and it was only with the publication of Thomas Reed's *The Art of Protest* (2005) that these neglected dimensions of protest began to gain increased recognition. Reed's focus on what he termed the "cultural dimension" (2005, xv) of social movements pointed to a lacuna in the resource mobilization paradigm. Citing Bogad (2010), Eyerman (2006), Flynn (2013), Haugerud (2010), and Hohle (2009), Juris (2015, 85) laid out his interest in the body and affect in light of work that connected movements, performance, and instances of artistic expression. This scholarship continues to grow. Edited collections such as *The Aesthetics of Global Protest* (McGarry et al. 2020) and *The Political Aesthetics of Global Protest* (Werbner et al. 2014) and books by Paula Serafini (2018) and Holly Eva Ryan (2017) complement art theorists' understandings of how art can intervene in the social (c.f. Weibel 2014; Sholette 2017; Thompson 2012; McKee 2016).

Much of this literature, from both the arts and the social sciences, has been influenced by the thinking of Jacques Rancière. Building on the discussions of Adorno and Lukács, Rancière's *Politics of Aesthetics* (2004) refuses to separate aesthetics and politics on the basis that aesthetics is the means through which the political is constituted and operates. Rancière's analysis is premised on his understanding of politics as the "distribution of the sensible," a "distribution and redistribution of places and identities, a reapportioning of spaces and times, of the visible and invisible, and of noise and speech" (2004, 12–13). Such an understanding gives a unique power to artistic practices because, as Rancière argues, art is not a privileged means of understanding "reality" but rather a "way of doing and making" that intervenes in the general distribution of what is visible or invisible, what can be voiced and what cannot (2004, 13). I return in greater detail to Rancière's theorization later in the book because such work proposes a useful apparatus to theorize aesthetic interventions. However, documenting such practice and linking it ethnographically to transformation is a different matter. To accomplish this, I suggest that any analysis of how art sparks transformation must place an emphasis on form. In this sense, form connotes both social and aesthetic configurations, and importantly, these connotations must be understood as connected. This contingency, or interlacing, is what I think of as form's double fold, the manner in which the aesthetic hinges on the social—aesthetic forms are shaped by social contexts—but crucially, the social also hinges on the aesthetic in that sociality can be reordered by aesthetic practice (Bell, Flynn, and O'Hare 2022).

In theorizing notions of form, it is important to note the long-established Latin American trajectory of artistic work that has explored the many ways aesthetics and social life are interdependent. The Brazilian artists Hélio Oiticica and Lygia Pape, for example, articulated embodied, experimental, and conceptual engagements of form from the 1960s on. Oiticica placed an emphasis on relations, seeking to overcome the mind-body dualism through his concepts of Crelazer and the Supra-Sensorial, and explored the notion of what he termed affective interflow through the embodied and kinetic dimensions of his Parangolé works. Through performance, he argued for the contradictory experience of an individual in the world, differentiated yet simultaneously collective: "the rediscovery of rhythm, dance, the body, the senses, which finally are what we have as weapons of direct, perceptual, participatory knowledge . . . is revolutionary in the total sense of behavior" (Oiticica 1992, 130). And Lygia Pape's performances, such as "Livro do Tempo" (1961) and "Divisor" (1968), conspicuously carried out during Brazil's repressive military dictatorship, hinged on the activation of public space as political metaphor, allowing groups of people to come together at a time when large congregations were prohibited due to the perceived threat they posed to order.

I was aware of such relational practice before I began fieldwork with the MST, and it was the culture sector of the movement that fascinated me most. Looking in from the outside, I wondered how a culture sector of a mass movement understood artistic expression and why the dissemination of a cultural identity had come to assume such importance in the wider struggle. When I began fieldwork in Brazil and started seeing the emphasis that culture-sector leaders placed on the construction of a collective identity, I perceived the importance of the relationship between creative practice, representation, and belonging. As such, I was broadly following the definition of the sector's activity that appears on the Friends of the MST website: "At demonstrations, marches, occupations, imprisonments, and commemorations of victories and conquests, music, poetry and dance are presented, expressing and strengthening the Sem Terra cultural identity" (Friends of the MST, n.d.). I became familiar with mística, a mode of expression unique to the MST, and I witnessed and heard of diverse movement activities such as instances of Theatre of the Oppressed workshops, the construction of murals, projects of memorialization, and visual art installations. What become clear, however, was that for MST members, articulations of creative practice to merely *represent* MST culture were considered limiting and reductive. Art theory with regard to participation emphasizes creative practice's constitutive and generative potential, and as I have argued elsewhere (Flynn 2015a), when art is imbricated in dimensions of the social, the elaboration of meaning is at stake. Over time, in the mística of the MST, I began to discern a multiple and contested elaboration of meaning taking place, pertaining to questions of human values, how members' bodies—particularly female bodies—could exist in specific spaces and times, and the position and direction of the movement.

Spending Time with the MST

I began fieldwork in May 2007, and this first period ended in April 2009. Over the subsequent years, I went back many times to spend time with people who had become close friends, principally to a settlement in northern Santa Catarina near the small town of Bom Jardim. These trips, lasting a few days or weeks, occurred in June 2012, January 2015, March 2017, and August 2021. In between these times, I maintained close connections via social media, online collaborations, and daily WhatsApp chats. When I first arrived in Santa Catarina, hardly anyone had a smartphone through which these kinds of connections could be made and sustained. In 2021, almost everyone had good internet access of one kind or another, and my ethnographic work shifted and developed in accordance with these technologies. The COVID-19 pandemic highlighted the value of online ethnography, with scholars such as Deborah Lupton collating valuable resources for researchers looking to pivot to non-face-to-face methods. And while the importance of virtual fieldwork has long been established (Horst and Miller 2012; Sanjek and Tratner 2015), it became clear to me how even though I wasn't physically in Santa Catarina, like many other social anthropologists, I never really left the place where I was conducting research (Shtyrkov 2022). Although I was away from rural Brazil, I remained a part of the rich social life of my interlocutors through long conversations and shared jokes and the exchange of videos, memes, WhatsApp messages, stickers, and GIFs. These virtual spaces were sometimes humorous, sometimes commonplace, other times profoundly moving. Despite the distance that separated us, these means of communication held us together, and different from a truly online ethnography, the notion of distance was always understood by us all as an obstacle to overcome as opposed to a component part of the relationship. As the years passed, I returned to spend time over and over again.

The manner in which social movement struggles were understood also changed dramatically over this period. The horizontalism, decentralization, and exuberant plurality of subjectivity associated with first the alter-globalization movement and then the Occupy movements marked a departure from the narrow analyses that characterized the early years of my graduate training. Discussions moved from a unified front of revolutionary progress to the racial connotations of protest (Campbell 2011), gender norms of activism (Eschle and Maiguashca 2018), and ableism in public protest spaces (Beasley 2020), and it was stimulating to engage with activist scholars working on such questions in 2015 at the American Anthropological Association's conference in Denver.

And yet, there was something fundamentally different about my work from an ethnographic standpoint that became clear in these conversations. Scholars like Maple Razsa, Jeff Juris, and Marianne Maeckelbergh were working in large metropolitan areas in the United States or in Europe whereas I was working in small rural communities in Brazil. For all that was written about the MST as a grassroots movement, the types of horizontal organization these authors described in their work were entirely different from the way MST members recognized and constituted authority. The activist actions that Razsa and others described—the confrontations with the police, the tear gas, the helicopters buzzing overhead—were less present in the lives of the people with whom I had spent so much time. Even if such actions did occur, they took on very different forms. I listened in on stories of activists putting themselves at risk on the barricades, making films of their confrontations, and then watching these films repeatedly as they psyched themselves up for their next street battles. By contrast, MST members feared the police and, even more so, the hired gunmen. Confrontations occurred, of course, but they were buried in the past, and people were reluctant to speak about them. On more than one occasion, women such as Clarice and Tais, an MST member living in a coastal settlement, recounted how in their childhood they saw their homes in MST encampments being destroyed around them in the dead of night.

Space and time also worked differently. Occupy encampments seemed fast paced and dynamic: the original Occupy Wall Street (OWS) encampment was in existence for roughly two months, whereas many of the MST members I worked with had been established on their land for more than twenty years and intended to stay there for the rest of their lives. And then there was the relationship to utopia. The whole framework of the alter-globalization and Occupy movements was premised on rejecting the politics of the vanguard, calling time on the notion of a revolutionary rupture that would bring about a new world, wholly formed, into which new social citizens would be ready to march. Maeckelbergh (2009, 54) makes multiple references to how activists no longer believed in the idea of social transformation through mass political mobilization, critiquing, "A theory of change where change occurs through the accumulation of people and size becomes the key factor in bringing about the revolutionary moment." And Razsa's interlocutors saw things from a similar point of view, putting aside "utopian ends and centralized authority of any kind" to embrace "forms of direct action that modeled change 'here and now'" (2015, 2). Maeckelbergh and Razsa's interlocutors were self-described anarchists who sought to distance themselves from mass mobilization. My MST interlocutors, by contrast, were members of a Marxist movement whose history, foundation, and continuing leadership training programs focus on the construction of an oppositional class character and the necessity for revolution.

Brava Gente, a book-length interview of João Pedro Stédile, the MST's most well-known national leader, conducted by Bernardo Mançano Fernandes, a professor of geography at Paulista State University (UNESP), details the MST's theoretical influences: Lenin, Marx, Engels, Mao Tse-Tung, Rosa Luxemburg, Fidel Castro, and Che Guevara (Stédile and Fernandes

1999, 59–62). On the one hand, the MST is a mass movement indexed by a flag, a hymn, and tight organizational structure, the whole bound together by a forceful collective identity. On the other, it is a set of autonomous rural communities in which people very much live their own lives. And it is partly due to this unique structure that counter-utopian practices have come to emerge within the MST: the creative gestures and embodied actions of MST members contest what it means to be landless from *within* a utopian framework. Such practices occur with reference to utopia, not despite it, pointing to the productive contradictions in play. The MST is a movement that insists its goal is to create a new society and overthrow neoliberalism but understands that the land it occupies must have ready access to urban markets and economic opportunities—a movement that once sought to oblige all its members to farm in a fully collectivized model and indeed still harbors visions of rural industrialization programs and yet will not force its members to produce in the manner it thinks best. When I asked MST members about the nature of their struggle, our conversations never ceased to surprise me. People spoke about their duty to their children, their desire to express themselves creatively, and the joy in working autonomously on a piece of land. Despite outward rhetoric, transformation, for these MST members, was not to be found in the notion of "cutting the wire," the moment in which everything would somehow magically shift from one state to another. But they did not fully disavow the dream of another kind of society, being the proponents of a tangible agrarian reform brought about in small spaces. Transformation in the MST occurs over decades and is constituted by how members make and negotiate an ongoing commitment to social justice. Focusing on transformation at a temporal as opposed to numerical scale, we can grasp how the creative gestures of small-scale community actions continually intervene to shape wider networks and, by extension, the forms through which future struggles can occur. This book analyzes transformation through the temporalities of the promised and the perceptible, illuminating how the struggle for social justice inscribes in the now a future as yet uninscribed and how a desire to remake a movement is also a decision to remake the world.

Positionality and Methods

My first encounter with the MST was a visit to an MST settlement near the Santa Catarina coastal town of Água Branca, arranged for me by Bernadete. On a sunny afternoon, I met Kleber, and we had a conversation about who I was, what I was hoping to do, and the possibility of spending some time in the settlement. Why the south of Brazil? The MST had originated in the south, and the first occupations took place in Rio Grande do Sul, the state on Santa Catarina's southern border. The movement formally came into being in Paraná, the state immediately to the north, and because of this proximity, many of the MST's leaders were from Santa Catarina. My initial aim was to work with the MST's culture sector, and Kleber mentioned that many cultural activities were ongoing in the south. I also chose the south because I wanted to be able to travel to various MST locations and understand the differences among encampments, settlements, and protests in the city. Santa Catarina is one of the smaller Brazilian states, and my plan was to buy a cheap car and travel around to gain various perspectives from within the state. This worked out to some extent. It's a thirteen-hour drive from the state capital, Florianópolis, where the MST state leadership is based, to the MST settlement Conquista na Fronteira in the city of Dionísio Cerqueira on the border with Argentina. These long drives became an intrinsic part of my fieldwork even as I became more and more settled within the coastal part of the state and the Planalto Norte, on the border with Paraná.

When I began fieldwork in 2007, my first objective was to attend the 2007 state meeting. Taking language classes at UFSC, I met Lyvia Rodrigues, who was involved with the Programa Nacional de Educação na Reforma Agrária (PRONERA). Lyvia mentioned me to Sonia, the state leader for education, and Sonia invited me to the state meeting in Fraiburgo. At that state meeting, I met Kleber again, and seeing I was on my own, he introduced me to the Alzemiro de Oliveira brigade. In this group of people, around eighty of who had traveled to the state meeting, I got to know André, a regional leader of the frente de massa sector—the most committed militants who run the movement on the ground—André's children, and Luizinho, a regional leader of the education sector. All of them lived in the northern settlement near the small town of Bom Jardim, and as time went on, this settlement became my main base.

Even though from the beginning I was warmly welcomed, questions of trust were important, and it took a long time for MST members to feel comfortable enough to speak openly. I was aware of researchers being accompanied by research assistants assigned to them by MST leadership at either the national or the state level. And it became clear through speaking to MST members, especially in encampments, that they had respect, sometimes bordering on apprehension, for the leaders in general and especially the frente de massa *militantes*, who appeared periodically in the camps to check everything was going smoothly. As time passed, I understood that sometimes people were reticent to speak out of turn because they were worried I would pass what they said on to the leaders. I became aware of trying to construct a neutrality in this sense, and part of that meant conducting my research with a certain independence from the state leadership based in Florianópolis. However, I wasn't always successful in being seen as a neutral presence. How could I have been? I was a doctoral researcher from an elite university in the global north, holding a United Kingdom passport with freedom of movement. In addition, I owned a car and was being paid a stipend, its financial weight further amplified by its conversion to Brazilian reais. Eventually, principally through living with Vera and her sister Lúcia, I became a sort of adopted member of the Fernandes de Castro family, an extended network that was present in the northern settlement near Bom Jardim.

I became more accepted, and people grew accustomed to seeing me around. Over time, we built trust. After a year had passed, people began to speak about tensions and problems. Many people articulated views about the movement. Some were positive, and some were critical. As I finished this first period of fieldwork, a serious confrontation occurred between the state leadership and the settlement where I was living. Due to the fact that I had a car and could travel to the secretariat in the state capital, I was asked to mediate. Throughout this crisis, I was clear that my ethical position was premised foremost on a belonging embedded within the family and friendship networks of the Planalto region. I will explore the reasons for this later in the book, but this situation would take years to resolve and sparked an ethnographic engagement that continues to the present day.

Over so many years, I have been privileged to experience many aspects of movement life. I have been invited into personal contexts, such as private conversations, people's homes, family meals, reunions, and celebrations. I have attended more formal encounters, such as rehearsed and choreographed movement performances, meetings, state events, protests and collaborative activities with other social movements. My research occurred in the state capital, Florianópolis, and its movement secretariat; the coast near the town of Água Branca; the Planalto, near the cities of Bom Jardim, Canoinhas, and Jaraguá do Sul; the interior of the state near the city of Fraiburgo; the *vale*, a series of towns founded by German immigrants near Blumenau; and beyond into the states of Paraná and São Paulo. It encompassed various settlements, principally what I refer to as the northern settlement, as well as the coastal settlement but also the settlement of Garuva and two encampments, which I refer to as Vitória and Novo Horizonte. The movement was my focus, and I settled happily into the rhythm of members' lives, going to local markets and community centers as well as more institutional spaces— for example, local union offices, councillors' offices, banks, and mayoral offices. I sought to gain an embodied sense of the movement through taking part in activities like demonstrations, chants, and solidarity events in the city as well as more rural activities like planting, digging, slaughtering, and sipping chimarrão (a tea made from erva maté). My first phase of fieldwork ended in April 2009, just as the confrontation with the state leadership to which I referred was playing out, and the world of which I had been such an intimate part seemed to be crumbling down.

In many ways, it was the worst time to leave, but over the ensuing years, I saw things change. From 2012 to 2021, I came to understand that what made me want to work with the MST in the first place was still present and had actually become stronger over the intervening period while I was in contact with the families of the Planalto. The new social movements scholarship and the ensuing work on movements like alter-globalization sought to understand anew how people come together to seek change, and being a part of such a longitudinal process has allowed me to document the incremental and yet radical trajectories that people like Vera and Clarice embody. An attendance to specificity of context and place of course amplifies the possibilities of what we can do as social scientists by deconstructing deterministic models, but articulating such considerations from within this extended temporal frame offers a unique perspective. Having been part of the discussions and the life of the MST since 2007, it is inconceivable to construct an analysis that solely focuses on the *massa*, the masses, and following Arturo Escobar (1992), I articulate a vital but marginal reality of social mobilization: for many MST members, the struggle over material conditions is secondary to struggles over meaning regarding how the world will change and what kind of MST will inhabit that world.

Structure of the Book

The temporal dimension of this story required a long-term ethnographic commitment. It has also prompted a different kind of ethnographic writing. The book is broadly divided into four scenes. The first scene, entitled "Promise," concerns the early stages of the MST and the founding tenets laid down at the Cascavel meeting in 1984 that underpinned the movement's rapid expansion across Brazil. Understandings of participation, time, and labor were established in this period, and I discuss how the promise of agrarian reform was structured by a utopian politics that has bestowed a legacy for today's movement and its ongoing struggle. The second scene, entitled "Contradictions," shifts the book's perspective to how the lived experience of MST members interprets and contests these abstract tenets. I focus on the question of productivity in the context of a settlement and concepts of time and space in the encampment to foreground the notion of counter-utopian practice. The narrative then moves to Vera's struggle for her land and family, pointing to dimensions of hierarchy and institutionalization that threaten to overwhelm her commitment to the cause. The third scene, entitled "Expression, Creative Gesture," examines the significance of artistic and performative interventions within my analysis of the counter-utopian. I suggest that the MST's mística has come to acquire a recognizable form, and I contrast this with how MST members are rethinking subjective expression through embodied practice. Performance, the body, and a repurposing of occupation as direct-action tactic call into question long-held conventions and normative social orders that generate a productive tension with broader organizational movement structures. The book's fourth scene is located in schemes of transformation and details how such tensions work to remake the movement from within. Through community spaces and counter-utopian practices, linking episodes from 2007 to 2021, the narrative presents a victory of sorts, a pause, and an understanding of transformation.

These four scenes are divided into sections, which are shorter than conventional chapters. Drawing on ethnography conducted over the past fifteen years, these sections trace the ebb and flow of life in the movement: people pass from this world; families grow; children are born. I chose to use an achronological order to reinforce a conviction that I express in the book regarding how the future is impossible to know and yet extant in the present: fragments emerge throughout the narrative in unexpected moments; people appear momentarily and make their presence felt through a gesture that registers as a lasting expressive intervention. The narrative is punctuated in this manner by *pausas*, which create deliberate exits from linearity. I ask the readers to allow themselves a sense of freedom in reading. As convention dictates, however, I begin at the beginning.

SCENE I—PROMISE

Utopia lies on the horizon. When I draw nearer by two steps, it is two steps further beyond. If I walk ten steps toward it, the horizon slips ten steps further away. No matter how far I walk, I will never reach it. What, then, is the purpose of utopia? For exactly this: to make us walk.

FERNANDO BIRRI[1]

Pausa

The very first member of the MST I met was Kleber. In the coastal settlement near Água Branca, I also got to know his wife, Marcia, and their daughter, Tais. One time, Tais told me a little of her experience as a child, moving from encampment to encampment. "It was in 1994. We ended up negotiating and three or four families came with us. Our family, Seu Salvador and his family, and another family that ended up not staying. You know, some people over time, they left. So when we started out, like encamped, it was really hard. We went hungry, it was cold, we lived in fear. There were many children around. We had really full-on confrontations with the police and those confrontations really left a mark on me. Because I was still a child, I only have fragmented memories of this. But I can't get away from them, it's like they're always with me."

I asked if she was talking about violence. She said, "You know I carried it with me so much so that the first time I left the *acampamento* to stay with an aunt in Barra Velha and there was a policeman outside her house, like just a normal cop doing his rounds, when I saw him, I had like a panic attack and I fainted. It took me a long time to live without fear, to become more used to the presence of the police because of the repression that I saw . . . my parents, my neighbors, people I knew. I was four or five years old. These things mark you—you wake up, there are policemen in the acampamento destroying everything, bringing down the *barracas*, ripping the polythene . . . the mothers running, carrying the children into the forest. You're isolated, in a place far from the city and so they can do what they want; they can't be held to account."

This conversation occurred early on in my fieldwork, and I wasn't really prepared. As an anthropology student, I had been taught to detach myself and analyze everything as data. Tais continued: "Ah! In amongst the policemen, there were always the landowner's men, there to beat people up. They didn't hold back, they didn't respect children, didn't respect anyone. One morning we woke up, encircled by policemen and the men were dragged out by their hair before being beaten up in front of the women and children. They threw tear gas grenades amongst our tents. They placed the women separate from the men in a tent for fifteen days. They gave the women and children only one meal a day. Many had to go to hospital because of malnutrition. It was brutal."

We were sitting outside the house in the coastal settlement where Tais lived with her mother and father. It had been designed in conjunction with the Federal University of Santa Catarina (UFSC) architecture department, and the pretty houses were set among flowers and rustic decorations. Kleber had commented to me at one point how the settlement confused people: "They come expecting to see war, but it's more like a holiday camp!" He laughed. It wasn't easy to imagine the military police mobilized with local thugs to destroy and burn. Tais was lost in her thoughts. I didn't know how to respond, so I echoed her last words. *The brutality.* She became matter-of-fact: "So, these are things that end up leaving their mark. Even today, I still feel a little bit of difficulty in dealing with this because like it or not, it was very painful. This thing of going without. I drank milk for the first time when I was seven, like I didn't know what it was, I didn't even know what milk was! We ate rice and beans when it came in the *cesta básica*, the basic food basket distributed to encampments by INCRA [National Institute for Colonization and Agrarian Reform]. Meat was very rare." She smiled. "I value what we have now."

"Of course," I responded.

"No, I value what we have now because we used to starve. Sometimes I laugh, like, today I really want to eat sweets."

"Like, to compensate?"

"Yes, sometimes we even joke, 'Let me eat! When I was a child, I went without, so let me at it now!' It's kind of sad, but at the same time, it's what I have, I can't let it go because I think it was a learning experience for me as a person. It contributed a lot to who I am today. So yeah. No regrets."

1

Landlessness

> We came from that history, from the land. It was
> instilled in us, domination and violence.
>
> LÚCIA[1]

L andlessness in Brazil, and its corollary, the huge concentration of
landholdings in the hands of the few, can be historically contextualized by three principal factors: a system of land distribution that
originated in colonial Brazil; a society that was until 1888 economically dependent on enslaved peoples; and the emphasis that Brazil has placed, first
as a colony and then later as an independent state, on the export value of
specific agricultural commodities.

In the early 1530s, the Portuguese crown was faced with how to possess,
administer, and profit from the newly "discovered" Terra de Santa Cruz (the
Land of the Holy Cross), the territory that would later come to be called
Brazil. Portugal did not have the resources or capital to effectively lay claim
to this land, whose expanse was beyond comprehension: demarcated by the
Treaty of Tordesillas, which divided Portuguese land from that claimed by
the Spanish crown, this so-called new world expanded inward from the east
coast of Latin America to a distant meridian in the continent's interior, located 370 leagues west of the Cape Verde islands. Driven by the impulse to
extract value from this vast area, the Portuguese crown decided to delegate
the process of ownership and exploitation by granting fifteen captaincies—
administrative divisions and hereditary fiefs—to private individuals mainly
drawn from the royal court (De Carvalho 2015). The captaincies comprised
tracts of land, or *sesmarias*, measuring roughly 175 miles from north to south,
and they were granted on the basis of usufruct: ownership resided with the
crown while right of use was granted to captain generals, a right that would
be forfeited if the captaincy was not profitably exploited (see Burns 1970;
Skidmore 2010). In this manner, the Portuguese crown laid claim to new

land, created a buffer against Spanish expansion, and retained the ultimate ownership of the land, all while outsourcing the cost and risks of the process to individuals given license to operate in any matter they saw fit (Dean 1971). Perhaps unsurprisingly, the captaincies foundered without state support and by 1549 had been subsumed into a new system, the Governorate General of Brazil. This reestablished direct royal authority over land and created the position of governor general, to whom the captain generals were nominally supposed to answer. Land, however, continued to be administered in a similar manner. The only captaincy that managed to turn a profit was that of Duarte Coelho Pereira in Pernambuco, which became legally exempted from the control of the new governor general (Dutra 1973). The fact that Duarte Coelho Pereira had made money though the cultivation and export of sugarcane gives an early insight into the production model that was envisaged more generally for the new colony.

The pattern of large landholdings and monoculture, the cultivation of a single crop in a given area, was maintained throughout Brazil's colonial period, from the 1621 partition of the Governorate General of Brazil into two colonies, the State of Brazil and the State of Maranhão, to the elevation of the State of Brazil to a viceroyalty in 1763, and to the eventual creation of the United Kingdom of Portugal, Brazil, and the Algarves in 1815, which put in motion the events that would lead to Brazil's independence in 1822. Despite the similarities in land usage in this colonial period and the present day, however, there are other factors that have shaped today's concentrations of landholdings in the hands of the few. As the Brazilian sociologist José de Souza Martins highlights, it would be a mistake to assume that the colonial system, based for three centuries on the granting of sesmarias, was the only important factor (2000).

In 1822, Brazil declared independence from Portugal, and, given the impossibility of another state's monarch continuing to grant land on the basis of right of use, this constitutional shift necessitated new policies. From 1822 onward, the land-grant system was suspended, but there was no accompanying process of agrarian reform similar to those being initiated in other former Latin American colonies. In Mexico, for example, through the Ley Lerdo of 1856, the vast majority of the property of the Catholic Church was confiscated by a liberal government (Bethell 1991), but in Brazil, the large estates continued to exist, made possible by a separate legacy of Portuguese colonial administration: the continuing use of enslaved labor. Since the earliest expeditions from the captaincy of São Vicente, explorers who became known as *bandeirantes* sought to acquire wealth, land, and prestige through the enslavement of Brazil's Indigenous population (Langfur 2006; Schwartz

1978). The captaincy of São Vicente, later renamed São Paulo after the city of São Paulo became its capital in 1681, was the base for these expeditions and resulted in a huge territorial expansion of the São Paulo state west of the meridian established by the Treaty of Tordesillas. These expeditions led to the creation of an economy that, along with Pernambuco, made a profit due to mineral exploitation and the trading of enslaved peoples between this captaincy and others in need of labor (Metcalf 2005).

Bandeirantes like Antônio Raposo Tavares conducted large-scale raids and sold the Indigenous people they enslaved to the *fazendas*, or plantations, of the Northeast. In this early colonial period, enslaved Indigenous people were crucial to the exploitation of the huge tracts of land made available by the Portuguese crown (Monteiro 2018). As the bandeirantes' focus shifted to the exploitation of mineral wealth, incentivized by the Portuguese crown's politics of the eighteenth century, the plantations instead came to rely on the Atlantic slave trade. Leslie Bethell states that more than two million people were transported from Africa to Brazil between 1800 and 1854, with three-quarters of a million of this total transported during the 1830s and 1840s (2018, 114). Although Brazil's sovereignty was established in 1822, the continuation and indeed acceleration of structures of labor that had been in place since the sixteenth century ensured the continued existence of the landed estates focused on monoculture production for export. Sugarcane was the first commodity to be exported in large quantities, and the success of this financial model provided the template for the subsequent cultivation and export of tobacco, cotton, rubber, and coffee. Land was important, but labor was key: Martins comments that the land grant in and of itself "was merely a secondary factor in the establishment of the large landholdings system" (2002, 304) as without preexisting notions of how to exploit labor in the production of a monoculture for export, the ownership of large landholdings may have diversified and been reformed.

Efforts to rationalize the administration of land in Brazil culminated in the Land Law of 1850, whereby the Brazilian state ceded ownership of land and granted full ownership and property rights to the purchaser. For the first time, land became a commodity: it could be purchased either from a private individual or from the state and thus traded, loaned, or offered as collateral. However, structural inequalities in gaining access to land were built into the new legislation's apparatus. Boaventura Leite describes how the first land law "effectively excluded non-Brazilian, non-white populations in an attempt to distribute public lands to 'Brazilians' and 'Foreigners' (European immigrants). This law inaugurated one of the most effective mechanisms for territorial expropriation: the law denied Africans and their descendants full Brazilian citizenship by placing them in the special liminal category of 'libertos' (Free Africans and their descendants), which under the law gave them only limited rights" (2015, 1231). In this manner, ownership become possible for some, but impractical in real terms for most; financial and racial barriers ensured that it would remain the preserve of a select few. Lígia Os-ório Silva's classic account of the 1850 land law, *Terras devolutas e latifúndio* (1996), demonstrates how powerful landowners, who in many cases were also lawmakers, were working to adjust the details of the coming bill to render it more favorable to their interests even before the law was formulated. The legislation's function was to envisage the fast-approaching reality of a society without enslavement, and intense lobbying efforts ensured that the law not only shifted ownership of land from the state to private individuals but also transferred the responsibility for sourcing the labor to work this land in the other direction. In other words, whereas private individuals such as the captain generals had previously worked state land and were obliged to fund the costs of acquiring labor themselves, under these new conditions—and signaling a shift to the modern—private individuals would now own valuable assets in theoretical perpetuity, and the state would shoulder the cost of finding people to work the plantations (Borges 1997).

Osório Silva (1996) details how, beyond restricting access to the purchase of land, the new law also sought to lock in preexisting favorable conditions for the accumulation of large properties. This was accomplished through repeated attempts to sidestep any transparent fiscal and legal system of redress regarding abuses of land use. When it became clear that zero oversight was not an option, the law was drafted so as to include a strategic ambiguity regarding how land could be used and what kind of measures could be applied to those owners careless enough to suffer sanction. Supposedly the law's universal provisions detailed various infringements by which land could be expropriated: "expulsions, removals, enclosures, the registering of 'vacant' lands, forced and arbitrary divisions of community and the seizure of lands for failure to pay taxes" (Boaventura Leite 2015, 1231). But through the power and weight of vested landed interests, enough uncertainty was built into the legislation so as to exempt landowners from any kind of state accountability, including a near total lack of taxation.[2]

Brazil was the last nation in the Americas to abolish slavery, in 1888, and from the perspective of the landowners, abolition created a critical labor shortage. The Brazilian state sought to address this, and thereby ensure the continuing existence of the land-use model, by initiating immigration programs targeted at European countries and later Japan. From 1877 to 1903, almost two million immigrants arrived at an average rate of seventy-one thousand per year (Levy 1974, 51). The Brazilian state had fulfilled its obligation to provide labor as envisaged by the legislation a generation earlier. Most of these Italian, German, Polish, and Ukrainian *colonos*, as they became known, were placed in estates in the state of São Paulo and farther south in Paraná, Santa Catarina, and Rio Grande do Sul. Moving to this system, in which immigrant laborers were held in quasi-servitude through debt, did not in any way accelerate land reform, and this new model of labor failed to address the inequality of access to land. In the three southern states, Paraná, Santa Catarina, and Rio Grande do Sul, a small family farming culture of colonos was beginning to take root despite all obstacles, and some of these immigrant families did manage to strike deals with landowners, often for their children's benefit rather than their own, in exchange for a lifetime of labor.

The Great Depression brought about the fall of the Old Republic of 1889 to 1930 and led to the ascension of Getúlio Vargas, a populist politician who served as president from 1930 to 1945 and from 1951 to 1954, with a period as dictator from 1937 to 1945. Vargas, despite his aims to modernize and industrialize Brazil, did little to address the concentration of landownership. Notably, he exempted rural workers from his expansion of labor regulations, which set the working day for commercial and industrial workers at eight hours, established a national minimum wage, and guaranteed pensions and paid vacation. Thus, agricultural workers were denied rights while other workers were gaining them.

Vargas's second period as president was characterized by increasing pressure around the notion of agrarian reform. There had been previous conflicts centered on the question of access to land, including the bloody massacre of Antonio Conselheiro and his followers at Canudos, Bahia, in 1897 and the four-year-long Guerra do Contestado in Santa Catarina, but the frequency and thematic similarities of fresh conflicts in the 1950s, noted below, were a direct threat to oligarchic landholdings. Martins (1994) describes how in this period a peasant struggle began to coalesce, a situation that placed landless peoples directly into conflict with landowners but also, because of a perceived communist infiltration of the land activists, placed landless people in confrontation with the Brazilian armed forces (Ribeiro 2010). The 1950s saw a series of conflicts between peasants and landowners in Porecatu (1950–51) and Francisco Beltrão (1957) in Paraná; in Santa Fé do Sul in São Paulo (1959–60); in Vitória de Santo Antão in Pernambuco (1955); and in Trombas and Formoso in the north of Goiás between 1955 and 1956, in which the military carried out violent repression as it had done in Canudos and Northern Santa Catarina decades earlier (Prieto 2017).

The situation came to a head in 1964, when left-wing president João Goulart proposed a series of reforms that for the first time would finally include the agricultural sector (Robles 2018). Among other socialist measures, Goulart proposed expropriating nonproductive properties larger than six hundred hectares for general redistribution. This proved to be a defining moment, and the Brazilian army staged a military coup, having gained explicit prior approval from foreign governments (Netto 2014). The resulting military dictatorship, which lasted from 1964 to 1985, immediately quashed any immediate possibility of reform. Instead, the dictatorship's strategy focused on transporting landless peoples to the Amazon in the remote north of Brazil, hoping to divert open conflict from more visible areas of the country while also benefiting by conducting a strategic occupation of the country's interior and creating "a bulwark against any possible foreign invasion" (Meszaros 2000b, 522–23).

Some of the MST's earliest members were landless people returning from these failed internal migration programs, and the movement's nascent acts of mobilization occurred in the dictatorship's latter period, a phase that was characterized by a gradual *abertura*, an opening of political possibilities. However, the advent of free elections in 1985 and a return to democracy did not presage any substantial reform of land, and more recent political climates have only reinforced the concentration of huge landholdings in the hands of the few. Government agencies such as the Brazilian Agricultural Research Corporation (Empresa Brasileira de Pesquisa Agropecuária, or EMBRAPA), which were founded under the dictatorship with a remit to make the agriculture sector more productive, signaled the military government's intentions to move Brazil toward more intensive farming models, and the administrations of José Sarney and, importantly, Fernando Henrique Cardoso favored large agroindustrial estates over family farms: Petras and Veltmeyer observe that during the 1990s, the Brazilian government's strategy regarding free-market farm policies led to the displacement of over 1 million peasant families (2002, 290). As a result, Sauer and Leite's data indicates that in 2005, there were 3.1 million families considered "landless people" (2012, 877) in Brazil.

The long struggle for agrarian reform in Brazil is now contextualized by the neoliberal market reforms of the 1990s: the loosening of regulations in the agricultural sector; the closing of government agencies and removal of the subsidies they had provided to small holders; and new technologies designed for large-scale production, such as satellite-guided harvesters and new agrochemicals and seeds (Welch 2006). Brazil's agribusiness sector has benefited and grown in this climate, and it gains a political significance from the fact that it forms an important part of the country's wider economy. Measured in US dollars, the value of Brazil's agriculture—including crops and livestock—grew by an average of 8 percent annually from 2000 to 2020. And the revenues from such growth are immense: the University of São Paulo's Center for Advanced Studies on Applied Economics estimates that Brazil's agriculture and food sector accounts for 29 percent of the country's GDP, valued at $1.8 trillion in 2021 (Valdes 2022). As such, successive Brazilian governments, including the left-wing Workers' Party (Partido dos Trabalhadores, or PT) administrations of Luiz Inácio Lula da Silva (2003–10 and 2023–ongoing) and Dilma Rousseff (2011–16), have counted on the sector's aggressive monocropping and intensive high-technology farming methods—all of which require large estates—for a positive balance of payments. Where once Lula made a public appearance wearing an MST baseball cap, Lula and subsequently Dilma have made concessions to what has become a powerful lobby group. As Sergio Sauer notes, politicians who support the agribusiness lobby have been included in PT cabinets, such as agribusiness insider Katia Abreu, the former head of the influential Brazilian Confederation of Agriculture and Livestock. Such arrangements ensured the temporary support of the rural caucus for the PT's legislative agenda but, as Sauer concludes, "prevented government action on land policies from producing more significant advances . . . and was critical in neutralizing and derailing structural land policies such as the expansion of expropriations for land reform" (2019, 118). In these hostile conditions—where unscrupulous landowners employ hired gunmen to guard unproductive land, the legal system is hampered by restrictive bureaucracy, and the legacy of slavery underpins pervasive landlessness—those seeking to redistribute land have few options. It is in this situation that the MST carries out strategic direct action.

The MST focuses principally on the occupation of land through encampment. In this process, landless people from a local area are recruited and organized by members of an MST sector called the Frente de Massa. Having thus joined the movement in an initial sense, people are directed to, or sometimes taken to, a piece of land that state-level MST leadership has identified as having potential for expropriation. MST occupations occur on both publicly and privately owned lands, and the encampment seeks to take advantage of a legally plural situation similar to that which landowners have exploited since the 1850 land law. In civil law, occupying private or government property can be construed as an illegal act, as it violates directives surrounding the right to private property and therefore constitutes trespass. Brazilian Civil Code Article 1.228 states that "the owner has the right to use, enjoy and dispose of his/her property, and the right to reclaim it from the power of anyone who has claimed it or possessed it unfairly. Actions that cause discomfort or discommode the owner of a property, or are motivated by the harmful intentions, are prohibited." However, under constitutional law, the MST argues that the encampment process is legally justified. Article 5, XXIII of the 1988 Brazilian constitution requires that land serve a "social function," and Article 184 specifies that if this function is not met, the government is required to "expropriate for the purpose of agrarian reform, rural property that is not performing its social function." A key detail of Article 186 is that the criteria for "social function" must be fulfilled in terms of "rational and adequate use," "adequate use of available natural resources and preservation of the environment," "compliance with the provisions which regulate labor relations," and "a use of land which favors the well-being of the owners and workers."

In this manner, one of the MST's principal justifications for establishing an encampment is based on what constitutes "rational and adequate use." Many MST occupations call attention to how large estates are often vastly underutilized, thereby contrasting land that is not being put to productive use with the impoverishment of local communities. Another important justification is a property's legal standing. According to INCRA (2015, 51), 729 individuals or corporate entities that own rural property in Brazil owe the state more than R$50 million each. In total, this group owes approximately R$200 billion, and their properties amount to enough land to settle 214,827 families—almost twice the number of families encamped waiting for land reform. When landowners have defaulted on government taxes and duties, a case can be made to appropriate.

Through establishing encampments on such estates, the movement aims to demonstrate how landless families can become successful small holders with access to basic conditions of housing and an income if land is made available for them to farm. As such there is an inherent emphasis on notions of productivity, and the MST's discourse on making use of land has echoes of John Locke's "Second Treatise of Government" ([1690] 2016), in which Locke argues that when man "hath mixed his labour with land" (27), that land may become his property. Such a precept anchors the MST's direct-action tactics through a clear assertion of the illegitimacy of owning land if that land is not put to use. In the MST, stories of landowners placing a pair of horses on a thousand-hectare estate are often recounted, and what constitutes productivity is a common topic of conversation. A second justification focuses on the constitutional requirement for landowners to preserve the environment. The movement encourages families to produce and become self-sufficient, but it encourages them to do so in what it terms an agroecological manner, eschewing pesticides, monoculture, and intensive farming methods. In this way, the MST offers a practical alternative to the models of Brazil's agribusiness sector that use genetically modified crops and high levels of pesticides, arguing that in the long term such practices are not sustainable, and thus such estates are liable for expropriation. Equally, the clause that specifies the well-being of both owners and workers opens up a clear pathway to occupy an estate if workers are, for example, being paid less than a minimum wage or the owner is not fulfilling other legal criteria surrounding employment conditions.

These openings and justifications for occupation are not a certain route to expropriation; rather, they are tactical maneuvers and opening gambits within a complex legal situation. Meszaros has noted that although the constitution makes clear the conditions under which the state can expropriate land for the purposes of agrarian reform, it does so through "an elaborate legal, administrative, economic and social web mediated by judges, administrative agencies [INCRA] and politicians" (2007, 8). Simply put, the constitution creates a terrain of possibility, but the onus is very much on individuals, groups, and lawmakers to explore how individual situations might be realized in practice. Landowners have, of course, been experimenting with this legal flexibility since the era of the captaincies: in Brazil, the total area of land that is suspected of having been falsely claimed and subsequently registered is approximately one hundred million hectares, four times the landmass of the United Kingdom.[3] And it is within this situation of legal ambiguity that an MST occupation seeks to make an incursion.

Once MST *acampados* (the term that the movement uses to describe people who are encamped) are established on the land, INCRA, the government department responsible for agrarian reform, is informed, and a *vistoria*, or evaluation, takes place to determine whether the land meets the criteria for expropriation. The process of occupation can be lengthy: I knew of encampments that lasted for the relatively short period of eighteen months as well as encampments that had taken eight years to be approved in Santa Catarina. If a case can be successfully made, land is devolved to the encamped families, an *assentamento* (settlement) is established, and families are given right of use (not ownership) to roughly ten ha (twenty-five acres) each. Devolving land is, however, just the beginning of the MST's commitment to landless people. Once the land has been won, those awarded plots are termed *assentados*, and it becomes a priority to provide the nascent community with access to education, for which movement actors lobby in local political circles. MST children may go to local municipal schools, or, if the settlement is large enough, a school may be constructed on the settlement itself with public money. Many different models exist at local levels: in the case of a settlement in Bom Jardim, the municipality constructed a high school focused on agronomy within the settlement's boundaries, but unlike other cases, the MST does not have a direct role in its governance. However, the school has an excellent reputation, and many children from the wider community attend alongside MST children. In this way, the movement attempts to fulfill a program of agrarian reform that goes beyond the mere devolution of land, recognizing that social inequalities are also rooted in a wider lack of access to schools and learning.

In undertaking such actions, the MST has made many enemies, not only in the countryside in which, as a rural movement, its land occupations are focused but also in the city, where its direct occupation tactics, such as roadblocks and occupations of federal government offices, seek to cause disruption. In the countryside, during the acampamento (encampment) phase, MST members are often threatened by landowners, hired gunmen, or police in efforts to force an eviction. If an eviction is judicially ordered, the movement usually organizes a reoccupation, but evictions vary, from families leaving peacefully on an appointed date to police or paramilitary forces arriving unexpectedly, clearing the encampment, burning possessions and crops, and leaving families with nothing. Historically, such violence has been common, and it continues today: according to the Comissão Pastoral da Terra (Pastoral Land Commission, or CPT), there were 976 murders of rural activists between 1985 and 1996 (Hammond 1999, 476), and more widely, the NGO Global Witness documented 753 killings between 2010 and 2015 relating to conflicts over land.[4] MST members sometimes live and work in extremely dangerous circumstances, and as the rural locations in which they are based are distant from any kind of oversight, many incidents are unreported or actively suppressed.

The MST coalesced at a very specific time and place, and its historical trajectory helps explain how the movement came to be so extensive in such a short space of time. The MST emerged at a particular confluence of events, contextualized by the smallholder farming culture that had taken root in the southern states and the fact that by the late 1950s there were already approximately 270,000 landless families in Rio Grande do Sul (Branford and Rocha 2002). The desire for agrarian reform was tangible but destined to be frustrated by the military coup of 1964. As the conditions of landless families became ever more precarious, their impoverishment drew the support of the local parish priests. The CPT had become more involved in people's struggles for land following the Second Vatican Council and the more general popularization of liberation theology, and certain elements within the

Catholic Church slowly became key allies for landless families in the struggle against the military government for agrarian reform, especially through the activity of Comunidades Eclesias de Base, Ecclesiastical Base Communities (CEBs). Indeed, before the coalescence of the MST, the CPT was already working with agrarian reform organizations like the Movimento dos Agricultores Sem Terra (MASTER) and the Movimento de Agricultores Sem Terra do Oeste do Paraná (MASTRO), the latter of which emerged in 1981 as a result of the construction of the Itaipu Dam.

Pressure was building, and key to the emergence of the movement that would become the MST at this juncture was the abertura, the relaxation of military government control that started to occur in the late 1970s. This period saw the first occupations by the nascent, as yet unnamed MST in 1979 in Rio Grande do Sul, with the assistance of Father Arnildo Fritzen, a local parish priest. More occupations followed, all employing the tactic of direct occupation, and in 1983 the governor of Rio Grande do Sul, Jair Soares, settled the families who had encamped by the roadside at a place that had come to be known as Encruzilhada Natalino. This victory was strategically important, and as it became clear that the tactic of direct occupation was proving effective against a weakened military government, more occupations took place. Finally, in January 1984 in Cascavel, Paraná, representatives from thirteen states met for three days to discuss the future of the still unnamed Landless Workers Movement.

Several important principles were established at this meeting, principles that Stédile has commented were "absolutely fundamental because they defined the conception of the movement" (Stédile and Fernandes 1999, 50). The meeting determined that the nascent movement should be autonomous, establishing independence from the church, political parties, and unions. The aims were defined as bringing about a more just society and an end to capitalism through the means of agrarian reform. As Branford and Rocha comment, the vision was "unashamedly utopian" (2002, 24), envisaging the "development of a new man and new woman" (25). To achieve this, the delegates argued, the movement should expand beyond the three southern states—Rio Grande do Sul, Santa Catarina, and Paraná—that had traditionally remained somewhat distant from the rest of the country.[5] Such expansion placed emphasis on organization, leadership, and tactical direction together with the creation of a collective identity. Item six of the meeting's "Practical Principles" outlines the justifications and motivations for this policy and details how "to expand the movement in municipalities and regions where it is not yet organized" (Debiasi 2022, 184). Following the MST's first National Congress in 1985, approximately twenty-five militants were dispatched "from the South and Southeast regions to other regions of the country, particularly the Brazilian Northeast, with the intention of structuring the MST on the basis of the organizational and productive experience developed in the South" (184–85). Many of these militants were from Santa Catarina, and in these early years the MST grew exponentially, expanding into faraway states, oriented by notions established at the outset. These militants were carefully chosen, and Debiasi details how the personal experiences of the militants sent to the Northeast were decisive in the structuring of the MST in a unitary manner.

Another key decision at Cascavel was the movement's name. Already known in media coverage as *o movimento sem terra*, the landless movement, delegates discussed opting for the Movement for Agrarian Reform, which was seen as less pejorative. In the end, however, class became the most important factor. As Stédile comments, "At the same time, we made a reflection in the sense that we should come back to an identity based on class. We are workers, we have a society with different classes, and we belong to one of them" (1999, 47). Delegates stuck with the name by which they had come to be known but added *trabalhadores rurais*, rural workers, to it. This change was significant. In the following year, the first MST National Congress built on the Cascavel meeting in clarifying and expanding the principle that land should be owned by those who work it. Work and labor became important foundational concepts and, in many senses, the legitimation for direct action and occupation. Agrarian reform came to be seen as dependent on work, and productivity entered a constellation of concepts that would structure the movement's future.

The movement's composition was also hotly debated. Reflecting on the role of women in the MST, Stédile comments how one of the ways in which the MST stood in contrast to the trade union movement was that trade union meetings were generally men only. Stédile envisaged the future MST as including the whole family—"the elderly, women and children"— and believed that this would become a strength: "because men, besides being sexist, are conservative and individualistic" (Stédile and Fernandes 1999, 32). The vast majority of delegates at Cascavel were men, and giving "equal rights to all members of the family" (Branford and Rocha 2002, 23) was considered progressive. A founding principle had been established: the MST unfolded around the notion of the family at its core, and importantly, a woman's rights were premised on her belonging to that unit.

Moving so quickly from a small organization in the south of Brazil to a nationwide phenomenon—what MST leaders refer to as the process of "massification"—the grassroots organization that had characterized the earliest

MST encampments was obliged to rapidly expand outward. Stevphen Shukaitis, David Graeber, and Erika Biddle (2007) refer to the friction produced by debates about bridging ideal and material worlds as a process of "constituent imaginations," and the legacy of how the MST's founding members envisaged the movement is tangible in contested terrain of what it means to be *sem terra* and how, in what configuration of time and space, transformation can be achieved. Such friction has produced contradictions. Understanding how these arose requires examining the MST's goal of creating a new society and how this was envisioned to be achieved—ultimately, this demands an analysis of the movement's relationship to utopia.

Pausa

It was my last day in the Vitória encampment. I woke up in the *barraca* they kept for MST people passing through. I was grateful for the shelter of the black plastic sheeting, as northern Santa Catarina sometimes sees a dusting of winter snow. The previous night, we'd sat around a fire in the middle of the forest, desperate to keep warm, relishing eating the hot roasted pine nuts, *pinhões*, that fell from the Araucaria trees all around us. Our fire was the only point of light among upward of 150 shelters. All around it was silent and pitch black.

Freezing cold, I got out of bed, an old mattress laid on top of a rough frame made from branches still fresh with sap. Paulo, a new MST *militante* who lived in the coastal settlement with Kleber, and the camp coordinators wanted to introduce me to some acampados. There were three of them, men in their twenties and thirties. One was wearing a black overcoat, shorts, flip-flops, and a black beret set with a red five-pointed star. The other two were presented to me as Polish. One of them, Polaco, took me around. We went to another barraca. There was a middle-aged woman inside who looked at me with a stern expression.

"Come sit down and eat," she said. On the hard earth floor, there was a large kitchen dresser. The woman placed some meat on a chopping board and started slicing it.

"Polish sausage," Polaco commented. I knew people were going hungry in the camp, but I didn't know how to politely refuse. So I sat down and ate. They insisted I eat first and gave me a bag of pine nuts when I left.

Paulo came to collect me. He wanted to visit the school, a building made of salvaged bits of old wood. There were about thirty kids there, and I taught them some English. At one point, Paulo performed a call-and-response with the MST *palavras de ordem*. He shouted "MST," and the children crooked their elbows at ninety degrees and formed fists with their left hands while shouting *"Reforma agrária já"*—agrarian reform now—in response. The children seemed to enjoy it, and there were smiles as they sat back down to do their work. Paulo talked to the class about the symbolism of the colors of the MST flag. He said there was discussion about changing the color of the white people in the flag. He said it should change as this depiction of MST members had nothing to do with reality. I admired him for this.

The time came to leave. I was exhausted and overwhelmed by the harsh living conditions; it was the first time I had stayed overnight in an MST encampment. I packed up my knapsack and went out to my car. The kids from the school were playing around. I chatted with them about soccer. All their questions were related to where I was from and where I was going. They found it hard to believe that I had a car and asked me to open up the hood. They gathered round, looking at the engine; they knew much more about the various components than I did. After a while, I realized they didn't want us to leave. We were new, something different, and a distraction. As I backed up the car, I looked at the kids' expressions. It struck me that they had no way out. I could just get up and go.

2

Willed Transformation

> Examples of the mode of "willed social transformation"
> can be shifted, in their essence, to the mode of "technologi-
> cal transformation," where the technology need not be
> only a marvellous new energy source, or some industrial
> resource of that kind, but can be also a new set of laws, new
> abstract property relations, indeed precisely new *social
> machinery.*
>
> RAYMOND WILLIAMS

Marxist notions of transformation were rooted in a nineteenth-century political thinking that was rich with visions of utopia. Henrietta Moore, in her analysis of the "good life," divides these utopias into two categories: first, the fictional utopias, or scenarios that proposed an inversion of present-day evils, thereby making a critique of contemporary society, and second, the utopia as a new world, "to be designed and planned and lived out in this life" (1990, 14). Raymond Williams's essay "Utopia and Science Fiction" (1978) emphasizes how these two different modalities of utopia can be read through the distinction that Marx and Engels sought to make between "utopian" and "scientific" socialisms with the latter a necessary and inevitable outcome of class conflict and the former a daydreamer's hypothetical vision of the future, abstracted from the necessity of revolution. As *The Communist Manifesto* states of the daydreaming "utopians," "Hence, they reject all political, and especially all revolutionary, action; they wish to attain their ends by peaceful means, and endeavor, by small experiments, necessarily doomed to failure, and by the force of example, to pave the way for the new social Gospel" (Marx and Engels 2012, 74). In distancing themselves from the writings of Charles Fourier (1971), Étienne Cabet (1840), and Robert Owen (1991), Marx and Engels sought not only legitimacy but also the impetus and justification for the element of willed transformation that was fundamental to their project: revolution was to entail a practical outcome, one underpinned by the conscious efforts and sacrifices of those involved.

For Thomas More, writing *Utopia* in 1516, the very notion of utopian possibility was deliberately specious and contradictory, and he expressed this through the way he chose to name the imaginary island that is the subject of the book. The word *utopia* is a dual pun on the Greek *ou* and *topos*, which translate as "no place," but also on *eutopos*, which means "good or happy place." More signaled further contradictions by naming the island's principal river Anyder (anhydrous translates as "no water") while the reader is guided by a narrator, Raphael Hythloday, whose name translates as "well learned in nonsense" (Sargent 2016, 185). Contradiction was characteristic to More's exposition of utopia, and utopian politics, in the mode of willed transformation, bears this legacy in the paradox it presents.

As Fernando Birri comments, utopia is always on the horizon. As you move closer by two steps, it remains two steps further beyond, forever out of reach. This is the utopian subjunctive; the new world must always lie just beyond the ambit of possibility. For Birri, this is utopia's true purpose, to oblige us to continue our struggle toward that horizon as we strive toward a place forever out of reach. In this sense, utopia is not a destination. Rather, it is the motor of a project of willed transformation, creating both an impossible goal and the conditions of necessary sacrifice and unity under which people must strive toward the unachievable. Utopia must therefore always be understood as articulating a *subjunctive grammar* in which the vision of the promised land informs and creates conditions for the pathway toward revolution. Importantly, this pathway is entirely linear in that it structures the necessary steps of the journey toward progress, how it will be undertaken, by whom, and under what conditions. What renders the temporality of the MST's utopian promise even more extraordinary, however, is the fact that MST occupations occur over long periods that often stretch into years, and to participate in a settlement is to potentially embark on a lifetime as an MST member and build a deep connection to the land. I discuss the relationship between space and time with regard to the MST in more detail in the book's second scene, but one of the most striking aspects of the movement is this very longevity: the fact that movement members live on settlements that become their homes, their means of production, their children's access to school, their communities, their social lives, their sports facilities, their places of worship, and, often, the sites of their extended family relations. Thinking about the notion of struggle across decades and related intergenerational questions points to a productive analytical differentiation between the MST and other movements, and the temporality of the utopian genre is an important consideration in this sense.

Utopias present worlds that point toward the future and yet must also be embedded within a recognizable version of the present. They hold a mirror to present-day realities by pointing to sunlit uplands, and these visions work as the very motor to realize conditions that can only ever be glimpsed in the briefest of moments. Contextualized by the evolutionary theories of Charles Darwin and Herbert Spencer, late nineteenth-century utopian visions were anchored in the notion of progress. A perception of society as malleable and an increasing belief that incremental societal transformation could be brought about by political will, as opposed to a divine power, placed greater emphasis on how such change might practically occur. Ruth Levitas describes how the emergence of an evolutionary view of society opened up a new role for utopia, which became the end point of a series of steps toward change. As Levitas (1979, 26) noted, "This role depends on an awareness of the future that makes possible a conscious, voluntary, and responsible choice between alternatives, a consciousness that society can, will and should be different and that man can direct the change." Levitas argued that the Marxist utopian vision was imbued with this linear temporality, with the road map to progress that it set out leading to the promised land of revolution. Placing Marx's vision of willed transformation in contrast with texts such as More's *Utopia*, Levitas suggests that the necessary condition for utopia to be a catalyst of social change is its placement in the future "and the belief that human effort can effect the transition" (27).

Two further notions are particularly pertinent in this regard: one, the idea of the "new man" as detailed by Karl Mannheim in a 1930 lecture where he affirmed that "as soon as utopia appears, a substantial transformation occurs, a new type of man comes into being" (2001, 24), and the other, the notions of discipline and unity. Early editions of the MST's monthly newspaper, *Jornal sem terra* (the Landless Newspaper), "were filled with discussions of the new 'social citizen' that the MST wished to create" (Wolford 2003, 505), an identity that was explicitly connoted with certain behaviors and values. Vices included "individualism" (where one person "puts himself above the organization"), "spontaneity," and "immobility" (which causes a person to not "involve himself with anything") (505). In the utopian tradition, the emphasis on new social citizens can be traced to the 1602 publication of Tommaso Campanella's *City of the Sun* (2010) and the emphasis it places on men and women to become "philosophers in common" (Ernst and De Lucca 2021). In the MST, the figure that held the most resonance regarding the formation of new subjects was Che Guevara. The Cuban revolutionary made a direct connection between the notion of a "new man" and the creation of a revolutionary subjectivity in his essay "Socialism and the New Man in Cuba." Implicit in this articulation was a sketch of what the revolutionary subject could and could not be and an argument that youth is the "malleable clay from which the new person can be built with none of the old defects" (Guevara 2005, 224). Influenced by a theory that established certain behaviors and values as more desirable than others, initial MST leaders began to entertain the notion that some members might be a better fit than others.

Such a formation of the subject is partially rooted in essentialization. Malcolm McNee comments on early MST visions of a uniformity of identity, describing how Ademar Bogo, an important early leader of the culture sector, idealized a return to peasant culture including "pacific coexistence, visiting neighbors, lending and borrowing, folkloric festivals, popular wisdom, and the true *sertaneja* music" (McNee 2005, 343). McNee argues that the politics of identity within the MST spoke to an inherent contradiction: On the one hand, there was a wish to delineate a clear vision of the MST "peasant" attached to folklore, authenticity, and the past, "embodying a timeless pastoral vision of harmony" (345). But on the other hand, the type of new social citizen the movement demanded was required to act as a revolutionary agent for change, "expanding enlightenment ideals of literacy, science and beauty into the Brazilian countryside" (345). The schools to train a new generation of leaders became a priority, and Gabriel Ondetti's (2008, 120) account of one such institution in Santa Catarina described how young activists were selected from across the country to take part in a residential school program: "The aim, first and foremost, was to cultivate a radical political perspective. Participants were taught elementary Marxist sociology, in classrooms adorned with images of Marx, Lenin, and Mao. They were also pushed to change their personal behavior, becoming more disciplined and less individualistic." Such training programs have been well documented (see, e.g., Kane 2000; Veltmeyer 1997; Wright and Wolford 2003), and while Branford and Rocha (2002, 120) wrote about a school in Paraná in 2002 as "no more than a boarding school . . . [with] normal subjects, spiced up with the MST's views on the evils of capitalism," it is important to note, as Ondetti does, that for the MST, the interdependent processes of transforming society and transforming the self were understood to depend on discipline and a sense of sacrifice to the wider cause. In his discussion of William Morris's *News to Nowhere* ([1890] 1897), Raymond Williams (1978, 209) calls attention to the notion of transition within utopian thinking and the conditions under which that transition must be realized: "What seems to me increasingly the strongest part of *News from Nowhere*, is the crucial insertion of the *transition* to utopia, which is not discovered, come across, or projected—not even, except at the simplest conventional level, dreamed—but fought for. Between writer or reader and this new condition is chaos, civil war, painful and slow reconstruction." Williams identifies dedication, discipline, and sacrifice as implicit to the utopian mode, and Stédile has made plain that preparation and organization have been central tenets of the MST since its beginnings (Stédile and Fernandes 1999, 81–82). What underpins such reasoning is the connection between the values of discipline and organization and the notion of "serious" attempts at mobilization, a connection that recalls the Marxist dichotomy between socialist and scientific utopias. The concept of a disciplined vanguard to bring about change stems principally from Leninist thinking: "The strength of the working class lies in organization. Unless the masses are organized, the proletariat is nothing. Organized—it is everything. Organization means unity of action, unity in practical operations. But every action is valuable, of course, only because and insofar as it serves to push things forward and not backward, insofar as it serves to unite the proletariat ideologically, to elevate, and not degrade, corrupt or weaken it" (Lenin [1906] 1965, 320–21). It has always been the justification of Marxist movements that organization characterized by seriousness is a necessary response to the impractical daydreaming of alternative models for social change. It is the heft of the opponent and the struggle to overturn the odds that call for the development of a revolutionary subjectivity: a worker's identity rooted in the centrality of productive labor and a realization of revolutionary consciousness. For Marx, this process was codependent on the development of capitalism in that there existed objective tendencies to the stages of capitalist development that would bring forward the inevitable revolution. The notion that history has a subject who traverses a path of events that is already configured and laid out is central to the utopian project of willed transformation, and the nascent MST's emphasis on organizational discipline reflected these notions of rigor and exactness while also holding them in tension with concepts such as participation and decentralization (Chaves 2022).

On one occasion during my first period of fieldwork, I was in conversation with Gaetano, a neighbor of Vera's. Gaetano was an elder who had been part of the northern settlement since its inception. He was descended from Italian immigrants, and he spoke a few words of late nineteenth-century Veneto dialect. Gaetano asked me with a smile what I thought was happening in Cuba. His son Alvise laughed—it was clearly a private joke between them—and it brought to my mind an argument they'd had with another neighbor, Juliana, as to whether Cuba was truly a successful socialist state. Without waiting for an answer to his rhetorical question, Gaetano complained about the leadership promoting a Cuban socialist paradise and commented how it was a useful vision with which to string along those in the movement whom he termed gullible and easily deceived, *os bobos*. Gaetano said that the vision of Cuba gave people an unobtainable target and kept them working toward something that could not be achieved. He became angry, and he called out the leadership's lack of responsibility toward the membership's lives and the movement's trajectory. He said the leadership always blamed someone else for the movement's predicament, be it the government, the state, or the capitalists; indeed, he commented, there seemed to be a new enemy every week.

Gaetano was known for his strong opinions, and in articulating a view of Cuba that he knew to be transgressive, he expressed something of the tension that exists in the maintenance of political coherence and unity, a building block of the concept of *massificação*. Seeking to massify its struggle, the MST expanded hugely in a short space of time, as Stédile explained in his interview with Fernandes (1999, 120–21): "The greatest challenge is to massify the struggle because there are millions of people involved. What the movement currently does is organize a few thousand. Today there are four million landless families in Brazil. It's not that the solution is slow. We believe that, if we massify the struggle, the solution will become faster, because it forces the state to also act quicker." Fernandes asked Stédile whether to massify meant to organize: "It's a word that can have various meanings. But in our case to massify means to incorporate huge populations, to involve millions. And to free them, which means, to construct a dignity for all. . . . Professor José Gomes da Silva used to say that agrarian reform could only be really considered agrarian reform if it was a program of massive, full and radical redistribution of the property rights of agricultural land. How can you achieve this without massifying the struggle?" (121) In the context of a social movement, the process of massification implies taking a reading of a social struggle at a community level and essentializing its core components before realizing its transposition to a bigger group of people. Massification is thus the device through which a diversity of agendas becomes a mass movement unified around certain key issues that both express and demarcate the dimensions of that struggle. Gaetano was frustrated when he made his comments and implicitly pointed to questions of permissible beliefs and structures of power that would enforce discipline within the MST. There is a consensus that the movement underwent a process of institutionalization as a result of its expansion (Martins 1999, 2000; Stédile and Fernandes 1999; Welch 2006), and seeking coherence can cause tension among the diversity of positions and beliefs that constitute the MST. Given its connection to the movement's wider legitimacy, a particular question that has been extensively debated in this sense is labor and the moral values that underpin it. To collectivize or not—that is, to move away from family-run farms and centralize production and distribution—perhaps seems to some like a technical decision. But for the MST, it touches directly on the heart of the sem terra struggle.

3

Productivity

If we have big cooperatives we will increase productivity, and political awareness of the importance of collectivization for the organization of workers. In this way, our settlements will not be "eaten by sharks." We are discussing a project to construct two large production and commercialization centers in Rio Grande do Sul by the end of the year. This will enable us to expand, and even to commercialize our products with other states and MST settlements. The intensification of agricultural cooperation in the settlements is not just about economic benefits. With this type of organization, we will advance in the struggle for agrarian reform. We will strengthen the internal organization of the MST, since we will be able to free up militants to organize the people's struggle. However, we have some vices that we must overcome. Individualism is something that is still very common. Collectivization, agricultural co-operation, does not arise as a direct consequence of the occupation. We must overcome individualism before we take more land.

Antoninho Mattes, *Jornal Sem Terra*, September 1989

By the late 1980s, the MST's national leadership was facing questions connected to the scale of the movement's expansion across Brazil. Production was more than just the practical consideration of planting crops. Defining and making tangible the notion of productivity went right to the heart of justifying the movement's existence, and in many cases, it was the legal basis for the devolution of land. If the movement could show that previously unproductive estates were being put to good use, it would be able to carry out future occupations highlighting how formerly landless families had become successful parts of the rural economy.

The MST faced great challenges in this regard. In the 1980s, access to credit was scarce, and landless families generally came to the movement with few material resources. Many landless families were also used to working on a subsistence basis and had little experience with working in a more organized manner, guided by targets and yields. MST leaders looked around for models of how productivity might be increased. Links had already been established with Cuba, and the movement began to study how Cuba had reorganized its agricultural sector as a potential way forward. In Cuba, agricultural production had been rapidly collectivized from peasant agriculture to large state-run farms. As Cristobal Kay (1988, 1246) wrote, "Cuban decision-makers are great believers in economies of scale and the technological superiority of large-scale farming. To them, bigger means better and large is beautiful." The pace of transformation in Cuba was stark. From a highly diverse system in the 1950s of larger and smaller estates owned by small farmers, large land-owners, and the state, in 1983 there were 422 state farms with an average size of 14,255 hectares, each maintaining an average labor force of 1,390 people.

The MST leaders who carried out technical visits to these state-run farms returned to Brazil with big ideas. Size was a preoccupation. The first acampamento in Santa Catarina, associated with what was to become the MST, appeared in the municipality of Campo Erê on a small estate called Burro Branco in 1980. However, the first lands to be devolved after the movement's official formation were in the region of Abelardo Luz and of a different scale. Beginning in 1985, a series of devolutions in Abelardo Luz resulted in the formation of twenty-two settlements consisting of approximately twelve hundred families. The total area of these lands was roughly nineteen thousand hectares. With this kind of area available for production, MST leadership began to imagine the possibilities of importing the Cuban model of permanent production brigades to Brazil. Perhaps they were also inspired by Fidel Castro's speech on the fifteenth anniversary of Cuba's First Agrarian Reform Law in 1974, in which Castro stated that there were two roads available to rural smallholders: "One path was their integration into the state farms, and the other was their transformation into producer cooperatives, i.e., collective farms" (Kay 1988, 1253). Gabriel Ondetti details how MST leaders envisaged models of collective production as industrialized cooperatives in which productivity would be raised and "members could exchange their 'peasant' identity for a 'worker consciousness'" (Concrab 1999, 11, cited in Ondetti 2008, 124–25). This shift would require the abolition of private land, and families would receive wages depending on the number of hours they worked in the co-op. The strategy was designed to socialize former acampados from lapsing into "anomic individualism once they gained land" (Ondetti 2008, 125; cf. Wright and Wolford 2003, 86) and to liberate assentados "for full time activism" (Ondetti 2008, 125). Settlement architecture would reflect this model of collectivization, with accommodation laid out in *agrovilas*, clusters of houses grouped together, based around communal facilities such as the kitchen, eating space, and nursery.

Eager to test these ideas, the MST created three collectivized farms in Rio Grande do Sul in 1989–90, and a consultation process regarding collectivization was carried out more broadly across the movement. In June 1990, the MST national leadership announced an across-the-board program of collectivization. *Jornal Sem Terra* defined the struggle as "to occupy, to resist, and to produce" (JST Editorial 1990, 3). From this point on, all MST settlements were to be fully collectivized, with capital-intensive systems of production employing large numbers of workers. Activities were to be focused on productivity "in such areas as timber extraction, the processing of agricultural commodities, agri-business, cash crops and so on" (CONCRAB 1999, 8, cited in Branford and Rocha 2002, 92). It was envisaged that such work would be premised on economies of scale and mechanization and be accompanied by a transformative social process. The movement recommended that settlements reconceive their notions of labor and activities in the domestic sphere. Collectivization meant not only a pooling of resources and labor but also the establishment of settlement crèches and kitchens and even collective modes of transport (a settlement car) and communication (a settlement phone line). The MST as an institution had long railed about the supposed vices—for example, individualism—of its members through the *Jornal Sem Terra*, and the collectivization program's social import and ethical ontology were intimately tied to a reconfiguration of labor relations and the means of production. As Douglas Mansur wrote in *Jornal Sem Terra*'s July 1989:

> Economic advancement is a fundamental factor in convincing the masses. In this case we have two general lines: possession of the occupied land and the development of production. These are the two material, visible elements from which the advance of the struggle can be sustained. The first is the concrete victory, even if not definitive, over the enemy (the bourgeoisie, the government, the landowners). The second makes it possible to develop new social relations, combating the pre-capitalist forms of production and making it possible to create a real basis for the ideological combat against private ownership of the means of production, the mainstay of capitalism. (Mansur 1989, 4)

A nationwide structure, the National Confederation of Agrarian Reform Cooperatives of Brazil (Confederação Nacional das Cooperativas de Reforma Agrária no Brasil—Concrab), was created to provide strategic guidance and technical assistance for the new settlements while the overall program was named the Assentados' Cooperative System (Sistema Cooperativa dos Assentados—SCA).

The program was roundly rejected by movement members. Collectives failed across the country, building up unsustainable debts and encountering problems with labor surplus or deficit and a general unwillingness of people to give up what they had identified as the most valuable facet of being small farmers: the autonomy it conferred. Just as in Warsaw Pact countries and the former USSR, there were many unresolved questions that emerged from the SCA debacle: How would leadership roles in such collectives be drawn up? How would roles be allocated—for example, who would work the land, and who would staff the crèche and kitchen? How would people who fell ill or those who retired be cared for? A forward impulse premised on productivity and rationality had overlooked such questions. Reflecting on that period a decade on, Stédile commented that the MST had learned its lesson and devolved power to "each state or each settlement" to decide the best form of organization for their own particular context (Branford and Rocha 2002, 95). However, the drive to tie revolution to productivity has been surprisingly persistent. In 2021, for example, at the MST's Second Virtual National Assembly, Busatto, the leader of the movement in Santa Catarina, was still insisting that the movement needed to increase production and harvests as a means to make a decisive contribution.

The settlement in the north was originally fully collectivized. Once the land had been officially devolved by INCRA, it was held in common by Vera, André, Gaetano, and all other members of the community. Agricultural labor and duties such as cleaning and childcare were put on a duty roster, agricultural produce was sold in bulk with profits divided up based on how many hours were worked, and a settlement kitchen, worked by the assentados, operated as a canteen. The settlement had been a full cooperative as an encampment and remained thus when it transformed. However, tensions began to surface, and the settlement split into two *núcleos*, one collectivized and the other composed of separate plots farmed by different families. When I first arrived in the settlement, there were only four remaining members in the collectivized unit: Roberto, Ana, Adenir, and the education leader, Luizinho. One night, in Gaetano and Silvia's outdoor kitchen, over baked polenta fried in lard, Gaetano told me what life had been like in the early days of the settlement's existence.

I'd heard mention of people falling out, and I'd always thought it odd that these four people were living at a distance from the rest. Silvia was good friends with Ana, however, and Gaetano said that anything he had to say about Roberto was purely professional. "He has his faults as a person, as we all do, right? But it's more about the way he thinks about the movement," Gaetano said.

When the settlement was fully collectivized, Gaetano told me, the person coming up with ideas and therefore giving orders was Roberto. Consequently, he was also the person who held the funding for any particular project. Gaetano told me proudly that he would not do what Roberto asked of him, and they used to have many arguments. Roberto, Gaetano laughed, liked to get his own way, and Gaetano's son, Alvise, who dropped in after finishing his shift, commented that this was a good example of how cooperatives looked good in theory but always failed in practice. "There is always someone trying to be the boss," Alvise warned.

Other people had similar views. On Roberto, Lúcia commented, "His ideas don't agree with mine. I would never work outright in any co-op run by him. He really orders people around, like he wants to be the *chefão* [the big boss]. He takes everything so seriously! 'It has to be like this!'" She smacked her first on the table. "Pum! OK, there are times when it's like that, but not the whole time."

Roberto himself remained a mystery. I never bumped into him in the settlement; he didn't play soccer or hang out in the bar, and I never met him at the community *churrascos*, the barbeques that happened from time to time. One evening I was talking with Luizinho at his house, and Roberto dropped in to have a beer. Feeling that this was a good opportunity to get to know him, I made conversation. We ended up talking about the market in Bom Jardim, the local town a few miles way. "Can I come?" I asked.

"Where?" he said. "To the market? Well, we start early, and I leave here at four a.m." So that was how I found myself sitting behind a freezing market stand the next morning with a hangover, selling eggs and milk. I asked how business was. It had been a slow start, and Roberto shrugged. "It depends. We deliver milk to many people, and that's money that we can count on. But sometimes we don't sell much at market, no? It's like that sometimes." Some people stopped to buy eggs. Roberto continued: "When you work collectively like we do, it's better for everyone, because even if you don't have that much, you always have the potential to do more, because you have more labor, do you see? For example, it's all about capital. A truck, a good secondhand one, costs R$12,000, and a tractor costs R$20,000. Alone, to buy that, it's complicated. In a collective, it's easier. For example, the assentamento of Garuva is collectively organized, everything is done cooperatively there. And they make money, with very little land."

There was a pause while I packaged up some eggs for more buyers. "So for me," Roberto went on, "this is the big challenge in the movement. It's organization and how we need to collectivize. Here in our settlement, for example, we have thirteen families and about thirty people. We could do a lot together, but it's not like that, we work individually. But it's a question of capital. For example, to start a collective which processes pork costs R$15,000 to R$20,000. You need three separate environments, refrigeration and so on. You need smoking equipment, sausage mixers, etc. These products sell for R$10 per kilo with a profit margin of more or less R$2 to R$4 per kilo. So you only have to sell seven tons of products to make the investment back. And I think we can sell a ton a month, so it frustrates me. Today I've sold just two liters of milk and twelve eggs. It's not a lot. If we worked together, it would work out better, but people don't want it. This is the biggest challenge in the movement, to convince people to work together and in this way increase production."

As we were talking, the market was packing up. I admired Roberto's vision of collective labor, and I felt that he was right: his products would sell. Santa Catarina has a tradition of German immigration. As I touched on previously, these colonos and their traditions are characteristic of Santa Catarina. From towns like Pomerode, where some people still speak a 1900s dialect of German, across the state to Blumenau, home of the world's second-largest Oktoberfest, to the local *kuchenhaus*, German traditions maintain a strong presence, including the wide availability of German sausage and cold meats. Roberto had done his calculations, and it seemed his whole plan was ready to go. He explained how the settlement would be divided into sectors. One sector would be dedicated to planting and harvesting the corn to feed the pigs. Cheaper than buying feed, he told me. Then another sector would be in charge of taking care of the pigs: mucking them out, feeding them, taking care of the piglets, and so on. Another sector would take care of the slaughter and butchering. Another would be responsible for the smoking, another the packaging and refrigeration, and another the logistics and delivery. On that bleak morning on the border with Paraná, Roberto's enthusiasm was tangible. He came alive when talking about his plans and convinced me of how the settlement could grow and prosper. The figures stacked up. He was talking return on investment, efficiency, livelihoods. It was a recognizable language—the language of rationality and reward, markets and metrics. The only problem was that no one in the settlement wanted to sign up for this vision.

When the MST stepped back from instituting a nationwide program of collective production, they did so with certain caveats. MST leaders reiterated their long-term commitment to collectivization as a "superior form of organization" (Branford and Rocha 2002, 95) but admitted that to work, such a production method needed specific conditions that couldn't always be guaranteed given the diversity of highly specific local conditions. An important development occurred at the Fourth National Congress in February 2000. In dialogue with the international peasant organization La Via Campesina about the connection between its struggle and environmental issues, the MST formally adopted an agroecological approach to production (Aliaga and Maranho 2021). This placed an emphasis on the training of a new generation of agronomists, the development of native seed banks, and, most importantly, a commitment to farming without the use of pesticides, monoculture, and other techniques employed in the maximization of agricultural value generation. In extending the socioeconomic struggle for land to include environmental questions, the MST hoped to create a progressive front with Indigenous peoples and *quilombola* communities and connect to the nascent organic food movement that was developing in the larger cities. It was a visionary move. Keen to develop training in partnership with the state, the MST created courses in around thirty schools in Brazil, the vast majority in its traditional stronghold, the south (Novaes et al. 2016). And indeed, my first contact with the movement came about due to the Programa Nacional de Educação na Reforma Agrária (PRONERA), which in 2007 took the form of regular classes for MST members at the Federal University of Santa Catarina (UFSC).

In Santa Catarina, the agroecological approach was broadly well received. Some people stuck with the old ways. A substantial proportion of the world's tobacco comes from the north of Santa Catarina, and I came across people planting tobacco, which requires intensive pesticide treatment. Such assentados were generally in need of money: the nearby Sousa e Cruz company was a guaranteed buyer, and the price per kilo for tobacco leaves was high. But many assentados embraced an agroecological approach even though they knew that planting without pesticides would be a challenge. In Santa Catarina, agroecology also fitted into the strong tradition of small family farms, and bulk commodities like beans, corn, and wheat were complemented by the production of organic versions of regional traditions: colono meats, cheeses, and sausages; pickled cucumbers and onions; salads and greens; and a huge variety of delicious jams, marmalades, and sweets. Agroecology came to mean eliminating the middleman, serving local markets with high-quality organic produce, and working to maintain the long-term fertility of the soil.

While the commitment to agroecology marked a departure from the intensive Cuban farming model the MST had been inspired by in the late 1980s, many MST leaders I spoke to were still in favor of collectivization but via the model of agroecological settlement cooperatives. Despite the failure of the SCA, Roberto was adamant, as was Luizinho, the lead for education at state level, that the main factor behind the members' rejection and continuing unwillingness to collectivize was a lack of *formação política*, political training. And they both believed that members merely needed to be better educated about the benefits that such a model could bring. In this manner, while an official commitment to collectivization across the board was dropped in the early 1990s, leaders in influential positions saw the membership's rejection more as a temporary setback. Luizinho explained in 2008 how he saw an agroecological collectivization in the form of what he termed "rural industrialization." I was to hear this term repeatedly over the coming years. Luizinho began by speaking about the MST idea of a "new person" and how this transformation could be accomplished through *formação*. I asked him what he understand formação to be.

He replied, "So the teaching of the theoretical has to be linked to practical matters. Work is really important. It's work that changes things, much more than teaching in a theoretical sense. Therefore it's this combined education that has as its role, constructing new human beings—people who think differently, who act differently, who have a different attitude during difficult times."

Conversation moved to what might constitute "difficult times," and Luizinho expressed a common concern of MST members: "There's a tendency, for example, for kids around here and in the movement in general to go to the city. It's the question of the second generation." He paused. "The city is always there, in the background. This is a concrete fact. The city has things that the countryside still doesn't have. The countryside doesn't have internet, it doesn't have cinema, it doesn't have cyber cafes, it doesn't have a load of advantages, good things that the city has. So this is what we're working on, to try to make the countryside more attractive. Give people a monthly salary, get customers. But it's not easy, and that's why I say that it is a challenge, and the challenge is to change the method of production."

"What would this change mean?" I asked.

"We're trying to change things," Luizinho replied, "but it's hard because often it's the farmers themselves, Mom and Pop, who inside their heads don't see this necessity to move away from planting in the field. But you have to get into other markets. When we say that collectivized farms are a necessity, it's because it will be to the advantage of the assentamentos, but it also will attract the youth. If we manage to create a form of industrialized collectivization in the assentamentos, to be able to produce our own inputs, our own raw materials in an industrialized way, for sure, the young people will stay more in the countryside. So this is the challenge."

I asked Luizinho if the model of industrialization would be similar to the assentamento of Garuva, which Roberto had referred to as a successful example of a fully collectivized settlement, paying its members an hourly wage to produce salads.

"Yes," Luizinho replied, "like Garuva or the cooperative in São Miguel which produces milk under the brand name Terra Viva. The kids need the courage to stay in the countryside, and it's a question of money. And these projects will make money, projects like making *cachaça* [a liquor made from sugarcane] or pork derivatives. And really, the idea is for each co-op to act as a hub of industrialization. This will increase production. And also when you have an industrial center like this in the countryside, it attracts other things, leisure activities, internet, cyber cafes, and so on. In this way, the kids will be able to find the advantages of the city here in the countryside."

Luizinho continued, "You have to find people who already have a cooperativist mentality." He paused again. "But this can also be taught." Luizinho's proposals for a new model of organization seemed similar to the movement's proposals for collectivization in 1990. He highlighted the prospect of greater productivity and the necessity to produce at levels beyond mere self-sustenance, which MST leaders have historically considered to be economically unfeasible (Ondetti 2008, 126). But there was also an acknowledgment of a need to commercialize: agroecology, it seemed, was envisaged to work within a market. Luizinho hinted at this when he argued that the MST's antagonists had changed over time and with them MST strategy. "Because up to ten, fifteen years ago, our enemy was *latifúndio*," he commented. "But from 1990 with the model of agroexportation and agribusiness, our enemy has become the big corporations connected to the production of food, seeds, pesticides: Monsanto, Syngenta, Cargill."

Luizinho's vision emphasized the connection between possibilities of employment and young people electing to remain in the countryside. He focused on the generation of profits through the aggregation of value and a consequent need to commercialize. We didn't really speak about the working experience, however. How did Luizinho envisage working for twenty or thirty years in such a scheme of production? The questions raised in the aftermath of the movement-wide program to collectivize remained unanswered. Many MST members articulated that the best things about being a small farmer was not having a boss and that patterns of work were dictated by the rhythms of the seasons as opposed to the precision of the clock. What might trading in one's identity as a peasant for that of a worker entail in practice? The lived realities of such a transformative program are complex, and the interpretation and contestation of these abstract concepts move us to the second scene.

SCENE II—CONTRADICTIONS

BERNARDO MANÇANO FERNANDES: The idea of a mass movement permeates the whole form of action and organization of the MST. If that's the case, do you think we can say that the MST brings fresh ideas? Do we need to rethink the very concept of a mass movement?

JOÃO PEDRO STÉDILE: It's possible. Maybe this is the major historical contribution that the MST can make to other mass movements: You have no future if you don't apply organizational principles, if you don't constitute yourselves as a political organization with reference to the class struggle as opposed to party politics.

Pausa

I was driving north with Paulo, a relatively new MST member who was living in Kleber's settlement down by the coast with his daughter, Jessica, and her partner, Douglas. It was April 2008. Paulo was new, but he was going places. He had worked for many years in Florianópolis as a trade unionist and had a house on the beach. We went there one time to watch a surfing competition and smoke some joints. Brought up in the city, he admired the MST and wanted to work with them, so in his late forties, he joined an encampment. He hadn't been encamped very long.

We arrived at the address Paulo had been given. A woman met us outside and led us indoors. A large MST flag was hanging beside the door. It was the first time I met Lúcia, and she seemed very serious. It was movement business. Paulo had been sent to get to know the north, the settlements, encampments, and leaders. Lúcia was his contact to facilitate this. She lived in a small house in Bom Jardim, adjacent to the settlement. I didn't know it yet, but she was part of the extended family of which I became a part. I'd already met her brother-in-law André; her niece and nephew Clarice and Artur; and her brothers Rui and José. Her sisters, Vera and Rosalete, lived in the settlement nearby while she took care of their mother.

Lúcia was a member of the movement. She had encamped, and some years back Kleber had offered her a plot in the Água Branca settlement, which she turned down. People didn't know that Lúcia was really sick. In 2007, just a year before our first meeting, she had a health crisis, and the priest gave her last rites. I used to drive her to a hospital in Florianópolis for her specialist treatment. She recovered. We went fishing; an army corporal fell in love with her, so we visited him at his barracks; we went to a military policeman's funeral together; and she swore vengeance on his soul when the guard of honor fired their rifles in salute. She was always cooking for her mother,

Dona Neusa, and her daughter Ana. I used to help out. Over the years, we became good friends.

One time, hanging out with Lúcia, I brought a chicken, and I watched her slice the bird up, separating the wings and thighs incredibly quickly. Her knife was razor sharp. "Old habits," she said. "In the factory, they gave us a sharpened knife every twenty minutes." She told me that before coming to the MST, she had worked for two years in a poultry processing plant. "We cut them so fast as they came down the line that after twenty minutes the knife was already blunt. I learned how to make the right cuts, so efficient, so quick, because there was a lot of pressure. We had to process a certain number per day, per person. They were watching us, you see."

Distracted, she nicked her left hand with the knife, and it began to bleed. She continued: "After a while I couldn't bear it anymore. My hands, my wrists and fingers were so tired at night. Doing the same thing day after day, like a machine. I wonder if I got sick there."

4

Human Values

O Chico caiu no poço, não sei como não morreu,
Por ser devoto das almas, nossa Senhora o valeu.

O Chico caiu no poço, do fundo tirou areia;
Ninguém tenha dó do Chico, que está preso na cadeia.

O Chico foi lá no poço com uma pedra no pescoço:
Ninguém tenha dó do Chico, que ele morreu por seu gosto.

Lá vem Chico, lá vem Chico, deixá-lo que venha, sim:
Eu não devo nada ao Chico, nem ele me deve a mim.

Chico fell into the well, I don't know how he didn't die,
Being a devotee of the souls, our Lady saved his life.

Chico fell into the well so deep he touched the bottom;
Don't feel sorry for Chico, he's stuck in chains and rotting.

Chico went to the well, his neck with a stone a'weighing:
Don't feel bad for Chico, he complained and had it coming.

Here comes Chico, here comes Chico, yes, let him come:
I owe Chico nothing, we're all square, quits, and done.
—CHICO SAPATEADO, A "GAUCHESCA,"
THE TRADITIONAL FOLK MUSIC OF
RIO GRANDE DO SUL[1]

D avi's house was in a less frequented part of the Bom Jardim settlement. When I first met him in 2008, he and his young family had recently left Roberto's collectivized unit, and they were still getting set up. When Davi decided that he wished to leave Roberto's collective, it caused a lot of tension. Roberto was angry and, in an assembly he called, moved that Davi be expelled from the assentamento and therefore the movement. When this motion did not pass, Roberto continued to harass Davi and his family. It was only much later, in 2015, that Vera told me the full story of how Davi's family came to find a solution. At that point in 2008, all I knew was there had been conflict, and the precarious conditions in which Davi lived communicated something unresolved. Davi and his family lived in a simple wooden house situated at the end of a rough track that became slippery with mud when it rained. It was a tight fit with four children, and I could see that Davi worked hard with the small amount of land he farmed. However, I usually arrived on the weekend and would find him leaning out of the window stirring a small glass.

"Do you want a caipirinha, Alex?" he would ask with a slow smile. The well-known Brazilian cocktail was rendered pretty potent in Davi's hands, and we would often sit around talking about Grêmio, the soccer club from Porto Alegre he supported, as the small glass was passed around and refilled. I never asked directly about what had happened with Roberto. Sometimes, it got heated at Davi's place in the evenings, when maybe the caipirinha glass had been circulating for too long. At the time, Davi's daughter, Juliana, was on track to become a militante, an MST activist, and just before I left Brazil for the first time in 2009, she moved to Paraná to attend a residential training school. Juliana had a strong personality and often took exception to the views of people like Gaetano when the subject of conversation turned to conditions in Cuba or the nature of the technical support the MST provided for its small farmers.

I knew that before Davi's family had joined Roberto's collective, they had been part of a bigger cooperative based in the settlement of Garuva. Roberto and Luizinho both encouraged me to visit Garuva as an example of what a collectivized space could achieve. Garuva's anniversary fell on October 25, which I had planned to visit, but disastrous flooding in Santa Catarina had rendered roads impassable. Three months of continuous rain, followed by a month's worth of rainfall occurring on November 22 and 23, left many cities isolated. The rain caused the death of 126 people—mainly victims of landslides and floods—and forced around 80,000 to leave their homes, so it was only in March 2009 that I was able to visit.

Traveling with Lúcia, I was surprised to find that in some ways Garuva resembled the Água Branca settlement down by the coast. There was an *agrovila*, a set of identical houses arranged around communal facilities, and people were busy tending to seedlings in large polytunnels (greenhouse-style controlled environments). When I arrived in Garuva, it was clear that the co-op had excellent transport links to big markets, and in speaking to people in the northern settlement, I understood that its collective system of production was dependent on this distribution system. The settlement itself was defined as ninety-five hectares, but of this only ten hectares could be farmed.[2] With the available land being enough for only one MST family under normal circumstances, and with fourteen families to support, the MST faced a huge challenge in making Garuva a viable project. It had always been a collectivized settlement, and over time the decision had been made to produce salad crops in an intensive manner, creating and nurturing seedlings in the polytunnels before transplanting them to irrigated fields specifically designed for a relative monoculture. Production in Garuva was done to a strict schedule, with allotted times for seedlings to grow and a program of a certain number of days for each type of salad to mature in the rows of the fields. The strict timelines reflected the fact that Garuva had a contract to supply salads to Angeloni, one of the biggest supermarket companies in the south of Brazil—a contract that, at the time in 2009, absorbed 90 percent of the settlement's production. Working to a carefully controlled schedule, the assentados living in Garuva were paid an hourly wage of just over R\$1 per hour, or US\$0.57 according to the exchange rate of the time. A typical month rendered a monthly salary of some R\$180. This didn't compare favorably to the monthly state minimum wage of R\$432, but living costs were less as most aspects of life were cooperativized. Beyond working together, the MST members living in Garuva ate together in a communal kitchen, and tasks such as food preparation and cleaning duties were on a roster. The canteen and provision of meals cost R\$20 per month per person, and collectivized services such as childcare were free. Members of the community also had access to collectively owned property, a communal phone line, and a communal car.

Even though wages were low, fourteen families were able to earn a basic living on the same amount of land that one family possessed in the northern settlement. Assentados were given one day off per week. Any additional day taken off work was docked from their pay, so work that was assigned on the schedule was effectively compulsory. Community members were also required to work from the age of twelve upward; children were usually assigned cleaning duties, which attracted critical comments from members of surrounding settlements. At the time, the settlement was constructing large pools to try to farm fish. When I asked why, one of the men working told me that parts of the settlement were so waterlogged that farming fish was the only possible productive use for the land.

I came back from Garuva with a lot of questions and happened to be going to Davi's place for lunch the next day. Lúcia told me that Davi and his wife, Jurema, had lived and worked in Garuva for a number of years. After making a caipirinha, Davi explained why they had left: "It was internal differences of opinion. The bottom line was that we got worried with this question of . . ." He paused. "Well, the future and what it's going to be like. For example, if I worked there for ten years and had to leave suddenly, I would leave with nothing. I mean, when we arrived there, they welcome you, they get you into it all and they tell you, everything here belongs to us. But it's 'us' in inverted commas, no? Because the day you leave, everything stays there. Nothing belongs to 'us.' It belongs to you only when you're inside."

I didn't really understand what he meant by "being inside," so Davi explained. "When you work there, you deposit money in the central bank of the collective and this money comes from the sweat of your labor. It's for the good of the group. So they've constructed a tool shed, bought a new car, new truck, two tractors . . . but this is my sweat! And when I leave? I don't even get one bolt of that tractor!" Davi spoke about how working in Garuva had made him feel. I could sense that it was difficult for him to speak about why Garuva hadn't worked out. He was deeply attached to the idea of working collectively—so much so that even after leaving Garuva he had moved to another co-op, Roberto's. As we talked, this contradiction became more palpable: "Look, collectivization is the best form of progress for moving forward. It's just that you have to have greater flexibility on the human side. Treating people like humans is not valued there. Being human there is just valued as labor, labor, labor. So when you get ill and you're not productive . . ." Again he paused. "I felt it badly, because I broke my arm, and I spent forty days out of action. And I picked up on not being valued anymore. It's an administrative thing. They wanted back the money from the hours I couldn't work. I really felt like I wasn't valued."

Davi's job at Garuva had been to deliver the salads to the Angeloni supermarkets in the settlement's truck. It was hard work; he woke up before dawn every day to do a two-hour drive to Curitiba, the state capital of Paraná, or a forty-five-minute drive to Joinville, the largest city in Santa Catarina. The accident happened while he was working. As he talked about driving the same route day after day, the notion that he was interchangeable was recurrent in our conversation, as was the notion of being human and its moral connotation. I asked Davi what he meant when he used the phrase "being human." "I don't mind so much contributing to the central bank of the collective," he replied. "You have to have this. Even though I left the co-op, I still think it's the best method, and it will eventually work out. The only thing I think is that there should be some changes in the internal politics. Like, lessen the investment in the capital side, to raise the investment in being human. Because treating each other well, being human, is the source of everything. And over there in Garuva, it has been forgotten."

We spoke for a while about how the settlement's administrators would consider going to a movement protest as a day off, and it would lead to a deduction of wages. At one point, Davi's wife, Jurema, came and sat with us. They both commented on how, with such focus on work and meeting the contract, people had forgotten about the wider struggle. At one point, Davi was even more explicit. "You know what? It's too much work, and they think twice before letting someone go on a demonstration. Because if they go, it creates a labor deficit and there, it's work, work, work."

I asked him who he meant by "they," at which point Jurema laughed as Davi replied. "There's always someone who speaks louder than others—it's useless to deny it. Down by the coast, it's Kleber, isn't it? He'll never leave. Garuva is Daniel. In the rest of the state as well, the other co-ops, there are always one or two people. So the other families come, they go, but these people stay. It's normal that there is someone who takes the wheel. Daniel, for example, he has the technical side. He understands how to plant the salads and how to prepare the seeds. And his wife, Nina, she does all the accounting, she knows how many hours everyone has done, so she controls the money. She has a computer, she does the Excel, she's taken courses. No one else knows how to do that. So they dominate."

Jurema commented that even after leaving Garuva, they had still believed in the co-op model. "I insisted," Davi said. "Come on, let's try Roberto's co-op. And I was certain that because the people were different, the politics would be different as well. But at the end of the day, the bottom line is that it always ends up the same, you know [cai na mesma realidade, sabe]? You can change the people, but the problems are the same. Someone gives the orders; someone makes the decisions. As a group you decide together, but this someone will always bypass this."

As we were speaking, Jurema became emotional. "I didn't like Garuva. I had just lost one of my children." She paused. At that time, she had been pregnant with twin boys, only one of whom survived birth. "And so I was really depressed, but I had to work in the crèche, and the noise that the children made? It was terrible for me. But I had to look after them even though

I didn't want to. Because I was a mother, because I had a child in the crèche, it was required. Whoever had children had no choice, the crèche was staffed by the mothers. I was stuck in the house all the time. I was depressed, I was having treatment. And there were twelve children, and I couldn't control them anymore. One day, I was just crying because I couldn't handle it and they could see I was suffering, but nobody. . . . It was like, 'No! You have to look after them as you're a mother!'" Davi nodded his head slowly. "It's a lack of humanity." Jurema crossed her arms. "I mean, if you're working and earning per hour. . . . Because you have to clock on and clock off. It's nothing but a factory. It's a salads factory."

*　*　*

Davi and Jurema had been members of the MST since 1997, and it had been a struggle. They had encamped together and worked collectively in two settlements before building their own small house. Making these critiques was difficult for them because even though Davi had ended up working his own plot, he maintained a commitment to the idea of collectivization as a morally superior form. It pained me to hear him talk about how things hadn't worked out in Garuva or with Roberto's co-op. Often, he insisted that these *divergências*, or arguments, had come about because of his own defects—that he was somehow not capable of working collectively. Listening to Davi and Jurema recounting their experiences in their simple wooden house with the wind whistling through the cracks in the walls was to be presented with the latent contradictions between what Davi termed "one of the best methods of organization"—collective living and production—and the types of connections and social relations it often engendered. That the reality of working in a collective might differ from accounts based in solidarity with a political stance is not surprising, of course. Sharryn Kasmir (1996, 2016), for example, has detailed the everyday problems of cooperative work and the disaffection of workers within the Basque country's Mondragón cooperative. She cites a worker questioning in one particular meeting, "What are the co-ops? . . . If they once talked about what it was to be human, now they talk only about profits" (1996, 184). And the manner in which Davi consistently emphasized the need for relationships to be conducted in ways that were "more human" echoes these preoccupations with what counts as labor, how notions of productivity are constructed and negotiated, and, fundamentally, how values of solidarity are held in tension with a rational application of resources and the hierarchies of management.

Jurema was specific about the consequences of such hierarchies. She identified how, despite having recently lost a child, she was obliged to work in the crèche because she was a mother. She pointed to the settlement's leadership team, a husband and wife who between them maintained technocratic control of production and compensation, as lacking the decency to see how traumatic her experience had become. The naturalization of gender roles dictated that beyond working the crèche, she was also obliged to work in the kitchen alongside another woman. For someone who was passionate about cultivation and planting, this was reductive for Jurema; she commented that if you were categorized as a cook, you didn't get involved in the planting side of the settlement. The assignment of roles based on gender was common across Santa Catarina. An overwhelming majority of state leadership from 2007 to 2019 were men, and female leaders commented to me that in general, the only opportunities they had were roles in the health or education sectors, spheres of activity that were viewed as more in line with women's capabilities.

For these leaders, as for Jurema, the gendering of labor went beyond the roles that were accessible or not. If we cast our minds back to Luizinho's analysis of the MST idea of a "new man and new woman," he placed a particular emphasis on how such transformation could be accomplished through the notion of *formação*, or political training. Luizinho, who became a national leader in 2010, believed there were multiple environments in which such a transformation could occur. But whether in the form of an encampment or a settlement, the common thread was a collective form of organization. As he commented, it was difficult to find people who already had the collective mentality, but it was a manner of thinking and being that could be taught. For Jurema and other women in the movement, if the roles to which they had access were limited, and work was so closely connected to notions of transformation, it was clear that only certain gender-normative pathways to self-realization were open to them. If work was how to learn to become a *sem terra*, what was Jurema learning in Garuva?

As I comment in the introduction, Marx and Engels's notion of willed transformation put forward the pathway to revolution, a realizable utopia, one underpinned by the conscious efforts and sacrifices of those involved. While Davi felt unjustly treated and not cared for by the co-op, what was at stake for Jurema was in many ways much more important. Striving toward a "willed transformation" as a worker laid bare the multiple contradictions that were inherent to this utopian projection, and the one Jurema felt most strongly was the unconscious association of her gender with the kind of worker she could be, and therefore the kind of person she could become.

What made the situation especially complex for Davi and Jurema was how one or two people could easily—and, in their opinion, inevitably—come to dominate a collectivized environment. In Garuva, they identified that the management team of Daniel and Nina were able to impose their normative vision of productivity because others didn't feel comfortable articulating alternatives. Jurema located the workers' sense of insecurity regarding technical matters as not knowing how to use the spreadsheet or oversee the growing process. And this situation also occurred in the Mondragón cooperative, where workers found it difficult to articulate their rights in meaningful forms (Kasmir 1999, 383).

Because Davi and Jurema had already participated in two co-ops, the question of how to leave a collectivized work environment was a sensitive one. Although during conversation it was not rendered explicitly, Davi equated "having to leave" with being expelled—just as Roberto had attempted to force an expulsion when Davi left his cooperative. And for Davi and Jurema, it was a question of thinking of their four children and of what would come next for them. Davi talked about Daniel and Nina's son to make his point: "We need to change the internal politics, not in all aspects, just some, in this sense of being more human, no? We have to value the family. For example, do you know Daniel's son? He was growing up when we were there, he was a little kid. Now he's eighteen or nineteen and married. But the marriage broke up because he had no opportunities. He has nothing, no hob to cook with, not even a sink to do his washing up in!" The problem for Davi and Jurema was that as all property was collectivized, there would be nothing for them to pass on to their children. By contrast, they mentioned that if they should ever have to leave the northern settlement, they would at least leave with some capital and have some assets to sell.

In these discussions, the notion of productivity was very much at stake, with differing visions being put forward. For certain elements within the MST, collectivization is the end point of a developmental pathway, and political training is the means through which people can evolve and cast off the "defects" that Davi attributed to himself. Speaking to Luizinho, it was clear that he and leaders like him thought collectivized schemes of labor, such as rural industrialization, could address various problems all at once. They would encourage mom and pop to shift from family-oriented autonomous spaces to regimes more tightly tied to wage labor, productivity, and political engagement. They would be the mechanism through which collectivization could be reintroduced onto the agenda and questions about financial viability tackled head-on. And rural industrialization in particular was a project very much geared toward a utopian future—an imaginary that was located somewhere in the distance but nonetheless would require a different kind of person to bring it into being.

Davi and Jurema, however, put forward a different vision. They questioned how productivity was understood and the way it dominated work and moral hierarchies, and they disapproved of the restrictive gender normativity that accompanied this. What kind of moral values were inscribed in a vision of productivity that, in Jurema's words, rendered the Garuva settlement a "salads factory"? What would a pathway to progress necessarily look like if it were to be premised on such values? Davi and Jurema repeatedly spoke of "being human" as a means of contrasting rational economic motives with the wider harmony and well-being of the collectives in which they worked. Such a perspective included immediate concerns such as caring for the sick, allowing people time off work, and supporting activism within the movement. But their contestation of productivity also points to the future as embedded in the present—for example, through the notion of what would happen when old age meant they could no longer work and, importantly, the connection they perceived between collectivized production and the assigning of clearly gendered roles within the collective. On this second point, Jurema questioned what kind of person she could reasonably become if work was truly transformative, given that she would be confined to crèche duties for long periods. And such contentions point toward differing visions of temporality that exist within the movement: a linear teleological understanding of time in which members clock on and clock off as rational economic actors and complex disaggregations of time and space that break with linearity and speak to the subjunctive dimension of transformation.

5

Time

I hesitated some time, not knowing whether to open these
memoirs at the beginning or at the end, i.e., whether to
start with my birth or with my death. Granted, the usual
practice is to begin with one's birth, but two considerations led me to adopt a different method: the first is that,
properly speaking, I am a deceased writer not in the sense
of one who has written and is now deceased, but in the
sense of one who has died and is now writing, a writer for
whom the grave was really a new cradle; the second is that
the book would thus gain in merriment and novelty.

MACHADO DE ASSIS, *THE POSTHUMOUS*
MEMOIRS OF BRÁS CUBAS, 15

TRANSLATION BY WILLIAM L. GROSSMAN

"We will never stop fighting for land. We are recreating the
struggle for land and building a new settlement model, along
the lines of a people's agrarian reform." This statement was
made by Busatto in 2021 on the occasion of the inauguration of a new settlement in São Cristóvão do Sul. Now housing twenty-three families, the land
had been occupied for three years before being incorporated as the Filhos
do Contestado settlement. In 2023, Busatto was one of the most influential
MST leaders in Santa Catarina, just as he had been since 1995. The ethnography that opened this book gave us a first glimpse of Busatto, giving a speech
in 2007. On stage at the state meeting, he set out defined objectives for the
movement in Santa Catarina over the coming year, breaking the objectives
down into three key points. Addressing over five hundred people, he told
us that our first priority was to take land, and second, we must continue
the struggle for agrarian reform. Busatto dwelled briefly on these first two

points before spending an hour outlining the third—the need to create a new society. He told us that an alternative to capitalism must be brought about and that the bourgeois must be confronted. A key principle in this would be education. It would begin through people's examples of character and the creation of a new man and woman. We were instructed that we must demonstrate sem terra values through our behavior and daily actions. However, during this long third section, the audience grew ever more distracted, and in the middle of his speech, Busatto suddenly stopped. He raised a clenched fist and shouted, "MST!"

The audience, suddenly awake, responded in the manner of a catechism: "Reforma Agrária Já!"

Again. "EMEE-ESSY-TAY!"

"REFORMA AGRÁRIA JÁ!" we shouted.

Busatto then asked us to memorize a specific phrase: *Os sem terrinha são a continuidade, a existência e a potência da mística.* (The young MST members are the future, the existence and the potential of mística.) The phrase was recited twice from the stage before we all repeated it at his request. Another one: *O movimento tem que superar o sistema do capitalismo—é possível realizar.* (The movement must overcome the capitalist system—it's possible to achieve.) As we chanted along with Busatto, I found myself not thinking too closely about the words themselves. It was more the rhythm of the phrase, the deafening volume, the collective fervor of being in unison with five hundred others that was so thrilling. Later that day I wondered if, despite our unified force, we really could overcome capitalism. How would this be accomplished? Busatto's words repeated themselves endlessly. There was something about the stages of the struggle that struck me. The first was so tangible, the occupation of land. The second was about continuation, the resilience of the ongoing struggle. But the third was broader, speaking more generally about the future. Listening to Busatto, this third stage seemed close but also far away, a promise that we could glimpse on the horizon but that retreated as we sought to approach.

Busatto's speech exemplified the utopian subjunctive of the MST. The promised world is a deferred destination that nevertheless lays out conditions of sacrifice and unity in the present day for the journey ahead. This subjunctive mode is entirely linear in that it details the necessary steps of the journey toward progress, how it will be undertaken, by whom, and under what conditions. Busatto broke down the journey into three stages and emphasized the kind of character necessary to be able to confront the struggle, the kind of new man and new woman to which such a struggle could give birth. And yet, addressing this—what Birri identifies as a utopia forever out of reach—caused visible discomfort during Busatto's speech. As the hour wore on and the dimensions of the struggle became ever more abstract, people lost attention and began to fidget and joke among themselves. It was only Busatto's oratory skill that unified us once again—a shrewd intervention and a moment of hard-won stagecraft—around the goal of overcoming capitalism and an affirmation that such an act was possible to achieve. Utopia in this sense points toward the future and is premised on a teleological, linear understanding of time. Busatto configured the MST's struggle as progress in the pursuit of inevitable victory and framed the revolutionary act as a conscious and voluntary choice. This was willed transformation, and we in the audience could opt to become agents of history and bring about change if we followed Busatto's fixed and visible path to victory.

And yet, there are other understandings of transformation that exist within the MST. These are nonlinear, work to a different notion of scale, and contest the moral connotations of the revolutionary subject. In the ethnography that opens this book, Clarice commented that it was impossible to create a new society in the manner Busatto put forward at the state meeting. However, this didn't mean that transformation was not possible. On the contrary, agrarian reform was entirely possible to bring about if people focused on the small spaces as opposed to a scale that could never be accomplished. Davi and Jurema also put forward differing visions, arguing against an agrarian reform in which productivity was equated with rational economic action above all other considerations, a mode of work that inscribed moral hierarchies and gender normativity.

Such differing understandings find expression through what I term counter-utopian practices. Blanes and Bertelsen (2021) question the ideals of utopia, but I am specifically interested in how transformation occurs from within contradiction, how such a counter-utopian practice exerts a powerful force that exists in tension with the utopian modalities of willed transformation. I argue that such practices bring about transformation from within a durational mode of time, rejecting a temporality of protest premised on rupture. In this minoritarian position, transformation occurs from within an experience of time that cannot be governed by its relationship to space and its demarcation of seconds, minutes, and hours of productive work. In the introduction, I touched on Henri Bergson's philosophical work on time and how it helps us to interrogate the linear premise of utopia. Bergson's perspective on transformation, premised on his understanding of time as duration, speaks to the experience of people like Clarice, Davi, and Jurema in their rejection of a single pathway toward revolution and the conditions by which that pathway must be undertaken. For Bergson, durational time is nonlinear. Feelings and memories from the past are active and influential in our present experience, which in turn is shaped by anticipation of the future. And such a position allows us to interrogate the differing visions of temporality that exist within the movement: a teleological understanding of time in which the trajectory to victory is mapped out and known or a disconnection between notions of time and space and the breaking with the subjunctive dimension of transformation. But how can we better understand this minoritarian understanding of time in the MST?

Where Bergson figures in the anthropological literature, it is often his theory of time that is put forward, whether in Nancy Munn's article "The Cultural Anthropology of Time" (1992), Alfred Gell's *The Anthropology of Time* (1992), or more recent work by Morten Pedersen (2012), Stuart Rockefeller (2011) and Matt Hodges (2008). For Bergson, time was intrinsically connected to transformation, and while this connection and emphasis are less apparent to us today, Bergson's writings deliberately addressed the evolutionary scientists of his era and particularly their theories of change. One of Bergson's most important ideas centers on his argument that the evolutionary theories of his day were *mechanistic*. Bergson argues that Herbert Spencer's theory of homogeneity to complex heterogeneity (1867), Charles Darwin's theory of variation and selection according to adaptation (1864), and Hugo de Vries's theory of mutation (1909–10) were all based on a set of assumptions inherited from classical philosophy and, as such, premised on a linear understanding of time. Such evolutionary theories placed themselves in an atemporal present. From this point of view, the past was necessarily anterior, becoming the present before ultimately arriving in the future. This linearity was precisely what Bergson sought to complexify. Bergson argued that in this conception of time, which he terms "spatialized" (1944, 233), time is understood as a series of intervals rather than a continuum, facilitated by our own inability to be able to separate time from space. Units of time, like hours, minutes, or seconds, are our ways of trying to grasp time, but essentially they are merely quantifiable measurements that derive from how our planet moves through space in relation to the sun. As Bergson writes in *Time and Free Will* of our common understanding of time, "We introduce [space] unwittingly into our feeling of pure succession; we set our states of consciousness side by side in such a way as to perceive them simultaneously, no longer in one another, but alongside one another; in a word, we project time into space . . . and succession thus takes the form of a continuous line or a chain, the parts of which touch without penetrating one another" (1910, 101). Bergson draws on the theories of physicist and mathematician G. B. R. Riemann to make this argument, particularly Riemann's distinction between *qualitative* and *quantitative* multiplicities. For Bergson, a quantitative multiplicity is composed of homogenous elements that can be numbered and distinctly ordered in space. The example he gives is a flock of sheep: each sheep exists in a distinct location and does not touch another sheep, and it is this discontinuity between sheep that allows them to be counted. In contrast, Bergson theorizes time as inherently continuous and interconnected in a processual sense: its elements (unlike sheep) are heterogeneous, cannot be isolated into separate moments, and cannot be counted—that is, time forms a *qualitative multiplicity*. This notion of time as *la durée*, commonly translated into English as *duration*, exits from the temporal ontology of Aristotle, Newton, and Einstein to lay claim to *time itself* as opposed to the measurement of time. Time is no longer the motion of a minute hand pausing over fractions of space. Instead, it becomes the fusion of the experience of nowness with that which will follow; moments that interpenetrate to become inseparable points of a single continuous, connected process; a flow, the "ceaselessly seething surd at the heart of things," in William Barrett's words (1968, 373).

Bergson does not dispute the empirical facts of evolutionary biology: his argument instead centers on *how* things change and the necessary adjustments we must make to our temporal ontology to comprehend this. His understanding of time, la durée, therefore captures "invention, the creation of forms, the continual elaboration of the absolutely new" (Bergson 1944, 14) whereas biological theories, trapped in their conceptualization of time as space, are inevitably *mechanistic* in their step-by-step, incremental linearity: "They understand (individual) development and (trans-individual) evolution as agglomerations or combinations or series of states-of-affairs" (Delitz 2014, 86), each in touching distance but without a discernment premised, as Bergson terms it, on penetration.

What is the significance of such a position? If we move from a linear "clock time" to la durée and its premise that time cannot be broken into separate moments, we must accept that it is not the case that each event is discrete and bounded; instead, each present moment interpenetrates—that is, it acts as a vessel for what Deleuze termed "the thought of the future" (1994, 7), inscribing, in a creative gesture, a future as yet uninscribed. Time becomes durational, a ground of possibility from which, as Clarice articulates, agrarian reform can take on a different form at a different scale and be structured by different values. Time for Clarice becomes "a dynamic field of potential relations without beginning or end, from which the present is actualized" (Pedersen 2012, 144), and this continual elaboration of the new sits at the heart of counter-utopian practice.

Spencer, Darwin, and de Vries may have explained the facts of evolutionary biology, but they could not address the nature of the evolutionary force. While a linear project "consists in cutting up present reality, already evolved, into little bits no less evolved, and then recomposing it with these fragments, thus positing in advance everything" (Bergson 1944, xxiv), for Bergson, the future is unknowable and yet already present in the now. How we arrive into that future, and the change necessary for that to occur, is fundamentally driven by an élan vital, a generative and creative impulse that *actualizes* life in unexpected and unknown directions, assuming trajectories that in their unpredictability can only be understood as possible in a post hoc analysis.[1] This quality to make anew speaks directly to the significance of Clarice's position. In the third and fourth sections of this book, I detail how MST members such as Clarice, Vera, and Tais articulate counter-utopian practices that perhaps seemed unimportant at the time but, within a community framework, took on significance and the power to shape the wider MST. And this is the productive and generative potential of the what-will-become, a continual elaboration located in the present that is the kernel of a durational struggle.

Another way to understand this process of actualization is to go back to the evolutionary theories that Bergson sought to confront. The problem with linearity, Bergson (2002, 232) states, is that we have to "resign ourselves to the inevitable: it is the real which makes itself possible and not the possible which becomes real." This is because, as Heike Delitz (2014, 96) argues, "prevailing evolutionary theories explain only *what has been selected*, instead of explaining what *arises*." Bergson's riposte is to put forward the notion not of how the possible becomes real but rather how the virtual actualizes itself: "Rather than awaiting realization, the virtual *is fully real*; what happens in evolution is that the virtual is actualized" (2014, 89–90). This concept and its pairings of the *virtual/actual* instead of the *possible/real* sit at the heart of Bergson's insistence on la durée as "becoming": if all elements are interpenetrable, in this flux, we can already recognize the presence of moments that are as-yet-to-be; the possible is no longer reality denuded of its existence, predetermined and finite, but is rather *virtual*, fully real, and merely awaiting actualization. This is "true" evolution, a process in which life "involves a movement of differentiation whereby the virtual is actualized in a creative process of divergence" (Ansell Pearson 2019, 20). In such an understanding of transformation, things are spontaneous and unpredictable. Mechanistic theories, on the other hand, "regard the future and the past as calculable functions of the present, and thus . . . claim that all is given" (Bergson 1944, 43).

With the concepts of duration and the virtual in mind, Bergson's thinking offers a unique affordance for discussion of the MST. I have argued that transformation should be understood as located within a durational mode of time. An understanding of time as a flow as opposed to a series of linear moments allows us to perceive how people negotiate an ongoing commitment to social justice. This mode of activism, rooted in duration, is characterized by the presence of counter-utopian practices, which bring about unexpected and unpredictable shifts in the wider movement. And to grasp the tension between the minoritarian and durational on the one hand and the mechanistic and institutional on the other is to comprehend the productive elasticity that underpins the MST's continuing resilience.

Busatto's speech normalizes the distant objective that is the goal of willed transformation—the overthrow of the capitalist system—but also highlights two further considerations: first, how the MST's teleology presupposes linearity and predetermination, and second, how this utopian mode is embedded within a *temporal dimension tied to space*. Busatto's explanation of the stages of the struggle allows us to glimpse the leadership's mechanistic theory of landlessness as evolution—that if the MST's program is carried out correctly, all is predetermined. Second, Busatto's stages are interconnected: land must be occupied, but this land can be won only if people invest their time; only through a long-term struggle can a new society be created. What Busatto presents here bears relation to Bergson's understanding of spatialized time except that for Busatto, time is not spatialized through the ticking of a clock or the movement of the earth around the sun but rather by how much land the movement will manage to claim, how many family plots can be demarcated, and how many hectares will be expropriated and devolved by the federal government. This very particular spatialization of time is premised on a calculus that the MST as an institution has developed with regard to the number of people necessary to occupy a plot of land, the time required to be invested, and the amount of space, measured in hectares, that such an investment will return. In this calculus, time and space are aggregated, and the result is a quantifiable measurement, an equation of time and space that determines resources allocated, years invested, and land devolved. Such a calculus underpins Busatto's third point, the utopian call for a new society. Busatto presents an evolution of the landless struggle based on linearity; he divides landlessness into stages that can be seen all at once from his viewpoint: an encampment will be followed by a settlement, and a settlement will be followed by many centers of rural industrialization until inevitably a new society will be created, and capitalism will be overcome. This is what Bergson terms a "false evolutionism" in which the future is posited in advance, and we are left only with what has been selected instead of an explanation for what has arisen. Durational activism, on the other hand, proposes the unforeseen and the unpredicted through counter-utopian practices that might be imperceptible to those focused on a linear pathway forward.

This disjuncture between temporal ontologies goes right back to the beginnings of the movement. Complementary to influences such as Che Guevara and Fidel Castro, the MST worked with many Brazilian Marxists. An important point of reference in this regard was the sociologist Clodomir Santos de Morais, who had worked in the 1940s and 1950s as a trade unionist and a journalist before becoming a member of the Pernambuco State Assembly and cofounder of the Ligas Camponesas (Peasant Leagues). Morais was a dedicated organizer and developed a mass training method for rural contexts that he termed the Organization Workshop (OW). While he was forced into exile after the military coup in 1964, the OW method was applied in Latin America, Africa, and Europe, and Morais studied in Chile before completing a doctorate at the University of Rostock in the then German Democratic Republic in 1987. When the political situation allowed Morais to return to Brazil, the MST was the first organization to invite him to conduct OWs. Taking place over a period of fifteen to thirty days, with a minimum of forty participants, the first of thirty OWs were held in 1988 in the Palmeira das Missões settlement in Rio Grande do Sul (Stédile and Fernandes 1999, 99). These *laboratórios de campo*, or rural laboratories, complemented an influential training document authored by Morais, in which he identified vices particular to the rural peasant, including "anarchism," "adventurism," and "self-sufficiency" and the necessity to address them (1986, 27–36). Seeking to build capacity among large groups of unemployed and underemployed people, Morais placed a particular emphasis on time and its connection to productivity: "Amongst the rural peasants (*camponeses*), for example, units of time are ill-defined, and in general, long: a *momentinho*, a moment, midday, a week, the next new moon, the harvest etc. Whereas for factory workers time is measured in seconds, minutes, an hour etc. With the development of a mercantile economy, time takes on value: as the English say, 'time is money.' . . . And this is why the biggest concern of the person who produces is to produce the largest quantity of goods in the least possible quantity of time" (1986, 8 my translation). Morais wished to bring about a new temporal ontology within the MST's membership. In criticizing individualism and self-interest, he placed a particular emphasis on spontaneity as a trait to be eradicated.

The spontaneous person is resistant to planning work or actions, much less acting according to a work plan. He prefers to carry out the tasks he finds most pleasant or convenient as well as to do them at the moment he finds most pleasant or convenient. He does not plan anything, he always lives the immediate moment according to his personal interests, because if he submits to a work plan he will not be able to attend to his pending personal matters. . . . Spontaneity has no timetable. For him, the clock is just a simple object of adornment. There is no time or date for anything. If an associate asks him: when are we going to do such and such a thing? he answers: any day, any time. The smallest unit of time he knows is "a moment." (Morais 1986, 31)

The notion of the rural poor living with a clock as mere adornment offers an insight into how important MST leaders framed productivity and temporality. And Morais's work led him to become a feted figure within the MST. In 2017, an encampment in Tocantins was named in his memory, following his death the previous year. Morais had been invited to work with the MST by its most senior leadership, and his observations of the people with whom he was invited to build capacity point to how the movement identified the persistence of a rural understanding of time within its members and sought to address this temporal "defect." To bring about a new society, efficient and massified schemes of production were earmarked as essential, schemes that necessitated ill-defined understandings of time to conform to a new linear paradigm premised on industrialized arrangements of labor. Just as Henri Lefebvre (2004, 99) identifies contested rhythms of time and space in the city as representative of the ways in which capitalism imposes itself on the human body, Morais sought to condition new members in an encampment context where time would be restructured to acquire a new meaning. As people learned how to be landless, it would no longer be acceptable for them to schedule "for after lunch, for tomorrow, for next week, next month, next year" (99). The path to revolution was impatient, spontaneity was frivolity, and the encampment awaited.

Pausa

In an encampment, money is a problem. Many things have to be bought: hygiene products, clothes, black plastic sheeting, tools, wiring. It all needs to be paid for. Many acampados look outside the encampment for paid daily work. The labor is hard and badly paid. People have little choice. Such a job might be working the harvest in a nearby farm. Paulo told me about work of this kind, what he termed a *serviço*, that he had performed: "I went one time picking onions. This is how the *bóias frias*, the day laborers, are exploited. I went with Jessica and Douglas and the three of us were paid five centavos [less than one US cent] for every three yards. Onions are planted in rows, you see. And we were paid five centavos per yard of onions that we dug out of the ground."

I grimaced. Paulo continued: "The work is really hard, like backbreaking, because you have to do it on your knees. You see, after a while it's impossible to pull them from the earth standing up. So you are on your knees in the soil using just your hands, no tools. This is debt bondage, *peonagem*. The work, it makes you feel like an animal."

Paulo told me that working all day, he and the other workers had managed to earn R$40 between them. I asked him if he knew the profit margin of the farmer. "There are around fifteen, twenty kilos [thirty-three to forty-four pounds] of onions per yard," he replied. "The farmer at wholesale gets around thirteen reais per sixty-kilo bag. So of that eight hundred yards that we dug up, he would have sold those onions for R$3,500 and he paid us R$40."

6

Encampment

In vital activity we see, then, that which subsists of the
direct movement in the inverted movement, a *reality which
is making itself in a reality which is unmaking itself.*

HENRI BERGSON, *CREATIVE EVOLUTION*, 248

It's 2008, and Lúcia tells me that André has some business to conduct
for the movement in the acampamento of Novo Horizonte. He wants to
check on some things and see Estela and her husband, both members of
the camp's *coordenação*. "Let's go," she says.

I collect my stuff, and soon, I'm driving with André, Lúcia, and Vera
from the outskirts of the city into farmland, down a federal highway jammed
with trucks, all laden with agricultural produce. We pass a John Deere
showroom, full of glistening tractors and machinery, and a huge, industrialized baker processing the wheat grown in the area. Leaving the agribusiness
behind, we pass a row of big 4x4 pickups and the visible signs of logging. I
ask what's happening here. Lúcia tells me that it's the *fazendeiros*, the big
landowners, carrying out illegal work. She explains that a strip of land on
either side of the federal highway is legally part of the *união federal*—that
is, it's public land. The trees on this land belong to the state, but the fazendeiros are logging them anyway. I ask why no one makes a complaint to the
authorities. Everyone shrugs. There is no point. A complaint can be made,
but it will never be listened to. The incumbent mayor is one of the largest of
the fazendeiros; his 4x4 is probably one of those parked by the side of the
road, André adds.

We chat about how the MST chooses sites for occupation. André is an
important regional leader, head of the frente de massa sector, and making
occupations happen is his principal job. He tells me it's important to consider a site's future economic viability. Factors include a site's proximity
to federal highways and nearby cities, and therefore its potential access to

97

markets. A site's general condition is important, he adds, as is the fertility of the soil. Disputed ownership is another factor that catches the leadership's eye—if there are any legal irregularities regarding its documentation, for example. Maybe the landowner has leased part of his estate without filling in the requisite paperwork, André says, and this makes it easier to put a case together for INCRA to expropriate. Novo Horizonte is highly productive land, it seems, but the owner has sublet the land without permission. André is keen to see how things are going, noting that the encampment sits on prime quality land with good road access to the city.

We have been driving for some time, and André tells me to slow down as we are approaching the acampamento. We cross a sweeping bridge, and at the top of the hill we climb is a cemetery. André instructs me to turn, and I brake, the car sliding over the rough gravel, leaving the asphalt of the highway. I see a roughly drawn hand-painted sign that indicates the estates that can be accessed from this dirt track. One of them is the Fazenda Barranco Alto, the land the MST are occupying. André tells me to be careful and mindful of the holes and rocks, so I slow down. He then chivvies me to speed up, commenting in a matter-of-fact tone that we don't want to be thought of as snooping or trying to arrive unobserved. I can see an MST flag in a tree and then another tied to a tall pole. There are freshly painted white gates, and I pull up in front of them. On them is black lettering that reads, "ACAMPAMENTO NOVO HORIZONTE MST." Written vertically is the legend "SEJAM BEM VINDO." Beyond the gates is a small hut constructed from pine branches and the familiar MST *lona*, the black plastic sheeting. This is the guard post, and next to it hangs a piece of iron and a hammer to strike it in cases of emergency.

As we get out of the car, I notice how the sky above us is a deep blue and the land is a verdant green. On either side of the track in front of us are a number of MST barracas, constructed in the familiar fashion for the south of Brazil, instantly recognizable. Each has a sloping roof and straight walls, and a chimney projects from the stretched black sheeting, smoke coming from a woodburning stove inside. Behind the guardhouse is a soccer pitch with goals roughly fashioned from branches. As we walk down the track, following André, we pass an abandoned barraca, scraps of the black sheeting still nailed to the branches that made up its frame. I ask if people are leaving the encampment, and André tells me there are always people leaving and new people coming. His answer leaves me unsure as to whether the hut has fallen into disrepair or is under construction.

A few people arrive to greet us, and we enter one of the nearest barracas. We're welcomed inside by an elderly man, Wanderley, who motions for us to sit down on his porch, sheltered from the sun by an overhang. The floor is hardened dry earth, and it's spotless, as is the whole area. Inside the hut there is a cooking space and behind that an internal partition of black plastic. As we sit down, Wanderley presents us with a heavy sack of *feijão*, which he offers to me as a gift. He says it's part of the camp's harvest, collectively planted and maintained. Knowing how short on food acampados are, I hesitate to take it, but eventually politeness dictates that I do.

Part of André's job is to organize protests in the nearby cities, and we start speaking about a forthcoming occupation of the INCRA offices in Blumenau. Holding a notebook and pen, André asks for Wanderley's participation and mentions that the minibus will leave at five o'clock the next morning. There's a slightly awkward pause while André waits for an answer. Wanderley makes an excuse, saying it's a long journey and he has to tend to the camp's crops. Standing up to get more hot water for the chimarrão we're drinking, Wanderley offers an apology and says he can't go. After he leaves, André tells me that he needs at least eight people from the acampamento to take part, but he doesn't expect it to be difficult to round up this number. Participation will count heavily in people's favor if and when the land is finally expropriated and divided up.

After leaving Wanderley's barraca, I wander around before heading toward the encampment school. Inside, a tall young man greets me. I recognize him; we met in passing at the 2007 state meeting. His name is Márcio. We say hello and then I greet his class, a group of twelve children aged seven to twelve years old. He tells me he is the schoolteacher, and the children are well behaved. The class laughs, and Márcio smiles as he tells them to take a break. Some of them go outside while others play on the dry earth floor on the other side of the room.

I ask Márcio how long he has been encamped. He tells me it has been six years. He seems glad to take a break. I ask him if it is hard work teaching the acampamento's children. He says that it isn't easy, that they have very little materials, and that the days can be long. It's dark in the schoolroom, with only two openings cut into the wooden boards. I wonder what they do when it rains, which it frequently does here in this part of the state. The walls have drawings of Brazil on them, and the rough chairs and tables all face his desk, behind which is set of shelves with a few books.

In the semidarkness, I look more closely at Márcio. He looks close to thirty, but he tells me he's sixteen. His face is prematurely lined and his clothes, like many people's in the acampamento, are faded from the sun shine and dust. He looks weary and tired. Sitting down, I ask him whether he has always been encamped in Novo Horizonte. He tells me that he and his father have been evicted from the encampment twice already and that in total, he has been evicted five times during his six years. I ask what it means to be evicted. Márcio tells me that landowners will forcibly evict you with hired men and the camp will be destroyed. However, in most cases, this is considered only a temporary setback: the movement will re-establish the occupation once they have reorganized the evicted acampados. When a forcible eviction takes place, the police can also sometimes be involved, and it might take place at night, Márcio relates. When it happens in this way, people have to leave with nothing; there is no time to organize transport to take your stove or furniture. You lose everything. Your barraca will be torn down, and your crops will be burned. Landowners can be ruthless, Márcio says. He relates a story I heard before about the acampamento of Vitória, where the landowner poisoned the water source with dead animals. It seems that incidents like this are common. Evictions can be frightening experiences, but the situation in Paraná, Márcio tells me, is much more dangerous than here in Santa Catarina. I tell him that I have seen some cars and even a truck in the camp. Márcio nods, saying that the truck belongs to Polaco, previously encamped in Vitória, but most of the cars don't run. Wearily, he tells me that this is the third incarnation of Novo Horizonte and that each time they come back they have to reconstruct everything—the water, the houses, the school. "Hard work," I say.

Márcio nods. "It's hard." There's a pause. "Six years." He shrugs. He doesn't know how long it will take for the land to be expropriated, and neither do I. It seems there is nothing more to do than stay encamped and keep on working. As I walk out into the daylight again, it strikes me that the whole of Márcio's adolescent life has been set to this slow rhythm of the encampment. Six years *debaixo da lona preta*, under black plastic sheeting, as they say in the movement.

It's time to leave. In the car, André is talking about the land. He's excited, saying that it's very good quality, that you can grow almost anything on it. I ask him how many families are registered as encamped. He says there are forty-eight families encamped permanently and another fifty or so who come on the weekends and live and work elsewhere during the week. It's good land, he repeats, and adds that three hundred hectares is good for twenty to thirty families.

"Twenty to thirty families," I say. "So each family gets just over ten ha?"

"That's right," André answers.

"What happens to the other families encamped on Novo Horizonte? The ones that don't get land?"

"They will have to move," André says in a matter-of-fact way. "Encamp again."

I think about something José, Lúcia's brother, mentioned to me: "The acampamento is where you truly learn how to be a sem terra. It's a great education."

* * *

February 2009. At Lúcia's house, there's talk of activity up at the acampamento. I hear rumors of a *divergência*, a serious disagreement. André is now in hiding from the police and worried for his safety. I ask Vera what happened. After much pressing, she finally tells me that Márcio's father has been causing problems in the camp and that Luizinho and André went up there last night to expel him from the movement. I ask her what kind of problems the father was causing, but she won't say. I ask her if Márcio had to leave as well, but she won't say. She tells me that Márcio's father, angry at the way he has been treated, has threatened to go to the police and reveal André and Luizinho's names and whereabouts. As regional leaders, these men are potential targets. Vera is worried for her husband. I immediately head to Novo Horizonte.

The first thing that I notice is that the school is locked up. There are few people around, but I see a group of young men gathered around a barraca, and I go to talk with them. They tell me they are from the outskirts of Joinville, the biggest city in the state. We are joined from inside the barraca by its owner, a middle-aged man named Marinho. After some conversation, I ask about Márcio and his father, but nobody will say anything apart from the fact that there has been an *expulso*, an expulsion. I press for more information, but no one will talk about it. All that the group will say is that the coordenação has expelled them. I spend a long time talking to this group of young men, and afterward we go and play soccer on the pitch. I start to think about Márcio again, looking at the empty school. Márcio worked hard for the movement. He taught full time and was present at all the important meetings, the *encontro estadual*, the *encontro dos sem terrinha*; he was interested, engaged, helping out. He had been encamped for six years, but since he had been expelled, no one even wants to talk about him. It is as if by suffering the expulsion order he has suddenly become unmentionable; in a way, he and his father perhaps never existed at all.

Back at Lúcia's house, I'm talking to Lúcia, Vera, and José. I ask them why the movement places more families in occupation on land than it can sustain as an assentamento. Vera tells me it is to do with security, that in the face of repression it's better to have greater numbers of people for the acampados' safety. José then returns to the notion of the encampment as an education. He tells me that the acampamento and the systems within it are how you discover you are sem terra. Numbers are important, he suggests, because the encampment is the environment in which your new identity is formed, and this is easier to accomplish when you are in a large group rather than a smaller unit. My mind flashes back to the encampment. We just finished playing soccer, and one of the young men was walking with me down the track. I was thinking about Márcio, of all that he gave and of all he had taken away. The young man stopped and indicated the acampamento, the earth, the black plastic sheeting, the gates, the crowded huddle of people struggling to get by. "*Nunca pensei nisso,*" he said simply. I could never have imagined this.

I recount the story to Vera in 2022. "So many things happened," she says. "Bad things." We talk about our memories of that time. Later I message, "Was that land ever devolved?" A short answer: Ñ.

* * *

The encampment is central to the MST in both strategic and practical terms. It is the principal means through which the movement exercises political power and maintains itself at the forefront of the struggle for agrarian reform. The ritualistic significance of encampment looms large: the notion that to become sem terra one must first undergo the process of encampment is strong, particularly among movement leadership. It is the primary locus of a social transformation, a process designed to empower members and make possible their rebirth as new social citizens.

From the beginning, when new members arrive at an encampment site and are organized by frente de massa activists, they are organized to work collectively. Tasks include building huts, digging latrines, establishing security, and choosing the camp's coordenação, the leadership committee. As André and Wanderley's interaction demonstrates, members in encampments are also expected to participate in marches and demonstrations in urban areas, which might include roadblocks or occupations of state agencies. On a day-to-day basis, nutrition is provided by the *cesta básica*. This delivery from INCRA typically comprises feijão and arroz, rice and beans, perhaps with sugar, eggs, vegetable oil, and milk. Those encamped add to this by planting crops. In the Vitória encampment, acampados planted fields of corn, salads, and root vegetables. Likewise in Novo Horizonte, there were collectively farmed fields of feijão in addition to other smaller plots. Water is often a problem in encampments, and most tend to use a tank to collect rainwater, which is then plumbed to various locations. Vitória had quarters for visitors with hand-fashioned bunk beds as well as a shower enclosure plumbed into the rainwater tank immediately above. Beyond washing facilities, drinking water can be problematic, as landowners have been known to contaminate streams from which the encamped drink. There is almost never electricity in encampments, and people rely on stopgap measures such as a truck battery wired to a single bulb; these truck batteries are recharged in local garages, and a single charge can last a month. Wired to a television, the charge may last ten days. It is expensive to recharge these batteries—the cost in 2009 was roughly R$15 per charge.

Once a camp has established its routine, monotony becomes a challenge. The encamped may spend years waiting for a federal decision to change their lives. In Santa Catarina, this lack of activity sometimes brought about fighting and other forms of restlessness. People played soccer for something to do, but tensions occur, and accidents happen. In Novo Horizonte, one of Wanderley's grandchildren drowned in a nearby small lake only a few weeks before my first visit. Living in an encampment is an insecure life, and people are desperate to gain a plot of land and begin a new chapter. As a member of the frente de massa, the former trade unionist Paulo was responsible for organizing the camps, and we spoke about how they were structured.

"Behavioral rules give a sense of security," he told me. "The acampamento is a space which we try to free from bad influences. All sorts of people go there with all sorts of bad things, so sometimes people fight amongst themselves over small things. Alcohol, sometimes they drink in the acampamento . . . so there are rules that you can't drink in the camp." I asked whether people obeyed these rules. "They obey. They obey because if they don't, they are invited to retire from the camp." He laughed. "In fact, they are expelled. We call an assembly. For example, it's not permitted to have any amount of alcohol within the camp. But there are people who arrive drunk, maybe they've gone to the city to drink, and they come back drunk. In the camp there are children, young people and so on, and so the drunk guy comes back and perhaps tries to be the big man, domestic violence and so on. In this case, the camp's security will take the guy and place him in what we call the *guarita*, which is a lodge where the security people congregate, a lookout post. So, there are rules."

For Paulo, life in the camps was characterized by structure. There was a period of silence and an alarm call to wake people up. Between six a.m. and ten p.m., people were free to make whatever noise they wanted, "listening to radios, messing around with pots and pans, whatever," he told me, but at ten o'clock, silence was enforced. And there was always a state of alert. "We have coded calls, done by the number of times the iron gong by the entrance is struck. For example, it might be that one strike is 'time of silence.' Two might be 'alert'—something strange is happening in the camp. Three might be 'assembly.' Four might be 'police in the camp' and then everyone will come out with their agricultural tools to defend themselves."

From 2008 onward, I noticed that camps were increasingly populated by younger people from the outskirts of cities like Joinville, Chapeco, and São José. As a former trade unionist from an urban background, Paulo was proud of his role in including people from the *periferia* in the MST encampments. He recounted that what he termed as the "*favelas*" were so violent, children were not able to play in the street. By contrast, the encampment was a safe environment in which to bring up children, which was a big motivation for his work.

"At six or seven p.m.," Paulo told me, "when night comes, people lock themselves in their houses and they can't come out until daybreak. This is the reality of the periferia. But in our acampamentos, it's exactly the opposite. People have freedom, they can chat and socialize much more. People play guitar, sing, mess around. Normally the children can play late into the night without fear of anything, without the fear of suffering violence or being hooked on any sort of drug."

Was it easy, I asked, for people to make the journey from the city to the countryside? "The difficulty is to communicate this vision to people," Paulo replied. "Not in words, but for them to believe and understand what it really is like." He paused. "I mean, even though the social transformation that we want seems delayed, even though agrarian reform is delayed, that people have to wait one year, two years, I don't know, four or five years encamped so that they can become assentados and have a better life in a different form— this period in which they encamp is much richer, much more satisfying than if they stay in the periferia."

The idea of "rescuing" people from the violence of the city was commonly held by MST leaders. On another occasion, Luizinho spoke of the transformative process that he sought to bring about in the encampments.

"I wanted to talk about the difficulty of working with the urban people," he told me. "Because from the urban people, not saying anything bad about anyone in particular, but they come with a ton of vices. Real vices: gambling, drugs, the vice of alcohol, for example. But on the other hand, the movement gives these people an opportunity to be human again, we take them and produce new people. So many of them, when they first came to the encampment, they were nothing, nothing had ever worked out for them, but after the encampment process, they became new people. And this is our challenge, to work with people in the encampments to produce new human beings."

I asked Luizinho about who the MST was recruiting. "As you know," he replied, "it's begun to change, because there are no more countryside people here, all of them have already gone to the city. And it's these people who've gone to the city who we have to bring back. So this challenge of working with urban people, it's necessary because in fact, we talk about agrarian reform, but there's few rural folk left around here."

In this kind of restricted space over long periods, Gabriel Ondetti (2008, 114) has suggested, encampments can function "as spaces for political indoctrination and collective identity building" in which members of the frente de massa sector "work the consciousness of campers, cultivating a leftist political perspective and loyalty to the goals, methods and symbols of the MST." And while Luizinho conducted political orientation classes roughly once a month in Novo Horizonte, these sessions could not be described as anything even approaching indoctrination. That said, for leaders like Luizinho and Paulo, discipline and clear rules were intrinsic to the transformative potential of the encampment, and the experiences of Márcio and his father demonstrate that MST leaders can wield executive power. In such situations there is no formal right to appeal, and because of this, the encamped have an incentive to obey camp coordinators and frente de massa leaders. There is also the question of how land is allocated if expropriation is achieved. Because more people are encamped than can eventually gain land, acampados have an incentive to make a good impression. When André comments that of the one hundred people registered in Novo Horizonte only thirty or so would be given land in any future settlement, Wanderley's calculation as to whether to go to the occupation becomes more tangible.

Nashieli Rangel Loera's book *A Espiral das Ocupações de Terra* (2006) confines itself almost entirely to the MST encampment, and her ethnography highlights how daily life in the camp consists of mundane as well as more significant moments: "exchanges, odd jobs, help, where people date, marry and separate, where conflicts arise and alliances are woven" (13). In among the everyday, Rangel Loera argues, "dependence and reciprocity" are created among the frente de massa leaders, the encamped, and those who live on nearby settlements, relations she describes as a logic of commitments and obligations. Putting aside notions of indoctrination, she suggests that "in the encampment, this discipline [the rules and obligations] is part of the 'contract' to which an acampado must adhere to be able to stay in the encampment and to be able to win land" (109).

The terms of this unwritten contract are at stake in the encampment process. In these early stages, the MST expects its members to obey certain rules, assume a political consciousness, and become sem terra through a praxis of the collective. In Santa Catarina, where many recruits are from urban peripheries, people are envisaged as leaving behind the violence of the city to be reborn as members of a new society, cleansed of the vices, both moral and physical, that previously held them back. But also at play in the space of the encampment is another unstated compact that underpins the movement's utopian vision: a linear temporality that aggregates space and time in the very act of occupation.

In encampments, a strict routine governs daily life. There is a morning wake-up call, a notification of silence, and a series of patrols that occur at night to guard the camp from intruders. These events structure any given day and divide time into repetitive blocks. Collective work further reinforces time as structure, allowing frente de massa leaders to pick up on which acampados in the encampment are succumbing to the vices previously outlined by figures such as Clodomir de Morais. Rangel Loera (2010, 290) suggests that time in the encampment also exhibits another quality, which she terms *tempo de acampamento*, encampment time: "This expression references the set of relationships and activities an individual engages in which are perceived as being related to their level of commitment, their dedication to their tent, the encampment, the movement in general, to their fulfilment of their obligations, as well as their demonstrations of loyalty." Time here is seen as a currency of dependability and a marker of status. It is more than a chronological measure of how long a person spends encamped; rather, it indicates prestige and "orders social relations within the camp" (Rangel Loera 2014, 195). Rangel Loera describes how those encamped "soon learn that it is not enough to have a barraca in an encampment to be a candidate for agrarian reform, a series of obligations and criteria must also be fulfilled" (196). And one time, while watching his soccer team, Grêmio, Davi explained to me how the leaders decided which acampados would be awarded land and which would not: "It's like, who's going to win this cup," he told me. "We put the names in and draw one. So it's done like that. The coordenação meet and discuss, they see which families have been there longest, which are most prepared . . . because there are a lot of acampados."

I looked squarely at him. Laughing, he made a gesture as if to admit defeat. "There are problems with everything," he continued. "So logically, the coordenação looks and evaluates. It's like this: Look, you're not ready to win land yet. If we give you some land, you aren't going to progress. You might be able to produce, to try, but not progress, because your head's not right yet—so you're going to have to stay encamped longer. We'll pick some others, *sortear*, those who are more ready, *firme na cabeça*, those who deserve it more!"

Encampment time connects time to moral participation. But there is another dimension missing from this analysis: space. Which particular acampados gain land is important to the MST as an organization: as Davi comments, the movement wants members who will be able to progress. But what also matters is that the movement keeps growing though the continual establishment of new settlements. Time, in this sense, is more than a fulfillment of a moral contract. It is the investment required for the acquisition of space, and this spatiotemporal relationship is a crucial underpinning of the movement's teleology. This majoritarian understanding posits time as spatially aggregated, as inextricably tied to quantitative measurement: the number of hectares that will be expropriated and devolved by the federal government.

The frente de massa leader Paulo acknowledges this understanding of time when he discusses the delayed nature of the MST's transformation. People might have to be encamped for up to five years, he comments, but it will be worth it to become an assentado, with "a better life in a different form." And even in this five-year period, he comments, life in the camp is infinitely richer and more productive than "if they stay in the periferia counting the days, watching the barbarity of life there happen around them." Paulo's vision of counting the days perfectly brings together the subjunctive grammar that is characteristic of the MST's utopian mode and the quantitative calculation that will result in a number of hectares of land being registered to a settler's name.

In this sense, the encampment is very much the social "stretched-out" of Doreen Massey's (1994, 22) theorization. It is a space in which people quickly learn how to become sem terra through adherence to values such as collectivization and productivity. The encampment is the tangible form of a spatiotemporal relationship that underpins the utopian compact: as the second hand moves around the watch, each increment brings the encamped—and those more fully aligned with movement values—closer to the realization of a dream: their own plot of land. And with each hectare gained, each settlement and quantitative data entry brings the MST closer to the realization of the dream of agrarian reform, the birth of a new society.

Pausa

I'm sitting on the grass outside Lúcia's house. We've arranged to meet, and she's really late. As the hours pass, I feel restless, frustrated, and annoyed. From time to time, people clap their hands from the pavement, signaling they want to come and sell something. The Quadrangular church has already passed by. The pastor's house is not far away; it's the largest house in the neighborhood.

Lúcia finally turns up. "Where have you been?" I ask. "*Porra*! I've been sitting here for ages!"

She grins and shrugs her shoulders. "Who wouldn't want to be sitting around in the sunshine for all that time with nothing to do?" Her reply strikes me. There's no comeback to that. I laugh, and we go inside.

Later that day, I ask Lúcia what she thinks about the MST leadership. We've joked about it a few times. Lúcia is a point of contact for visiting leaders as they pass through the north, and sometimes, she uses the word *chefão*, big boss, to describe them. They can be annoying, and sometimes they talk down to you, she says, but leadership is necessary.

"It has to be like this, no? If not, it would become a mess." She's busy sweeping her front porch. "They are kind of demanding—'Do it like this!' or 'Do it like that because it will work out better.' But sometimes it does work out better the way they say. You see, the people really look to the leadership. So, when there was that big conflict with the army at Papanduva, the people that had come from acampamentos and assentamentos went to Busatto and his brother, people like that, and they were saying, 'What should we do?' And what they are told to do, they do it, understand? 'Go up there!' They go up there. 'Stay down here!' They stay down here. People look to the leadership."

I ask if she thinks sometimes this discipline might go too far. "Perhaps sometimes it could be, no?" she replies. "But most of the time the leadership has got their feet on the ground. They know what they are doing."

7

Institutionalization

> To demonstrate the fundamental differences between
> housework and other types of work; unmask the process
> of naturalization this work had undergone because of its
> unwaged condition; show the specific capitalist nature and
> functioning of the wage; and demonstrate that historically
> the question of "productivity" has always been connected
> with the struggle for social power.
>
> SILVIA FEDERICI, *REVOLUTION AT POINT ZERO*, 4

On the occasion of the MST's twenty-fifth anniversary, there was a
ceremony to celebrate this important milestone. Held at the symbolically important Fazenda Anonni in Rio Grande do Sul, the
site of one of the movement's first occupations, João Pedro Stédile affirmed
the MST's commitment to a new type of struggle, one he termed *reforma
agrária popular*, or the people's agrarian reform. Standing on a stage with a
huge MST flag as a backdrop, he outlined how such a program needed to go
beyond the redistribution of land. It was necessary, he argued, for a popular
agrarian reform to establish collectivized working arrangements and small
agrobusinesses in rural areas. The first priority was productivity: the movement needed to focus on producing wholesome, natural foods derived from
native seeds. This required a program of education, and Stédile painted a fu
ture in which all rural people, young and old, would have access to scientific
knowledge. However, he stated, in taking this path, the movement would
make new enemies: Parmalat, Nestlé, agribusiness, and finally neoliberalism itself. He warned that the long-standing struggle of merely occupying
and settling land would be easy compared to the new lines of battle that
were being drawn. The frontier was now so large that the MST, more than
ever, needed to ally itself with other progressive forces—the unions, the

leftist parties, and all the activists who wanted change in Brazil—in order to defeat the capitalist model of domination. The speech ended with a typical movement ritual: Stédile led the audience through a renewal of vows to the struggle. With left hands raised, crooked at the elbow, hands balled into fists, the audience intoned, "We promise to struggle alongside the Brazilian people." Stédile then shouted, "Viva o MST!" to which the audience bellowed, "Viva!"

"Long live the working class!"

"Viva!"

"Long live the Brazilian people!"

"Viva!"

The commemoration, which took place in January 2009, was a significant event that occurred during my first period of fieldwork. After the event, the MST's website published some birthday greetings written by significant figures including actors, university professors, bishops, and union leaders. There was also a contribution by Eduardo Galeano, the Uruguayan writer: "The MST is the most democratic social organization that Brazil has or has ever had. It does not overlook the individual needs of its members, as political organizations usually do, and is capable of combining them with the broader needs of the struggle for land. Not only the struggle for land, but the struggle for the emancipation of Brazil. Not only of Brazil as a nation, but of Brazilians as people."

Writing in the early 2000s, both Branford and Rocha (2002) and Wright and Wolford (2003) described how the movement was designed to eschew a single centralized decision-making body, with decisions being made in the assemblies of MST settlements. Wright and Wolford (2003, xiv) stated how the MST sought to work through collective leadership, "scrupulously avoiding dependence on a single leader." And Branford and Rocha described how at the Cascavel conference in 1984, the organizational principles of the movement were defined to guarantee this: "The sem-terra were anxious to not let a clique of powerful leaders dominate the movement, so they decided not to create individual posts, such as president, treasurer, or executive secretary, but to run the movement as far as possible in a collective way, with a decentralised administration. . . . Delegates stressed the need to build a strong internal democracy. Leaders and coordinators must be permanently linked to the rank and file, they said, and every member should participate in decision-making through meetings and small group discussions" (2002, 30). Branford and Rocha identified the encampment coordination committee as the building block of the MST leadership pyramid. The encampment committee elected two representatives to sit on the board of the regional coordination committee, which in turn elected two more representatives to the state coordination committee. They described how this body was too large to function effectively, so the state coordination committee then elected the *direção estadual*, the state leadership, which ran all business on a state level. The state leadership then elected two further representatives to the national coordination committee, but "again it is the smaller national council, the *direção national*, made up of people which is the more powerful body" (253). Thus, in their understanding, the acampamento committee underpinned the entire leadership structure of the MST. To guard against entrenchment and to ensure that "new ideas from the grassroots are fed into the council," they noted that although national leaders had a mandate of two years and could then be reelected, "the movement encourages a turnover of about one third at each election" (253).

Over the years, various critiques of the MST's grassroots democracy have been articulated (Navarro 2002; Martins 2002; Calvo Gonzalez 2004; Gurr 2017). And perhaps it's the case that a vision in which acampamentos are ultimately electing the most senior leaders of the MST was an ideal to aim for rather than a reality that came to pass. The national leadership is generally not so relevant to everyday life in encampments and settlements. Declarations by national-level leaders are issued from one of the movement's bases in São Paulo, either the Escola Florestan Fernandes or the MST national secretariat downtown, and the content tends to be strategic or geared more toward national and international audiences. National leadership oversee the MST's social media accounts and overall strategic direction, but most of the important decisions regarding what happens in settlements and encampments are taken by state leadership. Tais commented to me that while she knew who some of the national-level leadership were, she didn't have any contact with them. The daughter of Kleber, a regional leader, Tais told me she saw more of the regional- and state-level leadership on a day-to-day basis. Because of her father's leadership role, Tais was used to socializing with leaders, but other MST members, especially the encamped, were often wary of state and regional leadership and the power they could wield.

State leaders decided where and when to occupy land, they structured the organization of new encampments, and they appointed people to leadership roles in their own sectors. In making these decisions, they relied heavily on the regional level of leadership—people such as André, regional head of the frente de massa; Luizinho, regional head of education; and Kleber, regional head of production. These three men had a great deal of discretion in selecting and forwarding potential leaders. For example, André appointed

the coordinators of each acampamento in his region. This process re-
volved around the interaction between André and his immediate superior,
Grimaldi, who was the one of the state leads for frente de massa. Grimaldi
worked closely with other state leaders who were well-known figures across
Santa Catarina. One was a gruff character called Osni, a huge man with a
ready smile. Another was a woman named Dona Franciele who, Lúcia told
me, had gained acceptance among the men of the frente de massa through
an incident in which she had hacked at a military policeman's arm with a
foice, the symbolically important long-handled scythe. Grimaldi would deliberate André's suggestions and, together with other members of the state
leadership, decide who would head the acampamentos in the northern and
coastal regions in Santa Catarina. Luizinho performed a similar role for education. He selected and vetted Márcio to be the schoolteacher in the Novo
Horizonte acampamento, and because MST education-sector workers are
state employees, this power had a financial connotation. Kleber's responsi-
bilities were more concerned with trying to ensure that settlements in his
region remained productive. And despite problems with productivity in his
own assentamento, which was collectively organized, he had held this role
since 2001. In fact, his presence acted as a barrier to Vera, who wished to take
on this role and had been his unofficial local-level deputy. Due to the time
Kleber had already served, however, he was considered unmovable, and entrenchment was a question within the movement. All the leaders I spoke
with in 2007 were still leaders in 2023, with the exception of André. João
Pedro Stédile was still a member of the MST's national leadership. Busatto,
first formally settled in 1985, still led the MST in Santa Catarina. Luizinho
still headed the education sector in the north. Kleber was the go-to figure
for production on the coast. But in Branford and Rocha's portrayal of grassroots decentralization, there is an unanswered question as to how what they
term the "old guard" of the movement might "eventually hand over power to
a new generation of democratically elected leaders" (2002, 254).

The tenure of leadership—and, on the other hand, a commitment to
grassroots politics—points to a contradiction within life lived in the movement. Like many other aspects held in tension, younger members wish to
have their say, and the entrenchment of leadership positions is subject to
ongoing critique. Because of her father, Kleber, and his leadership role, Tais
knew she was in an awkward position when she described the MST as a
gerontocracia, meaning a state, society, or group governed by old people. She
had a huge amount of respect for her father, but when Tais's partner, Wagner, described how the institutionalization of the leadership was a major
barrier to the emerging of new ideas, she agreed, suggesting that the leaders

had pulled up the drawbridge because they didn't want to give up the power they had gained. She pointed out that much of the state and national leadership were in their forties or older—that is, of the generation who were young men at the time of the conference of 1984 in Cascavel. Tais also mentioned that Maíra, a woman in her settlement, had taken to referring to the state leadership as dinosaurs, such was her frustration with their intransigence and lack of forward thinking. Such attitudes are not uncommon across the MST membership. Melinda Gurr's work with young MST members details how a member named Bea was disillusioned with the MST in São Paulo, principally because of its "antidemocratic tendencies, pervasive gerontocracy, and sexism" (2017, 148–49).

As I recounted earlier, Márcio and his father were expelled from the movement. After six years encamped, they left with nothing because of an argument Márcio's father had with André. Due to the fallout and people's unwillingness to speak about Márcio once he had gone, I was never able to discover the precise subject of the dispute. Expulsions occur in the MST. Elena Calvo Gonzalez (2004, 237) has written of tensions in a settlement in Bahia where members "face issues of hierarchy within the organization and witness the use of violence by MST leaders when assentados' actions are not what the hierarchical leadership expected." And Christine Chaves (2000) has detailed summary expulsions of those transgressing leaders' authority in her book, which describes an MST march to Brasília.

As Paulo and Luizinho make clear, there are rules in the MST, and it's unsurprising that the maintenance of order figures in the daily experience of life in a movement with over a million members. The MST as an institution has always prioritized order and unity, seeing a disciplined approach as the best way to achieve the movement's goals. Whether through the application of collectivized production, learning how to be sem terra in the encampment, or becoming a new man through hard work and political training, a normalized sem terra identity becomes apparent to many joining the movement. Wendy Wolford locates this identity as within "oppositional class character" (2003, 507), arguing that it has its own revolutionary genealogy, being discursively and aesthetically linked to Che Guevara; Zumbi, the Brazilian quilombola leader; and Antonio Conselheiro, a religious leader who led a rebellion against the federal government at the turn of the nineteenth century. Wolford theorizes sem terra identity using Benedict Anderson's (1983) classic notion of imagined community, and in her reading, a strong collective identity becomes a device with which to guarantee the continued involvement of those who have won land, thus fortifying the movement overall. Like Calvo Gonzalez and Chaves, Wolford also details the consequences of falling foul of the expectations that such an identity imposes, detailing infractions she encountered and consequent expulsions. She comments that "discriminatory membership is an important component of community—there would be little appeal to sacrificing everything for a movement that anyone could join" (Wolford 2010, 80).

Such a conclusion speaks to lived contradictions. Maintaining order with regard to petty infractions or expelling drunken troublemakers from MST marches is of minor importance. What seems more pertinent is how hierarchical instances of leadership, empowered to maintain unity and collective discipline, regulate, for example, the challenging of essentialized identities or gender norms or how social structures underpinned by an "imagined unity of identities that in everyday life are never experienced as a stable core of self" (Stephen 2001, 67) are regulated. George Meszaros has written about the movement's achievements while also detailing its paradoxes, describing it as "pragmatic" (2000a, 4). And pragmatism is an angle that Miguel Carter (2010) has particularly emphasized about the MST. Indeed, an unpicked thread in this wider contradiction can be perceived here in Carter's writing: "Within the landless movement, one can find some of the most relentless, no-nonsense practitioners of grassroots democracy in Brazil. Given the crude realities of Brazilian politics and harsh conditions under which agrarian reform must be implemented, one cannot expect the MST's contribution to democracy in Brazil to be anything less than muscle bound, forceful, and rough. By virtue of birth and necessity, the MST's distinct mark has been that of the tough touch" (2010, 211–12). Such gendered language—muscle bound, forceful, rough—speaks to a series of masculine tropes associated with the MST's "tough touch" and a long-unresolved tension in Marxist revolutionary politics. Since the 1970s, the feminist theorist Silvia Federici has asked why Marxist critiques of capitalism have failed to acknowledge unwaged work and the diverse forms of domestic labor that are taken for granted within a patriarchal system of power. Federici, together with Heidi Hartmann (1979) and Christine Delphy (1977), rejected the Orthodox Marxist notion that class is the only determining factor of exploitation. They contested the traditional Marxist feminist position that if class oppression were to be overcome, gender oppression would equally cease to exist. Rather, patriarchy is a phenomenon that exists separately from capitalism, and the feminist struggle must articulate a position separate from that of the worker. In this manner, feminism cannot be considered a subcategory in the struggles between economic classes, and as such, women's oppression cannot be subsumed within a broader class struggle.

By the 1980s, almost all major peasant organizations and rural trade unions in Latin America "had women's secretariats of some sort" (Deere and León 2001, 129). In Brazil, women in unions began to establish women-only organizations in response to concerns regarding being overlooked for positions of seniority. In the mid to late 1980s, the Rural Workers' Women's Movement of the Northeast (Movimento de Mulheres Trabalhadoras Rurais— MMTR-NE) was established in the city of Recife, and the Articulation of Rural Women Workers of the South (Articulação de Mulheres Trabalhadoras Rurais do Sul—AMTRS) was established in the south. Echoing Hartmann's notion of an unhappy marriage between Marxism and feminism, Deere and León (2001, 130) note that "while a number of gains have been made with respect to rural women's land rights, these have tended to take a back seat to the class-based demand to deepen agrarian reform."

Rute Caldeira's (2009) work with the MST posited the movement as having subsumed women's demands for the greater good of the class-based collective. In her analysis based on fieldwork conducted in the state of Rio de Janeiro, Caldeira argues that "despite the MST's public commitment to gender equality as a strategy to undermine what the movement leaders call a 'sexist capitalist model,' on the ground, women's issues are still seen as divisive" (2009, 249). She draws a comparison between what she understood the movement to advocate in theory and how it approached gender issues in practice, noting that between these two positions there was a "clear dissonance" (249). Caldeira suggests that sem terra identity came to represent a "class-in-itself" (250), a rural but increasingly urban worker at the margins whose needs as part of a working class were the defining characteristic of the struggle, and that "only the problems that clearly affect this community as a whole, as a collective or as a class-for-itself are given priority" (250). For Caldeira, the existence of a gendered class-based identity meant that women and their concerns were easier to ignore in the MST than they might have been otherwise, as women had no primary identity within the movement. She states that "the family unit is central for the strategic struggle against the forces of neo-liberalism and imperialism" and that the "MST does not separate women from the family unit" (250), concluding that "it is not the will of the movement to develop [a gender-oriented policy]" (254). Caldeira's ethnography highlights how women who were heads of households or lived alone found it difficult to orient themselves in settlements or encampments as they didn't fit into a traditional family structure. Indeed, such "women without men" (253), as she termed them, perceived themselves to have strayed so far from the path that they became apprehensive of forming women's groups as they didn't wish to make themselves even more obvious than they already were. These women were faced with difficult choices. They often considered leaving the movement but were held back by the possibility of destitution.

On the MST's website and social media channels, encampments and settlements are almost always populated by families: families settled, families living in cooperatives, or families in resistance. On both the English- and Portuguese-language versions of the MST website's "About" page, there are references to the number of families, families articulating for education, and families occupying land. As I wrote previously, the centrality of the notion of the family goes back to the very beginning of the movement, to its formalization in 1984 at the meeting in Cascavel. Julia Guivant, a longtime professor at the University of Santa Catarina, draws attention to this emphasis and concludes that "the family is still the natural unit of reference for discussing women's issues. Problems faced by single women, widows, or separated women in settlements, or in gaining access to land, for example, are not considered" (2003, 27). Spending time in the northern settlement, I sometimes saw women wearing the T-shirts of the Movement of Peasant Women, the Movimento de Mulheres Camponesas, and often heard women laugh and joke about how they needed to "keep the men in check" or "remember the struggle of the MST women." Tais and Lúcia contextualized such throwaway remarks when they told me how difficult it was for women to become regional leaders, let alone state leaders. Women were guided down typically gender-normative routes such as working in the health or education sectors, but they were aware that the real power lay in the frente de massa, a sector to which they had limited access. The veteran Chilean activist Marta Harnecker cites an interview with a "Mass Front" leader, who describes the sector as "not just one more sector or activity, it is its very heart, it pumps blood to the whole movement" (2003, 39). One of the only female frente de massa state leaders in Santa Catarina was Dona Franciele, and Lúcia and I would laugh about the stories of how she had won her place as a militante on the front line. But in 2009, things changed, as did Lúcia's happy-go-lucky attitude toward the leadership. In 2017, many years after things unfolded, I found myself back in the northern settlement. Vera told me the women in the settlement knew I was staying with her. From her tone, I understood that she wanted to speak about something she considered a delicate matter. I asked her what she thought about all the things that had happened.

"You have to write about it," she said. "It's what happened!" "They all said to me, the other women. They know. They know what it's like. They said to me, he has to write about it, tell him to write about it."

I think back to those times often. They were not easy.

8

Ruin

Bianchini is feted as a *companheiro histórico*, a historic comrade. In an interview in 2021, he spoke about his youth: "The colonizers [people who 'cleared' the land of Indigenous peoples in preparation for its settlement] sold parcels of land," he recounted. "Back then, the colonizers, they made a classification: the Italians were put in a community, the people of German origin in another, the *caboclos* [a pejorative term for people of mixed race, typically of Indigenous descent] in another. So in that way, in our community, there were two caboclo families and there was a family of Polish origin, but there was a ton of us, all the same, *tutti Italiani*, all Italians." He laughed. He commented how it was difficult for his mother growing up in what was a chauvinist community. Joking lightheartedly with his interviewer, he recounted how he learned to wash dishes only when he was much older: "That was women's work," he said. "The bedroom, cooking, the bathroom, the kitchen."

* * *

November 2008. André seems distracted. Lúcia and I agree that he has been like this for months now, withdrawn and a little lost. When I first met him, André was dynamic and consumed by movement business. He was the embodiment of a regional leader of the frente de massa, and he traveled all over the state, organizing demonstrations, hiring transport, and collecting lists of acampados to participate in movement activities. Vera used to say that she more or less lived on her own: André spent that much time involved with movement work. She would comment that she was worried about him, that he wouldn't come home for nights on end, and she would be sitting at home imagining that something terrible had happened or that he had been arrested by the police. In the region, André was a regular visitor in the encampments, making sure that operations were running smoothly and that morale had not dropped too low. I first met him at the state meeting in 2007 and was impressed by his obvious passion for the movement. But Lúcia doesn't want to talk about André and his problems. Something's wrong. Lúcia has moved on, so I drop it.

Three months later. André seems to have given up on the frente de massa activity in the region. Vera has moved into Lúcia's house. I'm on the living room floor, Lúcia has one bedroom, her daughter and her mother have the other, and Vera is in the casinha, a wooden shed out back. I ask Lúcia if Vera has moved out of the house she shares with André, and Lúcia tells me they are having problems. Vera has left him before, but it seems that she won't go back this time. I ask Lúcia how many times this has happened. She answers that it has happened many times. I comment that this is what must have been behind André's strange behavior in the past months. Lúcia agrees.

"He has been fighting for his position," she says. "He was going to be dismissed as regional leader of frente de massa. So, he had to try and catch the leaders' eye, he had to do well."

After a while, Lúcia opens up. Last year at some point, André started an affair with a woman who was encamped in the Vitória acampamento. He was always visiting the encampment, always finding reasons to drop by, and he took no trouble to conceal things. This was humiliating for Vera, as talk began to spread. Her children found out, as did the state leadership. Lúcia tells me how the movement has a strict moral code. This is primarily enforced in spaces of potential tension such as acampamentos, but it can also be applied more generally. However, Lúcia is dismissive of how the moral code is applied. She tells me that despite the fact that it is prohibited to bring girls back to an acampamento, a lot goes on. The general rule, she tells me, is that if affairs are kept quiet, there's a tacit understanding that people will look the other way. Lúcia tells me that André has fallen foul of the state leadership: "He flaunts his mistress without taking the trouble to keep things quiet."

Lúcia says that members of the state leadership spoke to André. They advised him to put a stop to his affair. Lúcia says that Vera is well known and well respected among the state leadership, but the situation became more complex when André refused to heed his superiors. "He refused to give the woman up," Lúcia says, and tensions started to manifest themselves within the acampamento itself, with accusations of prioritization and favoritism leveled at André.

Lúcia is angry with this nameless woman. "She was divisive and caused problems by herself in the acampamento, even without her relationship with André," she says. Lúcia recounts how in the end, the woman was kicked out of the acampamento by state leadership, first as a means to neutralize a troublemaker and second to distance her from André. At this point, I ask Lúcia how long the woman was encamped in Vitória. Lúcia tells me she had been encamped for over a year.

However, this was not the end of the affair. Lúcia accuses André of using movement money, designated for frente de massa activity, to set the woman up in an apartment in nearby Bom Jardim. Lúcia describes André as *desviado*, having strayed from the path, using movement money for his own purposes. I ask her why the state leadership expelled the woman from the acampamento but left André incumbent in his position. I ask if this reflects where the blame lies. She responds that it is difficult to remove a leader, that a special meeting has to be called and attended by the state leadership in order for someone like André to be dismissed. Removing someone from an encampment is a lot easier. Lúcia says the leadership put André on some kind of probation, telling him to get things in order.

Lúcia is upset, and I think I know why. The decision regarding André's future was made at the recent state meeting, and she tells me he has been confirmed in his position for another year. I ask how this is possible given that everyone knows what he has done. Lúcia becomes emotional. She tells me that this is not the first time André has done this, that Vera has had to stay with her before. She tells me Vera has been beaten by André and that only the presence of so many other people within the community keeps him partially in check. Lúcia tells me of one occasion when Vera was receiving text messages of support from a male friend, and André, enraged, snatched her mobile phone and crushed it with his hands, hurting himself, saying that she was alone, that no one would help her. I recall at this point trying to call Vera in the past, not getting through, and her later telling me that her phone had been broken by her children. Lúcia tells me that André has lost his ideology; he has lost the enthusiasm he used to have for the movement in the early days. She relates how all the MST activity in this area was down to André's dedication to the cause. But things have changed. It is Vera who keeps André going now, says Lúcia; it is her passion and belief in the movement that forces him to do even the meager amount of work he manages to accomplish.

Later, I find time to be on my own. Rumors about Vera and André have been circulating for some time. I think back to when I first met them and they offered to let me stay in their home. We took a photo of all of us together, the three of us dressed in red MST T-shirts. This image seems so at odds with the violence that Lúcia describes, and I find myself not wanting to believe what I've heard.

It's late in the evening, a couple of days later, and I drop by the casinha looking for Lúcia. It's cramped and cold. A bare light bulb hangs from a wooden beam. Vera appears and tells me that everyone has gone to church. Lúcia is evangelical but doesn't ask me to come to service anymore. I ask Vera why she stayed at home. She doesn't answer. There's a pause before she mentions that Lúcia told her I know about her and André. She sits down. The first thing she says is that it isn't all André's fault, that his violent side is something he grew up with and has not been able to leave behind. She talks of the scar on his face and how he was permanently marked by his father beating him when he was a child. She asks me to understand that violence is difficult to escape, even when you join something like the MST, even when you try to become a new man. She tells me that André was shot through the hand when they were encamped and that even now he can't grip properly. I say that I find it hard to imagine him like that. I struggle for words. Strangely, for both of us, we talk as if the person suffering from domestic violence were someone else entirely.

Vera says marriages have to be worked on and that nothing comes easily, but this time she is most worried for her children. I tell her it seems that André has been granted another year as a regional leader, and I ask her what she intends to do. I know she is reluctant to stay in the casinha; it's not the right place for her and her family. She mentions that the leadership have suggested working in an acampamento school in Rio Branco. Her children are not keen as the encampment is sixty miles away from the nearest city, and it means going back to a way of life they have struggled so hard to put behind them. But it seems like it's the only option.

"It is not possible to go back to the house with André there," Vera says. "It's dangerous."

"Why does André get to keep the house and land?" I ask. After all, they both encamped together, and Vera built large parts of the house herself as André was often away on frente de massa business.

"Because I have left the house, it is complicated," she says. She tells me André wants her to come back, but she will not, which makes things worse.

A long silence. I ask Vera why André was granted another year in the leadership position when everyone knows he has broken movement rules and continues to do so. Vera says the leadership council voted against her mainly because they are men. She says the few women on the council are outvoted, but also, importantly, the men all know André. She says that a lot of them have backgrounds in the frente de massa, and she reiterates what other members have told me—that most of the senior leadership tend to come from this background and that it represents the sharp end of the movement, organizing occupations, recruiting new members, and so on. She tells me André has also had his time extended because she doesn't have enough support on the committee, despite some members promising to come and visit her, saying they know what is going on and that they will support her. Franciele has supported her, as has Kleber.

"If I have to leave the house, I will lose everything," Vera tells me. "I'm thirty-three, with three children. The idea of losing everything for which I struggled for eight years only to have to begin again is too much."

"What will happen?" I ask. She says the MST is not like normal life. Normally the house and land would be sold, and everything would be divided equally, but in the MST, land can't be sold. Someone must stay on the property. We continue talking about the possibilities, and gradually I understand that even though she is a mother to the children, because André has been validated once again by the leadership, because he wants her to come home, and because Vera has vacated, in the state leadership's view, he has a greater claim to the house and land and all that entails: the means of production, all the property, all the cash tied up in agricultural stock—in short, the sum of what she has struggled for her whole life. Vera tells me that leaving her house will mean leaving the settlement and leaving all her friends. She mentions that it might even mean leaving the state and having to start a new life somewhere else, outside the movement, because she can't take the children back to an encampment. I ask how she's getting by day to day. She says he's working at a motel, doing housekeeping for a minimum wage. It's hard, she says, going back to a type of work that means keeping her opinions to herself after being a sem terra for so long. At this point, for the first time since I have known her, Vera starts to cry. Vera is one of the bravest people I have ever met, with a tireless, phenomenal commitment to the movement. I watch as she reaches for a pair of scissors on the table and begins to snip away bits of skin on her hands. She draws blood before I can pull the scissors away. "If he takes my children, I'll have nothing left to live for," she says.

The next day I am driving to Florianópolis with Lúcia. We're going to the hospital in the city for her specialist treatment. Conversation turns toward Vera, and I ask Lúcia what the state leadership have done regarding the situation. She says the leadership are waiting for Vera to come to them with a plan of action to move everything forward. Lúcia says the leadership have let it be known that they can't help her unless she helps them.

Fala para ela, Lúcia says they have communicated, *ela tem que lutar, se ela quer nossa ajuda*. Tell her she has to fight if she wants our help.

* * *

The text on the gender sector page of the MST's website states the following:

Obviously there are gender inequalities within the MST; after all, the movement is not an island within society. The most important task of the

Gender Sector is to discuss and to contest gender relations within MST while strengthening the role women play in the organization. The MST believes that gender and class are intertwined, and the movement has set a clear direction to describe and expand landless women's participation.... The new woman and the new man are within us. But it is necessary to awaken them and let them bloom, to construct together a new way of society.

In 2023, the text has hardly changed since 2009. Among the listed targets are how activities involving education and training should maintain equal proportions of men and women and that the movement will work to ensure joint land-use titles. But even here the primacy of the family is tangible. There is a commitment to the "right to credit in the name of couples." And regarding projects of investment, how to produce, and financial matters in general, the text makes clear that such decisions should be "taken only with family participation." Back in 2003, Wright and Wolford noted that gender was perhaps the area where the movement had made the least progress, and little had improved in 2009, when Vera was forced to seek shelter with her sister Lúcia. Without access to her land, she couldn't generate any income and faced the loss of everything she had constructed. It was telling that in the MST's institutional response the state leadership required Vera to *lutar*, to struggle, fight, or perhaps, in this context, resist in order for them to help her. The onus was on her: being a survivor of abuse did not necessarily mean that the leadership would intervene on her behalf.

After going to the hospital for Lúcia's treatment, we went to speak directly with the state leadership in Florianópolis. Bianchini, an important and visible state leader, received us in the MST's secretariat downtown. He was in his early forties, and I recognized him from state meetings in 2007 and 2008. Setting up this meeting had been difficult, and so to start off I asked about his story in the movement. Like many MST leaders, his family were from rural Rio Grande do Sul but had moved to Santa Catarina, where he was born. His story with the MST in Santa Catarina started from the movement's very beginnings. Four of his brothers were part of the occupation that resulted in the Abelardo Luz settlements. The second youngest of eleven, he worked at the tobacco company Souza Cruz, living in the city, before finding himself unemployed. At this point, he was invited to work for the MST's nascent Santa Catarina office. But he was unable to financially support his young family, and after a few months they moved to a collectivized settlement where he worked until 2001, when the movement arranged for him to study for a law degree in Florianópolis. He missed the countryside, he said, but he stayed. We spoke about coordinating efforts in the city.

"It's a problem, bringing different ways of thinking together, it always has been," he told us. "It's difficult to unite the forces of the left. People of the left are by nature, people who like to, I don't know how to say this. . . . They like their own line of thought because they are people who don't accept received wisdom. It's always a problem."

Conversation continued. "This is a principle of the struggle of the masses," Bianchini told us. "If you can't do it with that unity, you have no chance, and you'll never last twenty-five years."

I asked if the movement needed organization. "It does," he replied. "It needs clear objectives; it needs to have principles. If you can keep that strong, then you've got something to work with. As soon as this starts to crumble, the movement won't be able to withstand. The Landless Movement has this condition to endure."

When I introduced the subject of Vera, the atmosphere between the three of us quickly became uncomfortable. I asked what typically happened on settlements when a marriage dissolved, what happened to the land in cases of a separation.

"What is possible as regards a sale is that you don't sell the land, but you sell what you have produced on it, the infrastructure you built. You have the right to sell this. So, what do people do in general? They make this sale and split it as they have to. But this isn't going to set you up. It's just to keep you going. Or in some recent cases, it's possible to relocate. I don't know, it's something that INCRA do, relocate the man or the woman to another plot, form another family. But this is a conversation you have to have with INCRA. So this could be a solution. Generally people make this sale, but these are rare cases."

I mentioned that Vera's health was deteriorating and asked if there was a possibility of dividing Vera and André's land and constructing another house on the same plot. Bianchini objected on the grounds that in the future, one or the other might acquire a new partner. It was noticeable that at no stage did he admit that André already had a new partner, and he seemed surprised when I pointed out that this situation (splitting the land and each person gaining a new partner) was something that had already occurred in the northern settlement with another family. When I insisted that the movement needed people like Vera, he commented, "In fact, this family problem has distanced André from the movement, and that's terrible. It's not that we need Vera, but we must respect her as a comrade, a militante, because of the skills she has, of articulation, organizing people, organizing the masses. So I promise to speak to her, to see if there is a possibility of her starting again."

Bianchini seemed to assume that Vera wasn't going back to the settlement and spoke generally about what she might do in the future. He highlighted her skill with health care. As the conversation meandered, I bluntly stated that I believed if André ended up staying on the land and Vera had to leave, this would be contrary to the principles of the movement. Bianchini nodded but said there would be difficulties involving INCRA: "Certainly, but if you speak with INCRA about dividing the land, they will be totally against this proposal, because INCRA have the logic that the land is theirs and it's all fine because it's already occupied by a family."

No one has to tell INCRA, I commented. Bianchini replied with a sarcastic tone, "No, and if they can produce and also lead their lives in this way on top of that, perfect."

I asked him if he could visit Vera. "I'll go there, first of all to assure her that she is not alone and then to start a dialogue between them. We are late to arrive, but we have to support her like this."

Insisting he would visit, Bianchini again voiced concerns about having two houses on one piece of land, despite the fact that this very situation existed with Vera's neighbors, about two hundred yards from her lot.

"Like I said, I see this danger, that if you think short term to solve something, you can create a problem in the future. You have to think of that, but I believe that I can create dialogue between them and create a possibility of reconciliation."

We seemed to be going in circles. I said I believed Vera was in physical danger. There was a long pause before Bianchini delivered his response: "In fact, I know our comrade there [André]. It's a calm relationship. What you say about André being a dangerous person, I wouldn't be able to agree."

It was clear that the subject was not open to discussion. And Bianchini didn't seem interested in why Vera might be in danger. He didn't ask for any details, merely describing the situation as *tranquila*, calm. In the silence that followed, I said that perhaps *perigoso*, dangerous, was not the right word. Another silence followed before Bianchini exclaimed: "OK, well! I think that it's important that we have dialogue. And to contribute to her beginning again as a person, as a human being, as a *militante*."

I said that if Vera were forced out of the movement, it would be a huge loss for her, as the MST was an integral part of her life. He smiled. "Yes, we must return her to her natural habitat!"

* * *

Bianchini never went to see Vera. When I finished my primary fieldwork in March 2009, Vera was living in the casinha with Clarice, her boys were on the settlement with André, and there were rumors that André's new partner was moving into the house. Both Lúcia and I emerged from our meeting with Bianchini in something akin to a daze. Bianchini had subjected us to multiple unquestioned naturalizations of gender; we had been beaten down by his projection of the transcendent moral force of the family and the necessity of its maintenance and cohesion. His continual insistence on the family as primary unit was all-encompassing: any mention of Vera was in the context of her partnership with André; when talking about their land, there was an ever-present emphasis of its occupation by a family; and when discussing the total breakdown of their relationship, he sought only to achieve some form of resolution through reconciliation. Vera was asking for protection, but Bianchini did not respond to this. Nor did he respond to the possibility that Vera might be in danger. He refused to engage in this issue to the extent that conversation, in fact, stopped.

I left Brazil with the feeling that Bianchini blamed Vera for leaving the house and thereby creating a difficult situation for him to resolve. It seemed that if the woman André had set up in an apartment were to eventually move into Vera's house, for Bianchini the matter would be over, as there would be a family unit on the plot. Vera might work in an encampment school somewhere, and life in the settlement would slowly go back to normal. For Bianchini, it was seemingly impossible to countenance a course of action in which Vera would live alone in her house.

Cristiani Bereta da Silva, professor of history at the State University of Santa Catarina, wrote her doctorate on gender relations in the MST. In a 2004 article, she notes how in Santa Catarina settlements, leaders often blamed women for the continued existence of gendered inequalities. Leaders argued that women had the power to make a difference yet for "cultural reasons" did not participate sufficiently due to a lack of willingness to engage in the struggle (2004, 275–76). The verb *lutar* here, to struggle, reappears as a vessel of plural unspecified behaviors that characterize the embodied dimension of being sem terra. In calling for Vera to struggle in order for them to intervene, leaders like Bianchini were drawing on a long-established compact between sacrifice and the promised land. Vera's situation revealed multiple contradictions of the pursuit of a utopian vision: the emphasis on unity as the motor of forward progression; the exercise of a verticalized power to dismiss an identity beyond that of the worker; the fascination with production as the vehicle of self-transformation; and of course, the maintenance of the family unit, independent of whichever particular woman might constitute it, as a constitutive building block. In articulating her rights and contesting normalized values, Vera seemed alone. Having devoted her adult life to the movement, she had been cast adrift.

SCENE III—EXPRESSION, CREATIVE GESTURE

Through our creation, our action, we affirm our beauty and our resilience. We will continue to say that we are beautiful, we are beautiful in what we produce, in what we do.

Luciana Melo, member of the Banzeiros collective, an MST theater group based in the Amazonian state of Pará[1]

9

The Culture Sector

In the movement's debates, culture was only related to art.
However, with ideological maturity, it was perceived that
the social movement itself is a modification of behavior.
The MST represents the sum of interests of different people who set out to discover new possibilities, new values
that generate new social practices. The movement changes
habits. In each occupation, people find themselves obliged
to create new habits, for the pressure of collective life
makes people eliminate old habits and absorb new ones.

ADEMAR BOGO[1]

When sketching out initial designs for this research, my principal
motivation was to work with the MST's culture sector. I found
its practice fascinating, and I sought to understand how the
movement approached creative expression and why it placed such emphasis on this work. In seeking the ambit of the culture sector, I was guided
by a definition on the MST's English-language website of its activities: "At
demonstrations, marches, occupations, imprisonments, and commemorations of victories and conquests, music, poetry and dance are presented,
expressing and strengthening the Sem Terra cultural identity." The more
up-to-date Portuguese-language version also emphasizes art and culture's
fundamental role in the MST, particularly in the construction of a "landless
identity, through songs and poems, panels, theatre and our symbols, such
as the flag and the anthem." For certain MST leaders, the culture sector's
role was closely intertwined with cohesion. In his interview with Bernardo
Fernandes, Stédile laid emphasis on the connection between culture and
"organizational principals," discussing how creative expression could be incorporated and applied to "achieve unity" across a nationwide movement

making "people feel good about participating in the struggle" (Stédile and Fernandes 1999, 129). For Stédile, cultural identity engendered a greater degree of resistance, and he drew a parallel between a ninety-year-old man embarking on a 750-mile march to Brasília and families facing a long period of encampment. He remarked: "The sacrifices are enormous. They bear with it so long because they have a mysticism and organizational principles, not just because they need land" (130).

In Stédile's reading, creative expression is configured as a form of political and ideological sustenance and a locus of hope and solidarity. Its role is to express and strengthen the sem terra collective identity, as discourse alone is recognized as not being sufficient to create lasting bonds. Discussing the role of the MST flag and anthem, Stédile states that "what builds togetherness is the ideology of the political vision of reality and the use of symbols, which . . . materialize the ideal, this invisible unity." He comments that for the MST, the maintenance of such harmony is vital, and creative expression prevents the movement "from splintering in a way that would hinder an original union and identity" (Stédile and Fernandes 1999, 132). And yet, despite such a utilitarian understanding of art and culture, Stédile points to an ambiguity, arguing that collective manifestations of feeling must not become overly formalized or stale: "Nobody gets emotional because they are ordered to get emotional; they get emotional because they were motivated by something" (130). Given the importance of the culture sector's work and this intriguing tension between creative expression as a space of subjective reflection and culture as a tool with which to forge a collective sem terra identity, I was keen to witness, and if possible participate in, cultural activities. I didn't have to wait long. At the annual Santa Catarina state meeting in 2007, each day opened with what MST members term a *mística*.

Waking up at six a.m., we were greeted by the smell of freshly baked bread and hot coffee. Spreading homemade jam over *pão frances*, I was having breakfast in the food hall with members of the Alzemiro de Oliveira brigade, looking forward to the mística, which was scheduled to start at eight. I washed my plate and headed to the main hall. There were a few people dotted around the huge space, one strumming an acoustic guitar on the stage and another leading a group of people into the area between the stage and the chairs. It was still very early. They began to rehearse a performance, led through their steps by Mariana, a culture-sector leader. Some of the participants were wearing blindfolds, and their movements were accompanied by the acoustic guitar. The rehearsal broke up, and I went back outside. A lot of buses had arrived in the night, and there were hundreds of people milling about, catching up with old friends. Slowly people started to filter into the hall, and I found a seat with my brigade as the mística started. People fell quiet, and everyone watched.

The guitar started first, with amplified, somber chords conveying a foreboding atmosphere. Accompanying the guitar, a group of people in the center began to move. They were wearing blue blindfolds, and they grasped at thin air, unsighted and helpless. More actors entered from a side door, carrying placards. One young man was carrying a tank on his back with a hose to represent the application of pesticides. Another was wearing a tall top hat colored blue, white, and red to represent the figure of Uncle Sam. The placards read *agronegócio*, agribusiness; *EUA*, USA; *Coca Cola*; *Bancos: BID, Bradesco*; and *veneno*, poison. Another figure was holding a box representing a television, decorated with the logo of TV Globo, Brazil's largest commercial network. These figures encircled the blindfolded, who were now squatting on the ground, and continued to pace around them, all the while accompanied by the ominous chords of the guitar. The placards were waved in the faces of the blindfolded, and the television was placed over one person's head. The scene continued until another group of actors appeared. They were dressed in MST baseball caps and T-shirts and carried agricultural implements such the foice, the long-handled scythe, and hoes and rakes. They carried MST flags, which they brandished in the faces of those threatening the blindfolded. In this battle, those representing the USA, the banks, and agribusiness were eventually disarmed, and the MST members removed the blindfolds of the actors squatting on the floor. At that point, the music changed, and a positive melody was played on the guitar with a soaring vocal accompaniment. The actors portraying the capitalists had been symbolically defeated and were left seated on the floor. Now able to see, the formerly blindfolded joined those dressed in MST T-shirts in a line and began to wave MST flags in time to the music. Further actors appeared to join this alliance, bearing flags of the Peasant Women's Movement of Brazil (MMC) and the flag of La Via Campesina. The audience clapped in time to the music as the guitar played a popular movement song. People around me stood to applaud this symbolic triumph; the day had begun.

* * *

The type of performance described above is the most common form of creative expression in the MST. Such performances may last up to half an hour and are almost always performed by an ensemble. While there may be musical accompaniment, performances rarely feature dialogue; actors put forward meaning through gesture and action. Performances at which

I was present occurred at large meetings, such as the state meeting, or the meeting of the sem terrinha, the "little landless," an event for MST children and young adults. These were generally staged in front of a seated audience, and actors wore recognizable MST clothing and used simple props with symbolic value: agricultural tools, MST produce, flags, seeds, and drawings. Performances were allegorical and spoke directly to the movement's struggle for agrarian reform.

In the performance described above, the message was clear: the MST liberated a blindfolded group threatened by agribusiness, large corporations, and other well-established antagonists. The performance began with an exposition of characters and reached a critical point with the arrival of the MST, and a denouement was reached through resolution; the group representing wider society had their blindfolds removed, and everyone but the antagonists joined together to wave MST flags over the vanquished. If these performances exhibit certain dramatic conventions, it is because they derive from a very particular theatrical tradition. The MST coalesced from agrarian reform movements closely linked to the Catholic Church and developed networks of solidarity with priests who had been influenced by the tenets of liberation theology—the idea put forward at the Second Vatican Council that there should be justice on Earth as well as in Heaven. In this formative phase, the MST was influenced by the organizational practice of the church (Ondetti 2008; Chaves 2021), and the structure of Catholic mystery plays that date back to the Middle Ages in Europe is tangible in these kinds of performances, (Lara Junior 2005; Löwy 2001). Such performances can therefore be understood as embedded within a particular historical context of an early vernacular drama that brought communities together outside of churches and away from Latin texts. Plays portrayed mysteries based on stories from the Bible and miracles based on the lives of the saints. The plays also depicted allegorical moralities, allowing audiences to understand abstract ideas—for example, their depiction of people's struggle against sin.

Anchored in a spiritual context, the form of these medieval mystery plays served as a model for how to express what came to be known within the movement as mística. Mística has been interpreted in various ways. For Bernardo Fernandes, it is the movement's "cognitive praxis" (1996, 232); for Daniela Issa, it is "a subjective experience in collectivity" (2007, 126); while for Christine Chaves, mística connotes the intangible: "It is the quality of confidence, courage, and firmness in the face of favorable or adverse situations in the struggle for land" (2022, 3). Despite diverse interpretation, performances of mística have coalesced into agreed dramatic forms and exhibit certain conventions regarding form and content. The performances I witnessed between 2007 and 2019 adhered to a series of principles, in large part shaped by an influential training manual from 1997.

> Performances should particularly develop the following values: - Humility - Honesty - Coherence/Conviction/Perseverance - Passion/Love for the cause - Spirit of sacrifice/Gratitude - Responsibility/Discipline.

> There must be present in the performance: - The symbols of the organization, flag, anthem, etc.—Words of order - Songs of struggle - The organization's historical militants.

> The performance must consider: - The subversive memory of the people: the situation that led us to struggle, the struggle for land, the organization of production, etc. - Our utopia (socialism) and our dream of transforming reality - The practice and historical struggles of the workers (those that took place in the past and those that take place today) - The people in the group (the grassroots) and the level of their consciousness. - The steps we need to take (in anticipation of the future). - Events in progress or what is happening: grassroots demonstrations, militant meetings, leaders' meetings etc.

> Performances must be: brief and profound - be serious and sensitive (touch the heart) - show confidence in the organization and the struggle - show conviction regarding the path (it is the right one). (CONCRAB 1997, 26–27)

Since the 1990s, culture-sector leaders have continually sought to refine the form through which mística is most commonly evoked and experienced. Daniela Issa relates how Ranulfo Peloso, a national MST leader of the culture sector, wrote to his colleague Ademar Bogo, outlining what he felt performances of mística ought to comprise. Peloso indicates that mística for entertainment purposes, to convey mystery or to shock, is not authentic; and to be beautiful, mística should be brief, solemn, and simple and should incorporate symbols, gestures, and personal testimonies. Further, there should be no surprises; mística should be prepared and rehearsed, and improvisation should be avoided (Issa 2007, 131). Beyond these points, Peloso makes further recommendations. It is important to avoid the use of mística to adorn a meeting ("Now that the mística is over, let's get down to business"). It should not become the task of "specialists," even though some are more creative and sensitive than others. It should not occupy one's entire focus ("I couldn't attend the course because I had to prepare the mística").

It must not turn into a competition ("Their mística was better than yours") (cited in Issa 2007, 131).

In part because of this standardizing work by culture-sector leaders, while mística was originally understood as a spiritual element, intangible and intrinsic to the MST's struggle, for many people in the MST, mística has become a particular type of performance that occurs at a specific time with normalized dramatic conventions. Here we can differentiate between mística as intangible power held in abstract (mística) and a performance that seeks to express this intangibility, which has become increasingly subject to convention (a mística). And indeed, these performances have become so emblematic of the MST that mística as an abstract concept has become almost indistinguishable from these theatrical performances. Scholarly analyses commonly fail to make this distinction. Mística has been described as pedagogical tool (Campos Martins 2022; Munarim and Medeiros 2002; Comerlatto 2010; Nascimento and Martins 2008) with connections drawn to the radical pedagogy of Paulo Freire (1975) and Augusto Boal's ([1974] 2000) theatrical method based on Freire's work. It has been put forward as a form of political and ideological training—for example, Issa (2007, 135) has cast mística as a "praxis of empowerment," a perspective shared by Branford and Rocha, for whom mística is a tool of "conscientization," a means employed by leadership to "drive home particular political messages" (2002, 251). And mística has also been theorized as a mode of communication: both Michael Löwy (2001) and Wendy Wolford (2010) have argued that mística works to connect members of the MST through the collective sem terra identity.

Mística in the abstract, however, cannot be limited to instrumentality; its subjective dimension exceeds attempts at delimitation. As Brazilian anthropologist Christine Chaves argues, mística is a performative space into which different temporalities can be compressed, allowing the audience to glimpse the value of collective struggle, the meaning of history, celebration of the past, and the value of sacrifice. In this sense, mística anticipates "the symbolic pleasure of utopia" (Chaves 2022, 16), allowing audiences *and* performers a glimpse of the world to which they strive and providing a temporary exit from utopia's subjunctive grammar. What is missing from analyses of creative expression within the MST—as opposed to the MST's creative expression—is an understanding of how mística underpins diverse forms and how, in noninstitutional contexts, mística furnishes a subjective space that is capable of creating an excess of meaning with radical potential. Mística in this sense is not merely a performance of sem terra values but a much more abstract concept that guides MST members to deeply connect with their movement's ideals and ethical stance. It sparks interventions in which gesture, as opposed to discourse, assumes powerful meanings and constitutes a point of contestation and even resistance. In this more abstract sense, mística encompasses a deeply subjective and reflexive expression of what it means to be sem terra, and in such a mode, MST members have come to question the more institutionalized mística performances that are rehearsed and revolve around predicable themes.

The tension between these modes is unmistakable. Members frequently questioned the performances of mística at large meetings. After a performance at the encontro dos sem terrinha I attended, Lúcia explained that the místicas she saw no longer had the same dynamism they had once possessed: "Ah, I'll copy that one, let's do that one that's already been done. There isn't that evolution. But before, ten, twelve years ago, mística was mística, do you understand? Because I came from there. It was, like, made from me; it came from inside, back in that time. It was what led me to understand the movement, and what made me want to join the movement." Lúcia had a serious long-term illness and had nearly died in early 2007. So when she told me about the force of mística and how it had helped her to survive, I struggled to understand how these two modes of mística could exist alongside one another.

One evening, I came back home to Lúcia's and there was a motorbike parked under the front window. Inside, a middle-aged man with gray hair was playing guitar. His name was Thiago, and he was a local *vereador* (town councillor) who worked with rural trade unions. Thiago's first contact with the MST was in 1992, but he had been involved in the struggle for agrarian reform since 1989. Admiring the MST's direct action, in 1996 he moved to live permanently on the northern acampamento, which eventually, after seven years, became the settlement on which Vera, Davi, and everyone else lived. Thiago described his involvement with the MST over cigarettes rolled with *palha*, straw, while drinking chimarrão.

"My first contact was in Rio do Sul," Thiago explained. Vera and her daughter Clarice had dropped by and were sitting with us in the lounge along with Ana, Lúcia's daughter. "It was through the CPT [Comissão Pastoral da Terra], the church. And I liked their philosophy and after '96 we did the basics with the farmers, and we carried out the very first occupation in the North Planalto."

Thiago was heavily involved in acampamento life, an environment that many MST leaders describe as being fundamental to the formation of the sem terra identity. However, he made a point of telling me that although he was closely linked to the movement, he was no longer a member: "I'd say that today I'm not part of the movement, but it's still part of my life, because it's a movement that is legitimate, comprehensive, strong. . . . But I'm not a member anymore, I'm an ally."

Thiago spoke about mística and the importance it had played when he was encamped with two hundred other families, struggling to get by without the cesta básica, the weekly delivery of rice and beans organized by INCRA: "The subjective side of things: guitar, poetry, music . . . this moves mountains, it transforms, much more than sometimes all of those words. And back then, we did this. Every Tuesday, after working in the fields, we wouldn't go back to work in the afternoon. One day we'd play guitar, another we'd study, another we'd plan the week, pray . . . because praying is also part of the subjective, it's also mística—Catholicism, but it wasn't really to do with this church or that church, it was a spirituality for the struggle."

Thiago echoed Lúcia's opinion that performances of mística had become too predictable. He pushed back on the notion that it served to create identity, describing this as *vulgar*, or banal: "Of course mística is something which unites people, gets them ready. It unites peoples' experience and gives clarity." He paused. "I reckon the movement grew really big, really quick. And we couldn't look to all its aspects, all the parts of the movement that deserved attention. Something was left behind, and I don't know if it's exactly this, but I reckon one of those things that got left behind was mística. It got put to one side."

Thiago insisted that the MST had "lost a lot of its mística" and even "lost itself" and that this loss would have serious consequences. When I asked about this, Thiago spoke of mística's intangible qualities and how it went beyond its use in the formation of identity: "The loss of mística makes the spirit go cold. You lose, I don't know. . . . Mística takes away fear, mística gives you a . . . I'm not sure exactly . . . it's more like you become hard-headed and solely pragmatic. I'm off here to earn some money, I'm off there to get hold of some land. . . . Mística purifies the spirit. I'm going to this place because of the people, the crowd, justice." His phone rang, and he smiled as he took the call.

Lúcia laughed. "*Correria!*" So busy!

Thiago sat down again. "It's really difficult to explain. You lose that human warmth; you lose your way, and in that manner, you lose your resistance. It just becomes meeting after meeting after meeting. And you don't come together to celebrate, be together. And you lose sight, you lose sight of the goal. It can be whatever goal in the context of the group because you're working to make the conditions of the group better and your group is always part of something bigger, our society. And that's what mística guarantees, that your group will be connected to other groups which is the network that is the greater good. The lack of mística brings this pragmatism as a consequence. Like, I'll be a part of the struggle as long as it's in my interests, but as soon as it's not, then I'm out. Mística is a vision of the future; it speaks to how you are part of something bigger."

Listening to Thiago speak about mística was compelling. What really struck me was the way he communicated its elemental force. He placed such emphasis on how mística had moved him, speaking with a deep conviction on how it could move mountains and transform the world through an unknowable power. Mística for Thiago went beyond an institutionalized form of performance. It was the subjective dimension of the movement, its conscience, the manner in which to express but also constitute transcendent objectives that entered into dialogue with a person's most human qualities. Of course, the performances through which it took form helped to construct community, and he acknowledged that it had helped to keep people strong in times of repression. But within its elemental nature there was an untrammeled, almost transgressive quality about mística that could not be harnessed, instrumentalized, or controlled.

Thiago indicated that without this dimension, the MST could be in danger of replicating elements of a society it was trying to move away from. He repeatedly spoke of pragmatism as a danger, the notion of winning land for the sake of it, planting land to accrue profits, measuring success in terms of how many or how much. Maybe I drank too much chimarrão that evening, but sitting around Lúcia's table with Vera, Clarice, Thiago, and Ana while Dona Neusa sat knitting quietly on the sofa, I felt the simple pleasure of being part of a family and the complex sense of Thiago's words wrapping themselves around me. Mística moves mountains, he said, and cleanses the spirit of the pragmatic, the transactional, the extractive. In Lúcia's simple house, washing the dishes, sitting around idly on the porch, I never forgot what he told me.

10

Mística, Light on Your Feet

I was talking to Tais in the coastal settlement. It was early 2009, and I'd just got back from Novo Horizonte, where I'd hoped to meet up with Révero Ribeiro, a theater practitioner who worked with the movement. Révero lived in Florianópolis and was known in the region for leading the Agitprop Clown Army and working with the movement's National Theater Brigade, Patativa Assaré. We had first met through the Programa Nacional de Educação na Reforma Agrária (PRONERA) in 2007, but his visit to Novo Horizonte hadn't worked out, and I didn't get the opportunity to see him again. Révero passed away in January 2022 and has been greatly missed.

I was disappointed that the workshop we had planned in Novo Horizonte hadn't taken place. Tais also seemed upset and told me that what was really lacking in the movement was investment in culture. I asked her in what sense. She replied, "Today we have these performances of mística in the movement. You go to a meeting for young people, to a state meeting, a national meeting, and the only thing you see are these performances. And it's a strong point of the movement, you know, but it's the only thing, and not everyone really feels in tune with that. There are people who sing, play guitar, play other instruments really well. Some people who love to dance, you know?"

I nodded in agreement. The místicas were very common. Révero's mischievous clown workshops, on the other hand, were strikingly different, and younger MST members really enjoyed his sessions. Tais continued: "This question of mística. We had a youth meeting, and each assentamento had to prepare a cultural presentation, an expression of mística. And me and a friend, we prepared a *dança do ventre*, a belly dance. I don't know why, but I've loved this dance ever since I was a child. So when I got this opportunity, I trained really hard, like every day. My mother didn't like it, but I got really good at it, training alone, and I learned the movements really well. Me and my friend put together a whole choreography; we even designed and sewed our own costumes. And in this meeting the idea was to present this dance to everyone. For me, it was such a highlight. The joy of the meeting was in this dance because it was something new. No one had ever done mística like that before."

Tais told me how other people's presentations for the meeting took the form of typical performances, along the lines of culture-sector recommendations. I asked her how her idea of a dance had gone down with the members of the state leadership, some of whom were present. "It was like this thing about contradiction," she said. "Because a lot of those male leaders saw a belly dance as something erotic, which was totally different from my vision. I mean, that's totally wrong. We were going to present the dance at night, but they wouldn't let us."

I asked why. "The leaders said it was because of the way people might see it, that they would see it as sexualized, like something vulgar." Tais told me that changing it was out of the question. "We'd got everything ready, like, everything. We'd made our own costumes, we'd dressed up, done our makeup, got into character for the performance, and we couldn't dance because the leaders of the meeting said that the audience would be scandalized by its form, that people would see it with that frame of the vulgar, and we would end up disrespecting the movement. I found it totally egocentric. They are so conservative!"

In negotiations, the leaders offered to let Tais and her friend perform the following day at midday, when presumably the audience would be less susceptible to, as the leaders saw it, the form's sensualizing movements.

"The girl who I was dancing with, she'd had enough and packed it in. But me, being so stubborn, I refused to give in. So I danced alone. Like, just me on my own." She raised her voice. "*Vou quebrar isso*, I'm going to break this. And I danced in front of various leaders of the movement."

I asked her what she thought of not being allowed to present at night. She replied, "It's one of those questions, like, I see it like this. It's this very conservative part of the movement. They invest a lot in consciousness, political training and such, but leave these cultural matters to one side. It could be so important to keep young people involved and also to win over more young people from outside." She sighed with frustration. "And this is the way, through music and dance. Guitars are seen by the leaders as to do with America, like rock music. So that's not possible. These performances of mística have become a method to communicate political things, like a tool."

I admired Tais for maintaining her position in the face of such adversity. Standing on an MST stage to present myself and my research in front of five hundred people at the 2007 state meeting, I had felt a sense of trepidation. But what Tais did went far beyond mere stage fright. Tais's body was subject to both a moral and political stigma, which she effectively faced down when she insisted on performing. Not only did she perform in the face of MST leaders who sexualized her performance, but she also asserted her right to communicate landlessness in the form she chose, even after being told that this form would be morally, and by extension politically, corrosive of the leaders' definition of sem terra identity. She was entirely vulnerable in that moment, making a series of movements and gestures with her body in front of people who had communicated to her that they saw her creative interpretation of mística as sexualized and sexualizing.

Such a conservative stance on creative expression was characteristic of Santa Catarina. Most large MST meetings finished with a party, and the music at these events was *gauchesca*, a type of traditional *gaúcho* (from the state of Rio Grande do Sul) folk music to which people danced in couples. Prior to this conversation, Tais had already expressed reservations regarding the movement's leadership. She had commented that the leaders were of an older generation and seemed to be permanently entrenched, and this frustration found expression through mística. Her performance was an attempt to do something different, and on some level she wished to confront the leaders with a performance of uncontainable movement and form.

As Tais mentioned, she had fought with her mother over the dance, and she knew that expressing mística in a different way from the institutionalized form would cause consternation. And yet this was precisely her objective. She wished to confront the movement with something new as a means of contesting what could be considered morally and politically appropriate. In choosing to perform a dança do ventre, she was challenging a leadership structure that she had identified as entrenched and patriarchal and daring them to censure her, thereby revealing their prejudice.

When her friend understandably gave up in the face of such pressure, Tais's bloody-mindedness became mística in and of itself, underpinning and inspiring the movements and gestures of her performance. Face-to-face with the leaders, her movements, her makeup, her costume, and the embodied dimension of her pent-up frustration articulated the uncontrollability of the elemental force Thiago had described. Tais didn't care in that moment. Her phrase "I'm going to break this" is ambiguous, and in Brazil, *vou quebrar isso* can mean many things. But in that context, I suggest, Tais was seeking to create a rupture with the moral conservatism to which she felt she was subject, an essentializing power that sought to control her identity, her body, and, importantly, what being sem terra meant for her. The leaders' request that the dance occur during the day, as opposed to at night, is revealing of the morally corrosive effect they felt Tais's expression of mística possessed. And they were right. Tais's creative expression did articulate a powerful and transcendent force, but it was not one that would sexually corrupt; it was rather the expressive force of her subjectivity, a subjective interpretation of mística as opposed to an institutionalized norm; a liberating force performed under duress that, if other people were to commune with a similar experience, might well "break" other structures of power in sympathetic resonance.

At the 2008 state meeting, all the plenary speeches were given by men. The only exception was a female activist for a free Palestine whose talk made a connection between the political repression suffered by the landless of Brazil and Palestinians in Israel and Palestine. Wearing a "Free Palestine" T-shirt and a hijab, she argued that Palestinians were landless people and urged her audience to act in solidarity. This call to add an international dimension to landlessness had a pronounced impact on those in the hall, and after the session ended, I heard many younger members discussing her talk. Tais was not present at that meeting, but she was deeply concerned with where the movement was headed and spoke many times about an aging leadership prohibiting more creative ways of thinking. She argued sometimes with her father, Kleber, about these questions, just as others questioned Kleber's control over the coastal settlement. Tais believed that until the leadership allowed a younger generation to create their own cultural understandings of their movement, the MST's mística would continue to stagnate. The task was to combat such inertia and address, as she termed it, the question of the "second generation."

"I reckon the biggest challenge of the movement is getting young people involved," she told me. "In the assentamentos and acampamentos it's getting more and more difficult to keep young people from moving on, more and more difficult to keep everyone living together in that environment, in that style of life. Why? It's like I was saying, you have to create new things because outside the movement there's a market that offers so much. So, it's difficult. So much so that myself, I understand this problem and how hard it is. I've gone to the city, and I got used to city life. For example, here in our settlement, there was a time when we had fifteen or sixteen young people, but today there is no one. The movement doesn't have any perspective. I want to work on this question of the second generation. The movement has a very weak plan regarding young people, regarding its work with young people. And it's not just here that I feel this but in many other assentamentos throughout the state. We should be investing more in the question of young people and principally in this question of culture. It's what is most lacking in the movement."

Tais's intention was to transform the movement from within, and one of her principal motivations was to ensure its continued relevance. It is significant that of all the avenues open to her, she chose mística as the space in which to articulate an alternative vision. Given its institutionalization, I wondered how such a process of transformation might take place and what particular kind of power Tais was seeking to enact when she danced alone and was confronted by the state leaders.

As we saw in the previous section, MST members understand mística in two senses. First, there is mística in the abstract, which refers to a subjective expression of what it means to be sem terra, one of the landless. Mística in this sense is open-ended with regard to content and form. It may be a performance but not necessarily; it could equally be a poem, a painting, a dance, a song, a text, or a gesture. As Thiago commented, it speaks to the subjective dimensions of the struggle and as such cannot be defined in set terms. Second, there are performances of mística, or what is known in the movement as místicas, that through their repetition and normalization of form have become synonymous with mística itself. These performances are generally directed by culture-sector leaders and express agreed-on notions relating to the MST's struggle. They often follow established conventions regarding themes, symbology, and affect and can serve a pedagogic purpose, connotating the MST with victory over various antagonists, including multinational companies, financial institutions, and multilateral organizations. Místicas in this sense are performed at certain places and times, typically at larger meetings, either to open the day's activities or to finalize things and draw a meeting to a close.

As such, in this second reading, such performances of mística have a ritualistic aspect. When the MST commemorates the massacre of Eldorado do Carajás with events including staged funerals and mourning, the movement is articulating a carefully constructed ritual that renders private sorrow publicly visible, evincing an externalization of grief in the context of systemic violence and therefore a protest in the face of a lack of institutional support from the state. Importantly, such events are planned in detail, and outcomes are accounted for in advance. What rendered Tais's intervention so different from this second understanding of mística was the manner in which her dança do ventre broke with convention. In her creative expression of mística, Tais pushed back on the agreed steps of the landless struggle. Her performance eschewed a linear pathway, instead opting for the unknown and unpredictable, calling into question how younger members might want to become sem terra and what behaviors this might suppose. Elaborated with her friend, Tais's dance can be understood as an instance of durational activism, a counter-utopian practice exercised through gesture and embodied action. Contextualized by an institutional framework, facing the state leaders with her body, she pushed outward into the space of distension and contraction that characterizes the MST, making an intervention into the forces held in tension that fundamentally constitute the movement and that impel it in unforeseen and unexpected directions.

To better grasp this moment and understand how and why Tais chose creative expression to take a stand, it is productive to reflect on a shift outlined by the anthropologist and performance studies scholar Dwight Conquergood (1989). Since the beginnings of anthropology as a discipline, analysis of ritual put forward dance and performance as cultural phenomena. Such manifestations were considered codes or texts from which understandings of culture and society could be discerned. Van Gennep's ([1909] 2019) work on rites of passage particularly laid out a terrain for other anthropologists such as Gregory Bateson, Claude Levi-Strauss, and Mary Douglas to follow, producing works that became cornerstones of the discipline. Conquergood argued for a different formulation, seeking a "shift from the study of 'cultural performance,' or 'performance of culture,' to the study of 'culture as performance.'" Such a perspective necessitated a "shift from thinking about performance as an Act of culture to thinking about performance as an Agency of culture prompting a reflexive turning back upon the conduct of inquiry itself" (1989, 82). In this mode of analysis, Tais's expression of mística should not be analyzed as a phenomenon that bears interpretation to better understand the "culture" from which she comes. Rather, her performance should be understood as a generative, relational, and processual act embedded within a larger context that must be understood, in Conquergood's phrasing, as "a paradigm for meaningful action" (82).

Conquergood's formulation of an anthropology of performance foregrounds a series of frames that I think are productive for an analysis of how MST members understand, perform, express, and contest mística. First, Conquergood opens analytical space for what he terms "poetics," foregrounding the "fabricated, invented, imagined, constructed nature of human realities" (1989, 83). Importantly, he identifies the kinds of things an anthropology of performance might focus on, things like festivals, dramas, and narratives, as profoundly reflexive genres that reveal how people are not created but rather creative actors. As such, poetics as a locus of analysis is to accept that creative acts are generative: they "hold out the promise of reimagining and refashioning the world" (83). Second, Conquergood identifies play and related terms such as improvisation, experimentation, and agitation as a means to disturb the certainties within any given social order in which categories have been defined and hierarchies agreed on. Play "promotes a radical self-questioning critique that yields a deeper self-knowledge, the first step towards transformation" (83) from within the Aristotelian frame of mimesis: a space that imitates everyday life sufficiently to connect to an audience, yet it is distanced enough from life that shock and surprise may occur. Conquergood's third emphasis is on process and notions of the emergent, temporal, and contingent. In contrast to positivism, Conquergood argues that analysis should focus on the process of any given phenomenon as opposed to the product that emerges from it. In this sense, "culture is transacted through performance" and must be interpreted as a verb as opposed to a noun. Last, Conquergood situates performance as a contestation of power. Listing terms such as politics, ideology, resistance, and subversion, he notes that because performance is public, it is therefore "a site of struggle where competing interests intersect, and different viewpoints and voices get articulated" (84).

The questions that an anthropology of performance puts forward—How does performance reproduce, legitimate, uphold, challenge, critique, or subvert ideology? How are performances situated between forces of accommodation and resistance?—speak to what I perceive to be the relational aspects of mística. I wonder what the connection might be between the generative potential of movement members articulating an expression of mística and the reflexive and intimate spaces where such subjectivity came into being and the latent force this might exercise in tightly knit community contexts. How might mística be at once deeply reflexive and yet also uniquely public? Reflexivity is surely at the heart of any yearning to transform one's immediate social world. And as I wrote with Jonas Tinius, "Any desire for change implies a conceptualization of the status quo and conscious envisioning and imagination of a desired state of being; the very possibility of reflection is derived from intersubjective interrogation" (Flynn and Tinius 2015, 6). Another question that confronted me related to notions of the individual and the collective, a dichotomy so present in the pages of the *Jornal sem terra*. If a member of the movement put forward mística through a creative gesture on their own, were they necessarily acting as an individual? And if so, what kind of tensions might that create with the wider collective? But thinking more carefully about the terms individual and collective, it strikes me how redundant they are with regard to creative expression in that no one performs mística alone. Even though she was alone on stage, Tais conceived of the performance and rehearsed with a friend and worked together to design their costumes and makeup. And even if a person were to be alone in the moment of performance, as Judith Butler has so elegantly phrased it with regard to gender, "[it] is performed for a someone, even if that someone does not yet exist" (2016).

In theorizing how a creative expression of mística might be transformative for the person who brings it forward but also for the wider context of the MST in which it is made manifest, any analysis has to start with the body. Mística is an embodied practice. Those who perceive it are affected by its immediacy and physicality. As Erika Fischer-Lichte (2008) makes plain, the materiality of performance must be considered at least equally, if not more so, than its semiotic attributes. Through their corporeality, performances cannot be simplified and dissolved to signs and meanings; rather, they evince a particular effect on the contexts in which they are performed that goes above and beyond any interpretation of their semiotics.

The body is all the more relevant to consider because traditionally, scholarship on social movements has overlooked its importance, conflating it to *bodies* in the plural—for example, through the usage of a term like *a massa*, the mass, commonly employed by MST leaders and political scientists working on the MST alike. Echoing the shift in scholarship on social movements, Susan Foster (2003, 395) argues that classic theories of social protest "envision the body as an agitated irrationality, propelling individuals into the chaos of mob performance." Subsequent resource mobilization models were equally lacking, as the body dissolves into pragmatic considerations of the leveraging of action for political or economic gain. In both approaches, the body is somehow present yet also redundant, a mere vessel for spontaneous uncontrollable anger on the one hand and on the other an appendage or potential useful instrument to serve rational opportunism. Foster comments that neither approach recognizes the body as an "articulate signifying agent" (396), and neither takes the care to analyze the choreography of bodies and intersubjectivities that are at play in any protest event.

As we have traced, theorization of affect and the body in social movement studies has developed in the field in recent years. Maple Razsa pays close attention to corporeal experience in moments of conflict on the streets, Jeff Juris analyzes dimensions of affect in the more carnivalesque moments of his field research, and James Jasper has made clear the case for an analysis of emotion with regard to social movements (Jasper 2011). And yet, bringing anthropological perspectives into dialogue with those of critical performance studies is productive: as Janet O'Shea (2022) has argued, while scholars who bring affect into dialogue with social movement theory may attend to emotion as experienced by individual participants, "performance studies examines the structure of protest [addressing] the physical organization of space as it relates to protest's symbolic meaning" (28). What is at stake for scholars like O'Shea is how activists "train their bodies, organize physical space, and convey the messages of protest through movement and gesture" (31) and not the signs and symbols that those present might wish to ascribe.

If we return to Judith Butler's seminal work on gender, one question it provokes is the distinction she makes between performance and performativity. In *Bodies That Matter* (1993), performance is connotated with a singular act while performativity is associated with the qualities of processuality: "The reduction of performativity to performance would be a mistake. . . . Performance as bounded act is distinguished from performativity insofar as the latter consists of a reiteration of norms which precede, constrain and exceed the performer and in that sense cannot be taken as the fabrication of the performer's 'will' or 'choice'" (234). As scholars have identified (Nealon 1994; van der Watt 2004), Butler makes this distinction to clarify what she feels to be misreadings of her earlier book *Gender Trouble* (1990), especially those that equate gender with some kind of superficial performance. As Butler writes, if that were the case, "that could mean that I thought that one woke in the morning, perused the closet or some more open space for the gender of choice, donned that gender for the day, and then restored the garment to its place at night" (1990, x).

The notion of performance as a single act that somehow sits outside process has been questioned in extensive dialogues in which Butler has participated since the early 1990s (e.g., Parker and Sedgwick 1995; Benhabib 1995), and Butler's position has changed in the intervening years, coming to acknowledge the intrinsically relational dimension of performance that means it cannot be reduced to a single agent committing a singular act. As she comments, "There are bodies behind and to the side of this body, and they are working together, even when that plurality sometimes collapses into the figure of the one, even when no one else shows up on stage when I do" (Butler 2016). This shift from a binary of performativity and performance has an important consequence for what it means to enact, bringing greater complexity and nuance to the notion that performance is voluntary and singular whereas performativity is citational, an ongoing, repetitive practice or process of becoming. Butler's shift turns on accepting that performance is necessarily located within a social dimension of a bodily being. And thinking of Conquergood's focus on power and contestation, the following must be true if performance is a relational proposition: "When someone suffers as a consequence of having broken with a cultural norm, or for having shown how the norm can or must be broken or bent, that person has entered into a cultural and political struggle whether or not one meant to, whether or not there are proximate signs of others in solidarity. An isolated act can, in fact, be a radical petition for solidarity, as if to say, 'Where are those of you who will support me now?'" (Butler 2016). In making this shift, Butler has undoubtedly been influenced by a body of work that seeks to point out the relational dimension of creative expression, visual art, and performance, or, as Néstor García Canclini (2014) has argued, how art practices based on objects have been displaced by art practices based on contexts. This literature shifts the locus of analysis from the artwork as object to the artwork as event, arguing for a sophisticated theorization of art's imbrication to social and political contexts. Nicolas Bourriaud, for example, has sought to understand a type of contemporary art practice that takes "as its theoretical horizon the realm of human interactions and its social context, rather than the assertion of an independent and *private* symbolic space" (2002, 14). With regard to embodied practice, gesture, and performance more specifically, Shannon Jackson (2011) argues that such creative expression is never simply singular but rather emerges from shared social worlds. Acknowledging that interventions may be ephemeral, Jackson calls attention to the notion that all performance nevertheless relies on and reproduces a set of social relations, practices, and institutions.

Such theorization allows us to understand the profoundly relational aspects of what is at stake when MST members put forward mística through a form that sits outside of the normalized. It reveals how no such intervention is ever enacted alone, how no performance is limited to a singular act devoid of outward resonance. Beyond the fact that performances are not conceived, prepared, or rehearsed alone, performances are always performed for someone, even if that someone is not physically present, because in its realization performance calls forth others into being. This is the quality of mística, which, as Thiago put it, has the power to move mountains, to transform "much more than sometimes all of those words." Anthropologists, performance studies scholars, and practitioners have sought to create theoretical frameworks to define such a power. We can think of "communitas" (Turner 1995) in contexts of liminality and ritual, the "autopoietic feedback loop" (Fischer-Lichte 2008) that exists between spectator and performer, performance as embodied knowledge transmitted through repetition and replication (Taylor 2003), and the politicization of the spectator inherent to Augusto Boal's Theatre of the Oppressed ([1974] 2000). But I return here to

Foster's *Choreographies of Protest*: "Agency does not manifest as the product of a transcendent state. Instead, the process of creating political interference calls forth a perceptive and responsive physicality that, everywhere along the way, deciphers the social and then choreographs an imagined alternative. As they fathom injustice, organize to protest, craft a tactics, and engage in action, these bodies read what is happening and articulate their imaginative rebuttal" (2003, 412). I like this formulation because it addresses the dichotomy between individual and collective by bringing together Paulo Freire's notion of self-transformation with a relational understanding of how those actions will reverberate with others. What we can perceive in Tais's actions is a bridging of that false dichotomy: her agency issued an invitation to those who witnessed her courage to perform in front of disapproving leaders, in a context in which she was deviating from accepted norms of what was appropriate for her to perform. This was a counter-utopian gesture in that it contested the very notion of what it means to be sem terra from within a utopian framework, and her intervention articulated the notion that the smallest of community actions can shape the largest of social movements. Importantly, although Tais was alone on the stage, she did not perform as an individual. Her performance was conceived, prepared, and rehearsed with others before being articulated in front of hundreds of people. To label Tais's dance as an individual act would be to fundamentally mistake the scale of the counter-utopian: an expanded temporal frame does not mean a reduced spatial one. Rather, the question here centers on being able to comprehend how different understandings of the collective might arise, understandings in which the collective is resolutely nonlinear and nonnormative.

In this manner, after her performance, while some leaders congratulated her and others turned their backs, relieved that she had finished, something extraordinary happened. Tais smiled as she related the aftermath: "From then on girls came looking for me to go visit their assentamentos, to give them dance classes, so that we could set up a group. I saw how excited the girls were about it and that was so cool."

And that's perhaps why some leaders were so worried by what she proposed while others congratulated her on her work. More than the semiotic content of her articulation of mística, its unpredictable form unnerved those of a more conservative disposition, those who felt it their duty to police how sem terra imagination could express itself. For those who congratulated her, however, there was perhaps a realization that change was necessary and important. I suggest that in that meeting, Tais put forward a performance that was embedded in the relationality of the moment in at least two distinct ways. She had reflected deeply inward, pondering the state of the MST and its future, expressing to various members of the community her dissatisfaction with the entropy of state leadership. Her decision to dance came from there; she had decided to "break something" and, unbending, did not care at all what sanctions she would face. But also, she issued a gesture outward, a willful intransigence, understanding that through her body, she could issue a choreography toward an alternative and connect to others who felt thwarted in similar guise. This was not the action of an alienated individual whose actions would never be able to achieve substantial reach. On the contrary, this was a relational act that echoed and resonated among a community, gaining ever greater traction. In her mística, Tais was light on her feet, and yet the earth still shook.

11

Occupy, Hold Firm

The artist's freedom has always been "individual," but true freedom can only be collective. A freedom that is aware of social reality, that breaks down the boundaries of aesthetics.

LINA BO BARDI[1]

I was visiting Davi and his family for lunch. Walking down that familiar track, I came upon a small building site with a cement mixer, roof tiles, timber, and some tools left on the ground. Davi and his daughter Juliana came out to meet me. I gestured to the construction, and they walked me onto the site with its rough breeze blocks and black tarpaulin. It was going to be a brick house, Davi told me proudly and pointed out the size of the entrance hall, living room, bathroom, and kitchen, all the foundations freshly dug out in the ground. We stepped into the living room space, and Davi showed me the view over the hills. It was winter 2021, and the earth was hard from the morning frost. I stamped my feet and clapped my hands, and after showing me the fancy windows that had already been delivered, we hurried to Davi's nearby house and the warmth. Jurema, Davi's wife, was cooking a big lunch of meat, rice, and beans.

"Who's the house for?" I asked. Davi replied that it was for Juliana, her husband, and their three children. Juliana was working in the city as a receptionist at the time, and Davi told me this would become their home. I first met Juliana in 2008. She was steadfast in her determination to become an MST leader. Her first ambition was to become a movement technician trained in agroecological farming. At the time Davi told me she could expect to earn R$1,800 per month in this capacity, roughly three times the state minimum wage—a good salary. Back then, Juliana argued with Gaetano and others when the discussion turned to their disappointments with the movement. One time, with about ten of us from the settlement sitting around Gaetano's

157

television watching *A Favorita*, a Globo *novela*, or soap opera, Juliana got so angry with the conversation that I saw her bite her lip and shake her head before she stormed off back to her parents' house without saying a word. She attended the Centro de Desenvolvimento Sustentável e Capacitação em Agroecologia (CEAGRO), an MST school in Paraná, and met her husband there. By May 2014 they had joined an encampment, again in Paraná, near Rio Bonito de Iguaçu. I met her again in early 2015 when she was back from the encampment for a weekend at home. She already had two children. I asked what the conditions in the camp were like, casting my mind back to Tais's and Vera's experiences. She must have seen the worried look on my face because she laughed and said that things were fine.

"It's not like it used to be in the old days," she told me. "We all have our trucks, we have heating. People have electricity, water. It's like a vacation camp!" She said she expected the plots to be demarcated and the land titles handed out by April. Most of those encamped were children of MST assentados, but the frente de massa activists were actively recruiting people from the highways because there were not enough people to fill all the lots. She was optimistic and said the coordinators of the encampment núcleos had the most say in who would be awarded land, so she was mindful about staying in their good books.

When I saw Juliana again in 2017, however, something had changed. She no longer talked so much about the movement, and the fervor she had always expressed, her commitment, seemed to have been lost. She had moved back to the northern settlement, abandoning her claim to land through the acampamento in Paraná. I could tell she was disappointed, and I asked what it was like up there.

"Dangerous," she replied. I pressed her a little more. "The people there have a quick temper. It's not like here. There is conflict."

Davi and Jurema turned in, and it was just Juliana, her husband, Marco, and me. After a while, Juliana said that the land was valuable and that people were planting soy. The harvests were good in Paraná, and there was money to be made. But over nothing, she said, people got into fights; they shot first and asked questions later. Marco didn't say much while we were together and remained quiet while Juliana said they had come back for their safety and that of their family. I didn't ask more, but I understood that they wouldn't be going back. With her mother and father close by, near to all the friends she had grown up with, the northern settlement was a safe place for her and her family.

I was surprised by how things had turned out because Juliana, like Clarice, had been marked out from an early age as a movement leader. Juliana had been on the pathway to be a technician, and Clarice had been recruited by Grimaldi, a state leader, for the leadership school in Rio Grande do Sul. They were driven and committed, but they also stood out because no one else in their peer group seemed to want to work with the movement. Of Vera's two sons, William went to work in construction while Artur became an IT technician, earning good money setting up broadband and Wi-Fi for local companies and for the settlement. Gaetano's children, Alvise and Marina, although they both built houses on the settlement, chose not to work with the MST. Alvise never wanted to get involved in movement politics and worked as a radio DJ while Marina got married, had two children, and worked in the local municipality's health department. There were maybe twenty children on the settlement when I first arrived in 2007, and only one—Enzo, José's son, Vera and Lúcia's nephew—went on to work the land. When I visited Enzo's plot in 2021, I was amazed. There were a myriad of fruiting trees, a complex irrigation system, and a huge harvest of cucumbers with which he supplied the best gherkin company in the state. When I left that time, he gave me some cucumbers he had pickled himself, and they were delicious.

All of these young adults had taken their own paths. Juliana had certainly taken a circuitous route, but I saw how happy she was to come home and how excited she was to be building her own house. Davi and Jurema's plot of land had changed a lot since I first visited with Davi grinning at me from his window, a caipirinha in hand. Their four children were all grown up, Juliana and Guilherme living on the settlement, Randolfo and Deise living in nearby cities. Seeing the building site reminded me of Davi's plot when I first arrived, the air of precarity and of something unresolved. This small piece of land was Davi and Jurema's home; it was Juliana's home and home for her three children as well. How had Davi and his family ended up on this plot when they were originally part of Roberto's collective? How had that situation resolved itself, and what had happened?

When the northern settlement was created, it was entirely collectivized in the sense that labor and its profits were shared, and cooking, cleaning, and crèche duties for the entire assentamento were assigned collectively. No one family held land, and all decisions were made by committee. Over time, things began to change, principally because of tensions between assentados like Gaetano and those who believed in collectivized production like Roberto and Luizinho. The settlement began to fragment into plots of land held by separate family units. Four families, however, adhered to the collective and built houses in the style of an agrovila. The story was told to me bit by bit. I heard a few details first in 2009 and then again in 2015. Talking with me in more depth in 2017, Vera cast her mind back to that time.

"Around 2000," Vera said, "the collective were saying to the rest of the settlement's families, 'Ah, you can't handle collectivized labor.' But it was more the issue of Roberto. There were people who didn't like his attitude, because he was sexist and really full-on. I mean, he's changed a little bit, but at the time, there was no point in hiding it. He gave the children a hard time, Luizinho as well, like 'you can't play here' and such. As women we wanted to make space for the children, and they implied that we, the women, we were spending too much time with the children when we should have been producing, working, being economically productive."

As tensions grew, the settlement divided into two forms of organization: a social collective made up of autonomous families and a fully collectivized unit with Jairson, Roberto, his wife, Ana, and Luizinho. Short on personnel, Roberto and Luizinho sought to recruit, and Davi and his family joined the collective from Garuva, the collectivized assentamento working with salads. Davi believed in collective labor and was hopeful of finding a good environment for himself and his young family. However, things didn't work out as expected, and toward the end of 2005, things had been at breaking point for months. Davi had worked in the collective for almost five years, but relations were deteriorating, and he wanted to leave. It was an uncomfortable situation as the members of the collective were all living with one another in the agrovila. There was a standoff that lasted some five weeks while they lived together as neighbors, and Davi refused to work the assigned roster of tasks. Vera explained, "They began to undermine him, like this: 'if you don't want to stick with us, then you don't have space here anymore, we'll bring another family to live here in your space, in your house.' So, then he said, 'I'm not leaving,' and from that moment the collective was totally against him. He had nowhere to go, he was living in the agrovila, but he was not welcome there, and this made him feel really bad, it made him really depressed, he was really down. He no longer had the strength to continue fighting for the plot, nor to even bring the subject up with Roberto, and he had also lost the strength to discuss things with us."

No one knew what was going to happen. Davi and Jurema packed all their belongings without knowing where they were going to go, and the state leadership was made aware of the situation. Luizinho, a member of the collective, was also a regional leader of the education sector, so the state leaders were kept well apprised. State leadership offered Davi and his family various solutions: they could encamp again, or they could work in another collectivized environment, in the cooperatives Cooperdochi or Cooperoeste in São

Miguel do Oeste. Either way it would mean leaving the northern settlement and starting all over again.

Davi dismissed these options, and a tense standoff developed. Grimaldi, state leader of the frente de massa sector, made it plain that the state leadership didn't want to take a position on an "internal" subject. However, in the leadership's instructing the settlement to resolve things on its own, its silence became in and of itself a position, empowering the collective to do whatever was necessary and yet avoiding any subsequent consequences for the state leadership; expelling a family who had been part of the movement since 1997 would undoubtedly be an unpopular decision. Roberto called a full settlement meeting and demanded that Davi be expelled. He wasn't contributing, Roberto argued, and he had come to the northern settlement to be part of the collective, so that was that. Where Davi went from here was his own problem: Davi may have worked for five years on the settlement, but they owed him nothing; they were all square. After Roberto left, there was a discussion among the families, and no one felt that Davi should have to leave. André organized a motion on a Friday, and it was decided that on the following Monday, Davi would become an assentado—he would be formally assigned a plot of land within the settlement. On Monday morning, at seven o'clock, nine of the settlement's thirteen families went to the plot of land where Davi's family live today. At that time, it belonged to the collective. Vera recalled how Davi was really afraid: "We tried to reassure him, we're your friends and comrades. And our attitude wasn't so much to undermine Roberto, it was rather to articulate for Davi. We didn't want him to be evicted. He had gone through so much, various evictions, he'd gone hungry. And then he got here, worked for five years, and his own comrade tells him that he doesn't have the right to a piece of land. This was what really led us to take action."

I asked what happened next. "So when we took this decision to act," Vera continued, "there was a big, big backlash." She laughed. "Interesting, right, that you fight collectively to make something happen, but then sem terra fight among themselves when dividing up sem terra land. Probably around ten a.m., Roberto arrived. I mean, it was exactly like the fight against the latifúndio, the landowners. Roberto turned up on a tractor with a machete in his hand. It's kind of funny thinking back now, but it was really ugly."

Vera described how people were occupied with various tasks when Roberto arrived. Because the plot was in disuse, there was no shelter, and the families were busy using their experience of MST acampamentos to set up an encampment for Davi and his family. The families had brought horses, tools, rope, and tarpaulin to construct a basic shelter. Some were in the woods chopping down branches, others were digging foundations, and others were taking care of the children. The families had left no one at home, including infants and babies.

"Thank God nothing happened," said Vera. "We arrived at seven a.m., and Roberto arrived soon after. It was dangerous. We were like thirty people, and Roberto drove toward everyone on his tractor with a machete in his hand and shouted, 'What are you doing?' It was an occupation! He was like a landowner! So he asked everyone, and no one replied, and then he confronted Davi. Why was Davi there, what was he doing? And then André, with all his craziness, said, 'Leave here, because this land belongs to our comrade.' André stood up and said, 'We're doing this because Davi will become an assentado.'"

Vera described how the families stayed with Davi until nightfall. They set up a barraca, the shelter built for an MST occupation, and sent a horse and cart to fetch Davi's belongings from his house in the collective's agro-vila. Vera told me they tried to calm Davi; he was ashamed and thought he was doing something wrong. The families talked to him and convinced him that this was his right. He had suffered evictions from MST encampments in Papanduva and Garuva, and the families told him he wouldn't have to suffer that again. I asked more particularly about the moment when Roberto arrived. Vera said, "It really was an occupation. We were doing something that we had done before, all of us. The only difference was that we had never done this in our own settlement! It was historic. It was something we knew inside out, building an encampment, and we knew someone would come. When Roberto did arrive, everyone came together, close to one another, and we made a circle around Davi. We protected him. And we did it also so that when Roberto was asking that question, like what are you doing here, no one would have to answer, like he would understand. In that way it was very similar to what you do in a real encampment."

I asked what she meant. "When the police arrive, or the owner of the fazenda arrives, we close ranks so we can negotiate better or make demands. And we knew we could count on each other in that moment of tension, because we just knew. That decision to close ranks, it was something that came in the moment, it was the spirit of belonging, like a mística, a unity of thinking. It was tense but a pacific act."

Vera's invocation of mística to describe the act of occupying land to stand up for a friend echoes the shift discussed previously, the notion of moving away from performance as cultural phenomena to be interpreted, toward an understanding of performance as a generative and relational act embedded within a larger context: a paradigm for meaningful action; a choreography of an imagined alternative. Susan Foster (2003, 397) makes plain the kind of questions (here abridged) a critical performance studies scholar might ask: "What are these bodies doing?; what and how do their motions signify?; what choreography, whether spontaneous or predetermined, do they enact?; what kind of significance and impact does the collection of bodies make in the midst of its social surround?; how have these bodies been trained, and how has that training mastered, cultivated, or facilitated their impulses?; what do they share that allows them to move with one another?"

Thinking with these questions, we can perceive that what happened on the collective's land that day recalls in close approximation people's actions in MST encampments across Brazil. The settlement's families took a decision to support Davi and occupied a part of the collective's land to which they felt he was entitled. Starting early, they built an MST encampment in a very particular manner. Davi's temporary shelter was built from stout branches from the nearby woods, tightly wrapped with the black polyethylene sheeting that is so intrinsic to the movement. In occupying the collective's land, the families were drawing on an embodied knowledge that had been built up through many years of being encamped, being evicted, and having to set up all over again.

The barraca they were constructing for Davi was instantly recognizable. The design incorporated a sloping roof and straight walls with a chimney projecting from the sheeting, the smoke coming from a woodburning stove inside. As I have written elsewhere (Flynn 2018), the aesthetic of the MST encampment is iconic, coming to visually represent the very essence of MST landlessness. What occurred on that day, however, was a twist on expected proceedings. The families were acting in defense of one of their friends against a fellow MST member, putting to use a series of steps that they knew intimately how to reproduce. This was a spontaneous choreography that drew on years of practice, a means to enact the kind of world the families wanted to live in, one in which *alguém da luta*, a comrade in arms, would not be left bereft and homeless just because he was no longer economically productive. The impact these bodies made in the midst of their social surrounding was striking. Roberto arrived enraged, brandishing a machete, and it is significant that in the moment of his arrival, people already knew what to do. Drawing again on their past experience of violent occupations, they acted decisively when Roberto drove his tractor toward them. Roberto became the landowner in that moment, and the families immediately closed ranks, just as they had done many times in the past when confronted by a threat, whether that be hired gunmen, a landowner, or the military police.

Their bodies had been trained for this eventuality, and they all knew the drill, closing ranks to protect Davi, their own children, and themselves. They brandished the foice, the symbolically important long-handled scythe, in the face of the enemy, and in occupying the collective's land, they resignified the notion of occupation, asserting an outcome that contradicted the wishes of Luizinho, an important leader and member of the collective, and the broader state leadership, who had refused to take decisive action in support of Davi's case.

This was durational activism characterized by counter-utopian politics. In putting forward an embodied knowledge and creatively appropriating the movement's own direct-action tactics, the families put forward a powerful creative gesture to enact their understanding of mística, one that asserted the terms of the kind of movement they wanted to be part of—one that drew on the affective bonds of comradeship rather than the balance sheet of rational economic activity; one that forcefully articulated what being a true sem terra really meant. Reflecting together with her mother, Clarice commented on the day Davi became an assentado: "It was a symbolic act. To occupy is to resist. If you want to confront someone or something head on, we occupy. Usually it's a landowner, not a sem terra, but this was a sem terra who didn't understand the social dimension."

Clarice was a child when the occupation happened, but she had a very clear memory of the day. She remembered playing with the other children and being frightened when the tractor drove up yet also being part of a happy and joyful atmosphere. "To occupy the land of the collective was a revolutionary act," she explained. "To help Davi out in that moment, which was so difficult for him, was an act of mística. To make a connection between what he went through, why he was in the situation he was in, and how he was trapped . . . this was mística."

Vera interjected: "Our worry was on the human level. This guy had gone through everything that the struggle implies, and he was going hungry inside the assentamento without any possible way out. So we occupied. That's the truth. It's a symbolic act, an act that constitutes the movement. The idea of the act is to confront landowners, but we changed it, we took the movement's own act and turned it on the landowner mentality. It's just that this landowner mentality happened to be in a sem terra."

The families got their way. Thwarted by their solidarity, Roberto accepted defeat and left. The families remained with Davi and prepared a communal dinner that night to celebrate Davi finally becoming an assentado. Vera shook her head, and her tone changed. "They were so downtrodden, that family. There comes a moment when you just don't have any more energy to fight. I don't know if you've already felt this, being so powerless in front of a problem, you know, it's so difficult as a woman, when you are made powerless in a particular reality. I couldn't go to Florianópolis to argue with the leaders in 2009, I was powerless. The cost of travel, having to stay here and look after my children. But in that moment, the attitude was different. It made me happy to act and help Davi. It's like, fine, he might not be so productive in this financial sense, but we feel the ties of friendship. Davi is a good guy."

Listening to Vera, I understood that she was making a connection between Davi's situation and her own in early 2009. At that time, when in fear for her life, she ran from her husband, André; she left the home she had built on the northern settlement. Like Davi, she had been cast adrift by the state leadership, an older generation who washed their hands of an internal difficulty by allowing normalized behaviors and moral positions to resolve a problem in which they were unwilling to get involved. She continued: "And you know, sometimes I think, how many families were thrown out of acampamentos because a group didn't come together to say 'no, these are good people'? Everyone in the region knows the story, but I've never heard of this happening elsewhere in the movement. It was a gesture of solidarity."

Vera's comment made me think of Márcio and his father, expelled from the Novo Horizonte acampamento after being encamped for six years, and even the woman I never met, thrown out of her encampment by the state leadership for being André's lover.

Clarice got up. "So you see, Flynn, the movement is the people." She used the words *as pessoas*, and not the more common MST formulation, *a massa*, the mass. "You shouldn't have to sacrifice yourself for the collective. There is a big difference between the místicas you see at the meetings, the things we act in, and the mística of the everyday. Because in this *mística*, you join the past, present, and future. And that's what we did that day."

* * *

Members like Vera, Clarice, and Tais make plain the difference they perceive between the institutionalized performances of mística—"the místicas"—that occur at MST state and national meetings and what they understand to be mística in the abstract: a subjective expression of landless identity; a spiritual force; or, as Thiago understood it, the very conscience of the movement. Where the former has taken on a defined form, the latter can manifest itself in a variety of ways; while one is tasked with the construction of identity, political mobilization, and the promulgation of certain normalized sem terra values, the other is minoritarian, community-based, and, as I suggest, the locus of counter-utopian practice.

I previously wrote about the philosopher Henri Bergson's differentiation between time as it is commonly understood—"spatialized" time—and his notion of time as la durée, "duration." For Bergson, time wasn't just the watch's minute hand pausing over fractions of space; rather, it was the experience of the now with that which will follow, a flow of moments that interpenetrate to become inseparable points of a single continuous flux. Temporality was central for Bergson because of his interest in how things transform. Duration was characterized by the creation of forms and the continual elaboration of the absolutely new whereas biological theories, such as Charles Darwin's, were limited by their conceptualization of time as linear: theories of evolution might be able to map out how change took place step-by-step but could not explain from where the impulse to transform came forth.

I've argued that within the MST there are two discrete understandings of time: first, a linear and teleological mode in which the victorious outcome of the struggle is predetermined and given; and second, a minoritarian understanding in which space and time are disaggregated and from which transformation, unexpected and unpredictable, can come about. I describe this second understanding as minoritarian because of the efforts of early MST leaders and militants like Clodomir de Morais to impose a mechanistic temporal ontology on the MST membership. In their writings and activities, such leaders sought to cultivate an understanding of time as linear to increase the movement's productivity, to bring forward the revolution, and to root out people like Davi. Their intention was to address the manner in which rural people regarded the minute hand of the clock as fundamentally unimportant and in doing so eradicate the "vice of spontaneity" by defining time in seconds, minutes, and hours as opposed to the cycles of tides, harvests, and seasons.

Institutionalized presentations of mística often put forward a narrative structure that reinforces such a linear teleology. These performances consciously link the movement to revolutionary folkloric figures and events from the past, historicizing and contextualizing the MST's struggle. These include Zumbi dos Palamares, the quilombola leader executed in 1695 by the Portuguese colonial government; Antonio Conselheiro's Canudos rebellion in Bahia, which was suppressed in 1897; the Guerra do Contestado in Santa Catarina, which was brutally put down in 1916; and the emergence of the Ligas Camponesas in Pernambuco in the mid-twentieth century. The presentations of mística that take place at large MST meetings seek to reinforce an ideological position by harking back to such heroes and martyrs but importantly do so by creating a linear timeline of resistance in which the MST becomes a natural continuation of these historic movements. In this sense, the movement affirms itself as continuing a struggle of the ages before creating a presentation of a victorious future in which those present will surely arrive. In part influenced by the lasting influence of Christian theology in the movement, the performances that occur at large MST meetings represent the promised destination of the revolutionary journey, as opposed to materializing it in the here and now.

In this manner, institutionalized performances do not bring about transformation; rather, they merely *represent* it. And this, I argue, is what renders the interventions of Tais and Vera so powerful. In putting forward their own creative expressions of mística, they articulate a subjective interpretation of what it means to be sem terra, and their interventions bring about, in the *now*, the kind of movement they wish the MST to become. In this mode, the future-as-wished-for is not merely represented; it is made tangible and fundamentally enacted. In institutionalized performances, by contrast, the future is not made real; it is a mimetic construction, the imitation of the real.

For Tais and Vera, something *changed* in the moments they communed with mística: Davi gained land, on which his family still dwells almost twenty years later; for Tais, her dance set off a complex series of events, an unforeseeable transformation, which I describe further in the following section. As Clarice mentions, in mística, past, present, and future are joined; mística, as an abstract notion, is rooted within durational time. As such, when mística is evoked, the intervention it inspires does not map out the future: there is no vision or projection, only a series of experimental gestures that issue a starting point whose ultimate end is unknown.

When mística takes form in the creative expression of a member of the MST, it brings about something transformative that is premised on that temporal ontology. Vera and Tais bring about transformation from within durational time; they make something happen in the now. I often think back to Clarice's comments on the MST's politics as a utopian dream and how she considered the creation of a new society an unrealistic objective, something that lay outside of the movement's control. The interventions that Tais and Vera put forward are fundamentally counter-utopian, not just in the sense that they break with established norms and conventions about, for example, what kind of dance can be thought of as sem terra or on what basis land is awarded in the MST, but also because they demand an exit from the notion of the subjunctive, of transformation held in the suspension. Mística and creative expression in this sense allow us to grasp how an understanding of social justice as durational practice impels these struggles in new and unexpected directions.

Pausa

In Novo Horizonte one time, I was chatting with some encamped people. There were two guys I recognized from the Vitória encampment, Polaco and a friend of his. It was common to be moved from encampment to encampment. Vitória had been cleared by judicial order; the local frente de massa was looking to reestablish it, and the men were here in the meantime. We were talking about where we were from, and I asked whether being both of Polish origin, they supported Brazil or Poland at the World Cup. After laughing about it, both men said Brazil. We continued to talk lightheartedly about soccer and pierogi, a type of filled dumpling, until Polaco suddenly told me that soccer was a device of the bourgeois to make the working classes lose their focus on the necessity of social revolution.

At first, I thought it was a joke, a *zoeira*, so I said that I thought soccer was just a game. Polaco's friend then weighed in and told me that I should be careful about playing it too much or getting too involved in supporting a team. Unsure, I thought it better to not say anything. While I nodded along, they both started laughing, and eventually, I did as well. I guess it was a zoeira.

Polaco kept on appearing in my life. Another time in Novo Horizonte, I was sitting around and not doing much when I heard shouting in the distance and people running back to the encampment. They got closer, and I saw Polaco. He was covered in blood.

"*Que porra é essa?*" What the fuck? I shouted.

"It's his thumb, it's almost taken off," one of the men said. "Chainsaw."

Polaco was securing his hand with a bloody rag. "I let my boy use the chainsaw, he lost control. You've got a car, right?"

171

I took Polaco to the hospital, driving as fast as I could with him bleeding in the back. At first I kept checking the rearview mirror, and I saw him sitting there grim faced. But it wasn't long before he was making jokes. About his boy. About his thumb. About soccer.

Polaco's name was Miguel, and he died landless in 2018, crushed by a falling tree. He was with his son when he died.

SCENE IV—
TRANSFORMATION

[Agrarian reform] is possible to discuss, but in these small spaces, not the big ones. Because the MST is not totally utopian, I mean, you get land. You achieve agrarian reform in small spaces.

CLARICE

12

Remaking the Movement
from Within

Se não tivesse havido muita chuva que choveu, se não
tivesse havido muito sol que queimou, esta tarde de hoje,
possivelmente não ocorreria. Foi preciso que alguns mor-
ressem, foi preciso que alguns desistissem, foi preciso que
fortalecesse sua coragem de briga e iluminasse o seu sonho
de refazer o mundo.

If there hadn't been so much rain that fell, if there hadn't
been so much sun that burned, this afternoon today pos-
sibly wouldn't have happened. It was necessary that some
people passed away, it was necessary that some people gave
up, it was necessary for you to strengthen your fighting
resolve and illuminate your dream of remaking the world.

PAULO FREIRE IN A TALK GIVEN AT
ASSENTAMENTO CONQUISTA DA FRONTEIRA,
BAGÉ, *JORNAL SEM TERRA*, SEPTEMBER 1991

The actions taken by Vera and Tais necessitated conviction and courage. Pushing back on normative understandings of what it means
to be sem terra, their embodied interventions called into question
two foundational tenets: the right to land being premised on a rational understanding of productivity and a set of transcendent conservative morals
embedded within a patriarchal system of power. Tais frequently expressed
frustration with the entrenchment of power in the movement, referring to
the leadership as the gerontocracia. And in this manner, the social context in
which Tais lived made a powerful impression on the aesthetic form through

which she chose to take a stand. She simply decided to not back down and instead insisted on doing something new: vou quebrar isso, I'm going to break this. In her choosing to subvert what was expected of her, the social forms of hierarchy and its constraints shaped the aesthetic form she put forward.

Tais's intervention provides a good example of what the philosopher Jacques Rancière considers the indivisibility of aesthetics and politics. For Rancière, politics isn't about deputies and chambers, political parties and manifestos; in *Aesthetics and Its Discontents*, he asserts that politics is rather "the configuration of a specific space, the framing of a particular sphere of experience, of objects posited as common and as pertaining to a common decision, of subjects recognized as capable of designating these objects and putting forward arguments about them" (2009, 24). This configuration is typically a realm of social order, "a set of implicit rules and conventions which determine the distribution of roles in a community and the forms of exclusion which operate within it" (Sayers 2006). This order is founded on what Rancière terms the "distribution of the sensible," an apportioning by those with power of what is visible and invisible, what is audible and inaudible, and what counts as speech and what is merely noise (2004, 13).

Such a framework determines what can be thought, made, or done and prescribes what is acceptable or not, including or excluding actors as a consequence. Politics occurs when those who sit outside this configuration decide to intervene in the established order, thus contesting the rules around what can be made visible, permissible, and possible and thereby proposing a redistribution of the sensible. To put forward dissonant aesthetic forms in this sense is to contest the political, for example, by articulating that which has been silenced or invisibilized or, as Tais did, by situating a body where and when it is not typically acceptable to be seen. Such interventions can challenge a social regime of order that seeks to maintain degrees of inequality and exclusion leading to a reordering of what is permissible and where.

Aesthetics is therefore the means through which the political is constituted and operated, but it is also the means through which the political can be contested. For Rancière, aesthetic forms are not necessarily elite forms of art but more simply "ways of doing and making that intervene in the general distribution of ways of doing and making as well as in the relationships they maintain to modes of being and forms of visibility" (2004, 13). To recognize the indivisibility of aesthetics and politics is to express the idea that politics is "primarily conflict over the existence of a common stage and over the existence and status of those present on it" (1999, 26). The political dimension of aesthetics meanwhile rests on its power to reconfigure who gets to be on stage and how.

In Rancière's understanding of a realm of social order, well-established conventions normalize and structure hierarchies of sensitivities, objects, and roles. Pierre Bourdieu (1979) makes clear how aesthetic judgment and taste are conditioned by social factors in his study of the French middle classes. Bourdieu's ethnography details a relationship between aesthetics and politics with which we are all familiar. This relationship—how social forms determine aesthetic forms—can be termed the *aesthetics of politics*. Conversely, what Tais's intervention puts forward is how aesthetic forms reorder the social—and this politics of aesthetics underpins this fourth section of the book. Together with Lucy Bell and Patrick O'Hare (2022), I have written on the ethnographic importance of form and how it can be productive to expand anthropological research on this term. In English and other Germanic languages, the word *form* denotes shape, format, or arrangement. In Portuguese and Spanish, however, *form* also means way or mode. For example, in Brazil, people refer to *uma forma de fazer*, a way of doing. If we think about the anthropological consequences of such an expanded definition then we can establish a connection between forms of action (ways of doing things, of changing things, of shaping experience) and aesthetic forms (ways of shaping objects, words, and experiences) (Bell, Flynn, and O'Hare 2022, 101). In this expanded reading, there is a necessity to grasp how form has both social and aesthetic connotations and, importantly, that such connotations must be understood as connected. This contingency, or interlacing, is what I think of as form's *double fold*—the manner in which the aesthetic hinges on the social. Aesthetic forms are shaped by social contexts, but crucially, the social also hinges on the aesthetic in that sociality can be reordered by aesthetic practice. First, I discuss how Tais's performance was informed by its social context. How did Tais's performance reflect events that were playing out in her own settlement? Second, I discuss how the social hinges on the aesthetic and describe how the coastal settlement in Água Branca changed as a result of Tais's intervention and continues to change today.

* * *

The coastal settlement in which Tais lived was an anomaly in many ways. It had its beginnings in 1994 with an encampment on the land of a local landowner, Seu Humberto. Its uniqueness, however, stemmed from the fact that it was Humberto himself who advocated for the encampment and supported the landless families while negotiations with INCRA took place. Humberto had been involved in land disputes in Santa Catarina for many years, and his first contact with the MST was when he lent a tractor as a gesture of solidarity to an MST occupation carried out by sixty families in Garuva. When I met Seu Humberto in 2008, he told me that the coastal settlement was a direct result of the Guerra do Contestado and that he felt it necessary to offer part of his land to counter the war's ongoing legacy of dispossession. However, negotiations with INCRA to formally expropriate the land were complex. INCRA conducted a soil analysis and, encountering a high proportion of sand and a lack of nutrients in the topsoil, deemed its composition unsuitable and therefore inappropriate for agrarian reform. After a long process, which Humberto and Kleber jointly led, INCRA finally agreed to expropriate, and an area of fifty hectares was demarcated, envisaged for the settlement of ten families. Kleber quickly took on a leading role within the settlement and, in line with MST policy of the period, organized a collectivized model of production to try to make the best of the challenging conditions.

At first the settlement was populated by only five families, and even after the construction of the settlement's agrovila—brick-and-mortar houses built with assistance from the Federal University of Santa Catarina—the settlement struggled to attract recruits. Word had spread, first about the infertility of the soil and second about Kleber's insistence on collectivization. Even when the settlement's houses were full (I slept in an empty house when I spent time there), there was always a high turnover, as families never stayed long. This created many difficulties for Kleber, who was committed to self-sufficiency and a collectivized system of work but lacked a consistent labor force to get things done in the way he thought best. Indeed, the conditions in the coastal settlement were such that many families found it difficult to adapt and ended up leaving for other settlements or even decided to return to living in the temporary shelters of an encampment with its attendant dangers.

When I returned to the coastal settlement in 2008, a year after I had first visited, change was in the air. The settlement had moved from full collectivization—cooking, cleaning, and crèche duties—to a simpler model where only agricultural labor and its profits were collectivized. However, more than that, a new family had moved in: Paulo, the trade unionist from the city; his daughter, Jessica; and her partner, Douglas. I asked Douglas how they had come to move to Água Branca. "Me, Paulo, and Jessica were in an acampamento," he told me. "There were sixty families there. And you know what the conditions are like, no? Life is complicated. So then, Kleber arrived, and an assembly was called. He said that there were *vagas*, vacancies, here and asked if people wanted to come.[1] Out of the sixty families, we were the only volunteers."

Douglas, a young man, told me that no one in the encampment wanted to work collectively because people wanted their own plots of land. On top of that, people knew that the coastal settlement's poor soil quality meant it would be difficult to make a living through planting crops. The situation was perilous. Because nothing substantial could be planted, one of the settlement's key sources of income had become the manufacture of bricks, which were sold to local construction firms; each pallet of one thousand bricks cost 450 reais. These were made from straw, shaped in a manual press, and baked in a kiln. One time Paulo showed me the backbreaking effort it required to make one brick and dismissively commented that no one ever made money in the manufacture of raw materials. Other sources of income included selling artisanal cheeses and providing labor to build houses in the nearby town of São Caetano. In short, the assentamento was in dire straits, and three out of eleven houses were almost always empty.

Paulo and his family quickly understood that things had to change and began to think of more sustainable ways in which the settlement's families could make a living. In doing so, they were issuing an indirect challenge to Kleber, not only through their presence but also because Paulo and his family unit were different from Kleber's typical recruits. Paulo had experience in the trade union movement and was being fast-tracked for leadership. More broadly, Paulo, Jessica, and Douglas were from an urban background and brought a different economic rationale to the settlement that ran contrary to Kleber's ideas about self-sustainability, agricultural work, and the gendered roles associated with such a model.

The new recruits initiated a series of discussions within the settlement's committee to propose new ways of working. Among the ideas suggested was taking advantage of the settlement's proximity to a major highway and using it as a base for a restaurant themed around *café colonial*, a type of buffet featuring a variety of cakes, breads, pickles, and cold meats associated with the German immigrants of Santa Catarina. Another idea was to create nature trails in the surrounding *mata atlântica*, the Atlantic coast rainforest, with observation platforms overlooking the sea as part of an ecotourism project. The latter foundered because of the lack of capital and intensive labor required to construct the necessary trails. The idea with the most traction was using the bricks the settlement produced to manufacture barbeques for resale at supermarkets and small businesses. Paulo argued forcefully that the settlement should take advantage of the bourgeois system of added value, the additional economic worth that goods and services acquire when they are transformed during the production process. However, none of these ideas gained Kleber's support as he found involvement in a wider capitalist market deeply troubling. For Kleber, settlement land was to be worked collectively for agricultural purposes and not to be used as a base for capitalist enterprise. As tensions grew, the situation became untenable, and Paulo, Jessica, and Douglas left the assentamento.

At stake in this dispute were notions regarding the use of land but also the gendered roles associated with collectivized labor models. Kleber was comfortable with sales of artisanal cheese and batches of bricks, but he didn't want to sanction a more regularized interaction with the market. While the dispute was largely amicable, the urban cohort's perspective was on occasion something of a culture shock: Douglas's suggestion that he manage the roadside restaurant while everyone else cooked and served went down particularly badly. But Kleber's reticence to countenance change fundamentally came down to how such plans might reorder relations in the settlement and specifically how the mutually constitutive relationship between gendered labor and collectivized production might be called into question. In the original collectivized labor model, women took care of children in a settlement crèche, ran the kitchen for a settlement's workers, and brought new workers into the world through reproduction. Men, on the other hand, planted the land and carried out the harvest, producing agricultural commodities that would be used directly in the settlement kitchen, thereby ensuring sustainability.

Such clearly delineated gender roles were foundational to this regime of productivity, and Kleber, as a regional leader of production, was simply implementing long-held best practices. In the coastal settlement, however, this kind of production had become unsustainable, and the financial difficulties the settlement faced revealed the contradictions of such a model. As Tais commented to me one time, "We often end up laughing about this question of capitalism, you know? Sometimes someone will say, 'Ah, I need to go buy some sneakers, I need to go buy some jeans.' Then someone else will say, 'Ah! Are you taking part in capitalism?' The movement preaches one thing, but like, you are forced also to be part of a capitalist system."

Kleber felt a strong duty to ensure financial viability for the settlement's families, but he was also wedded to notions of collectivized production as put forward by his immediate superiors in the state leadership. For all the misunderstandings and everyday disputes, the departure of the urban cohort of Paulo, Jessica, and Douglas ended up revealing an essential fault line: any shift from collectivization to individual lots would have a direct impact on understandings of productivity and its attendant moral values. Within the ideas outlined by Paulo and his family lay the beginnings of a new understanding of women's bodies and labor, reshaping wider notions of what it meant to be productive.

Tais's performance interrogated these gendered norms of sem terra identity by insisting on a female body out of place. Informed by the fundamental connection between the movement's moral conservatism and notions of productivity in the settlement in which she lived, her performance questioned what women were allowed to do and where, pointing to what was permissible or not. Thinking through how aesthetic forms are shaped by social contexts is the first element of the double fold, and Tais's performance was clearly informed by what was happening in the coastal settlement. But the social also hinges on the aesthetic, in that sociality can be reordered by aesthetic practice, and in the time since Tais's bold performance, the coastal settlement has undergone significant transformations, unfolding along the fissures and possibilities her intervention brought to the surface.

The period in which Paulo, Jessica, and Douglas arrived in the coastal settlement was a time of flux. The composition of the assentamento was shifting, and another assentada, Maíra, was also pushing for change, albeit in a very different manner. Maíra had also moved to Água Branca at the beginning of 2008, but different from the urban cohort, she was a long-term MST member, having joined the movement in 2000. Married to Maicon and the mother of two children, Maíra was one of the stronger voices among the families who were pushing for a move away from full collectivization. At the time she was comanaging a medicinal herbs project with the Federal University of Santa Catarina and had been appointed a regional leader of the MST's health sector, working across four settlements in the region. One day in 2008, as we walked around the settlement, Maicon gestured to the sandy topsoil, commenting that it was difficult to grow anything; Maíra told me how the recent floods had damaged what little planting had taken place. It seemed their solution to this bleak situation was the medicinal herbs project, and Maíra spoke about her objective: to produce herbs and deliver them in dry-leaf form direct to the consumer. She had technical support from professors in the department of public health of the Federal University of Santa Catarina (UFSC), and they met once a month to coordinate. We were walking toward a polyethylene tunnel where the plants were cultivated. As we entered, Maíra stopped and commented, "You said you'd like to see our plot, right?" I nodded, and she continued. "So, just to be clear, it's not mine, it's the movement's. It belongs to everyone. Just so you understand."

The question of who owned what was clearly a delicate point, and afterward, in their home, Maicon mentioned that it was difficult to make ends meet. Not all the settlement houses were occupied, and there were only three families signed up on the collectivized work roster. I asked how people were getting by, and he said people relied mainly on the Bolsa Família, a welfare payment from the Brazilian government.[2] When I asked Maíra about her work as a leader, she commented that it was a challenge to balance it with the expectations in the settlement. People in the region commented that Maíra was ambitious, but as I got to know her better, I understood that she simply had no interest in making cheese, making bricks, or taking care of young children beyond the two she already had. Her ambition in this sense was articulated in a much less confrontational manner than Paulo, Jessica, and Douglas: she was mindful of Kleber's insistence on collectivized production and agricultural work, but she also understood there was no future in toiling away on unproductive land.

Collaborations with local universities offered a pathway forward. In 2012, Maíra led a workshop on the cosmetic uses of medicinal plants as part of a broader two-day seminar on traditional medicine and phytotherapy organized by UFSC, the Santa Catarina Association of Medicinal Plants (ACPM), and the nearby municipality of São Caetano. Maíra's session was one of the most oversubscribed events in the program, and she conducted a brisk trade at her sales stand throughout the event. In 2015, she became a project partner of a joint UFSC and INCRA initiative to develop agroecological projects in rural locations across the states of Santa Catarina, Paraná, Rio Grande do Sul, and São Paulo. When I saw her again in 2017, she had been successful in her application for four years of funding from the Banco do Brasil and INCRA, and she had extended and developed her polyethylene tunnel production. Maíra told me how she was selling products derived from medicinal plants at local markets and fairs. I didn't ask about Kleber's stance. It was clear that relations had shifted in the settlement, and through persistence, the application of public funds, and careful networking, Maíra had been part of a process of transformation that Paulo, Jessica, and Douglas had not been able to realize. Indeed, the assentamento's organization had changed entirely over a ten-year period, with each family unit acting autonomously, much in the same manner as the northern settlement. By 2022, Maíra had founded a multifaceted business on the sandy soils of Água Branca offering Reiki and other healing therapies, holistic workshops, and beauty products created from medicinal plants, all from within the space of what she marketed as a "rural retreat" whose facilities included camping, fishing, and hiking. Her therapeutic space directly faced the main road with an ornate drive and gateway to welcome in passers-by—a marked contrast to my first visit to the settlement some fifteen years earlier, when the busy asphalt road had been a dusty track, and the settlement was almost entirely hidden from the road by a screen of trees and vegetation.

Maíra's trajectory was intimately connected to Tais. They were neighbors and shared confidences that they kept to themselves. When I met Tais and her partner, Wagner, they openly criticized the leadership, saying it was a major barrier to the emergence of new ideas, and it is significant that Tais referenced Maíra as sharing the view when she labeled the leaders "dinosaurs." Tais supported Maíra in her desire to progress the settlement and often found herself in disagreement with her father, Kleber, on questions of how the settlement's land should be used and the role of women in work. When Tais performed before state leaders, one of her central provocations was the way a woman's body could embody and assert the MST's struggle. Her performance catalyzed the interest of many other women, who sought to engage with mística in ways that resonated with their own interpretations of the movement.

Tais's actions sparked widespread discussion throughout the region. Her confrontation with state leadership was particularly notable given her own positionality as a leader's daughter, drawing further attention to the situation in the coastal settlement. Central to her performance was the body as a site of resistance, challenging gendered norms within sem terra identity. Through her actions, she directly contested the intersection of the movement's moral conservatism and its structuring of roles within the settlement, asserting a woman's right to embody, practice, and express herself differently.

This insistence reverberated in the years that followed, shaping both personal and collective trajectories. As Tais and Maíra's relationship deepened and Kleber distanced himself from collectivization, Maíra forged new partnerships with universities and community actors. Yet at the core of her engagement was the body itself—her training as a Reiki practitioner informed a healing practice that redefined the possibilities for women's roles within the settlement. Departing from a framework in which women's labor had been confined to cooking and cleaning on settlement duty rosters, Maíra rejected conventional schemes of collectivized production. By breaking the link between productivity and gendered labor, she demonstrated how a practice centered on Reiki and medicinal plants could constitute a different, yet equally generative, form of production within the context of agrarian reform.

Alongside her partner, Maicon, Maíra not only reconfigured labor but also reshaped the physical landscape of the settlement, creating spaces to welcome local communities and those invested in agrarian reform and healing. She asserted her right to work autonomously while remaining in dialogue with her neighbors, modeling an alternative mode of engagement.

Tais's performance was a catalyst—by taking a stand, she emboldened Maíra and many other women in the region to assert their own forms of expression, reconfiguring social relations both within the settlement and beyond.

A more conventional analysis might interpret Tais's dancing body as ephemeral, a fleeting gesture within the sequence of linear time. However, I argue that in that moment, she articulated something with enduring and transformative impact—an assertion of the kind of MST she sought to belong to, one that unfolded in lived time, not as a fixed event but as a movement within duration, accumulating ever greater meaning and resonance. It was a vision of an MST whose forms of labor allowed women's bodies to perform fundamentally different tasks and, in turn, allowed women to become fundamentally different people.

And she was not alone. Tais's intervention was part of a wider paradigm of youth culture that was unwilling to continue evoking sem terra culture by performing partner dances like gauchesca that exalt and reinforce very defined gender roles (Biancalana 2014). In the period when Tais was breaking rules in Santa Catarina, John Muller, living on a settlement near the city of Ribeirão Preto in the state of São Paulo, was starting out with the hip-hop group Veneno H2 alongside two other assentados, Césinha and Mano Fi. Veneno H2 was becoming known for what its members termed *rap da roça*, rap from the fields, and just as Tais faced a conservative moral reaction, rap da roça encountered similar resistance. Janaina Moscal (2017, 192) has detailed how MST leaders, "especially the older or religious ones," considered rap music as music for "criminals and layabouts." MST radio stations were subject to campaigns calling for them to cease broadcasting "music for criminals," and just as with Tais's dance, what was threatening to MST leaders was the form through which these young people were choosing to express mística. Veneno H2 performed in contexts where spontaneity was a recognized aesthetic component: a duel of MCs, for example, where the group had to improvise responses in a freestyle rap against an opponent. The spontaneous form through which they chose to evoke mística allowed the group to bring difficult questions to the fore but also challenged more conservative leaders who sought control over what kind of message was being put forward (Bastos 2016). From the track "Vinheta Militante":

Quem somos por essa terra?
De punho esquerdo estendido ao alto,
Unindo as forças do campo e do asfalto,
Do leste, do oeste, do sul e do norte,

Preparam os guerreiros para bater de frente e encarar o choque.
Somos todos Sem Terra!

//

Who are we for this land?
With left fist stretched high,
Uniting the forces of the countryside and the street,
From east, west, south, and north,
Get the fighters ready to take it head on and take the hit.
We are all landless!

When Veneno H2 rapped about the connections between the MST and urban peripheries, they articulated a different way to understand the landless struggle. Just as with the notion of gendered labor, the question of the urban peripheries is a thorny issue within the movement. Is the MST still a rural movement? Should it consider itself such? How have ideas about what is rural changed since 1984, the year of the movement's foundation? Veneno H2's performances put all these questions and more into the space of public discussion. However, unlike Tais, Veneno H2 was able to gain a degree of acceptance, which culminated in their performance at the third National Assembly of Landless Youth as part of the MST's Sixth National Congress in 2014. As Melinda Gurr (2017, 2) notes:

> Once assembled, we watched a collaborative musical performance from Saci Arte, a country-rock fusion band from Paraná, and Veneno H2, a hip-hop trio from São Paulo state. The performers were twenty-something males, rising stars of a new generation of MST militant-musicians. Visually, they did not conform to stereotypes of rustic rural people. Instead, they reflected both the countryside and the urban periphery, indexed stylistically by their choices of appearance, speech, and song. Levi sported a large "black power" afro, Fi paired a Corinthians soccer jersey with a Palestinian keffiyeh, and John Muller had a shaggy hair cut and was prone to infusing his song lyrics and speech with urban slang (e.g., *ta ligado*? Ya know what I'm saying?). The musicians did not perform selections from the MST's extensive catalogue or classic *caipira* (traditional rural music). Instead, they began by covering a Brazilian rock classic, Legião Urbana's "Que País é Este."

Veneno H2's form of expression was challenging for leaders steeped in gauchesca. And just as with Tais's performance, the aesthetic forms they proposed resulted in a reordering of the social forms of their context—in this case, the National Congress itself. Following Veneno H2, a series of leaders gave speeches, but they were delivered from the floor as opposed to on the stage, which is the norm. And the first speech was given by none other than Miguel Stédile, son of João Pedro Stédile, the most visible MST national leader. As Gurr notes, Veneno H2's performance, with its urban connotations, lyrics, and stylings, brought about an "explicit attempt to foster less hierarchical group dynamics" (2017, 4). The sheer informality and energy of Veneno H2's aesthetic intervention made it impossible for Miguel Stédile to return to a more formal modality; to do so would have seemed out of step and inappropriate. And such a reordering is another example of how aesthetic forms—in this case those of a hip-hop group—can have a direct impact on the social forms that structure everyday lives and experiences.

Tais's act did not find the same kind of favor in an institutionalized context; in that moment in 2007, she was obliged to perform alone. But again, it is important to note that this was no individual performance; paraphrasing Judith Butler, Tais's dance was performed for someone, even if that someone had not yet come forward. The poetics of Tais's gesture—of a defiant daughter who loved her father and was proud of what he had accomplished— speak to the forces held in tension that contextualize counter-utopian practices within the MST. When I first visited the coastal settlement in 2007, its future and financial viability visibly weighed heavy on Kleber as he sought to square his position of regional leader of production with his leadership of a settlement that people knew was failing, a settlement that people encamped in the harshest conditions preferred not to join. As things changed, so did he. Kleber was one of the few MST leaders who supported Vera in her struggle for justice. And the nickname that people somewhat jokingly called him behind his back, *chefão*, big boss, began to disappear. The families of the northern settlement even began to spend their holidays over carnival in the empty houses in Água Branca. Vera and Lúcia sent me WhatsApp photos of twenty members of the Fernandes de Castro extended family happily playing soccer, cooking up barbeques, and generally causing mischief on the beaches with Kleber smiling in the background. A decade had passed, and Tais's creative expression of *mística* had prompted a transformation from within.

Pausa

October 2008. We're walking through small streets in downtown Florianópolis, the state capital of Santa Catarina. The island on which the city is
located is known as the Ilha da Magia, the Magic Island, but this is a dense
urban reality. The streets end in a single road that begins to slope steeply
upward toward the Alto da Caieira, one of the so-called *favelas* or *morros*
that constitute the Morro da Cruz neighborhood. I'm walking with some
350 children and 70 adult monitors for the fourth Encontro Estadual dos
Sem Terrinha, the junior equivalent of the MST state meeting. Our destination is a social center at the summit run by the Maristas, a Catholic religious
order. All the children are wearing identical MST T-shirts with the MST
badge, and the file winds up the hill, an unbroken stream of red.

I'm walking with Luizinho and Lúcia, who have helped organize the
event. As we climb ever higher into Alto da Caieira, Luizinho explains that
he sees this trip as an opportunity for the children to see that while many of
them desire a move to the city, with its malls and cinemas, often the reality
of migration from the countryside to the city is different from the dream. He
points out that for most of the people around us, the bus is too expensive,
the mall security will not let them enter, and the cinemas are far beyond the
reach of all but the wealthiest.

After an hour's walk, we arrive, and the director greets us in a large hall.
A street theater project run by the center performs a play about the problems
that the young people of the morro encounter. It is remarkably similar to
the kind of místicas we see at the MST state meetings. The performance
depicts a young boy getting involved in a gang and finally being killed in a
shoot-out with a rival gang. It isn't long before it's time to go. The children
are excited because we're heading to the beach, and for most of them, it will
be the first time they have ever seen the sea. As we walk down the hill, my
group begin to sing: "Bandeira, bandeira, bandeira vermelhinha, educação

189

do campo para todo sem terrinha!" (Little red flag! Rural education for all the little landless!) We arrive at the Praia do Forte. The Atlantic Ocean is an azure blue and lies sheltered from the waves. A long beach of fine white sand sits under a rocky bluff, dense green vegetation reaching up to the cliff path above. An eighteenth-century fort frames the summit, its embrasures silhouetted against a clear sky. It's a hot day, and the children run screaming into the ocean. Lúcia laughs, and even Luizinho, usually so serious, has a broad smile.

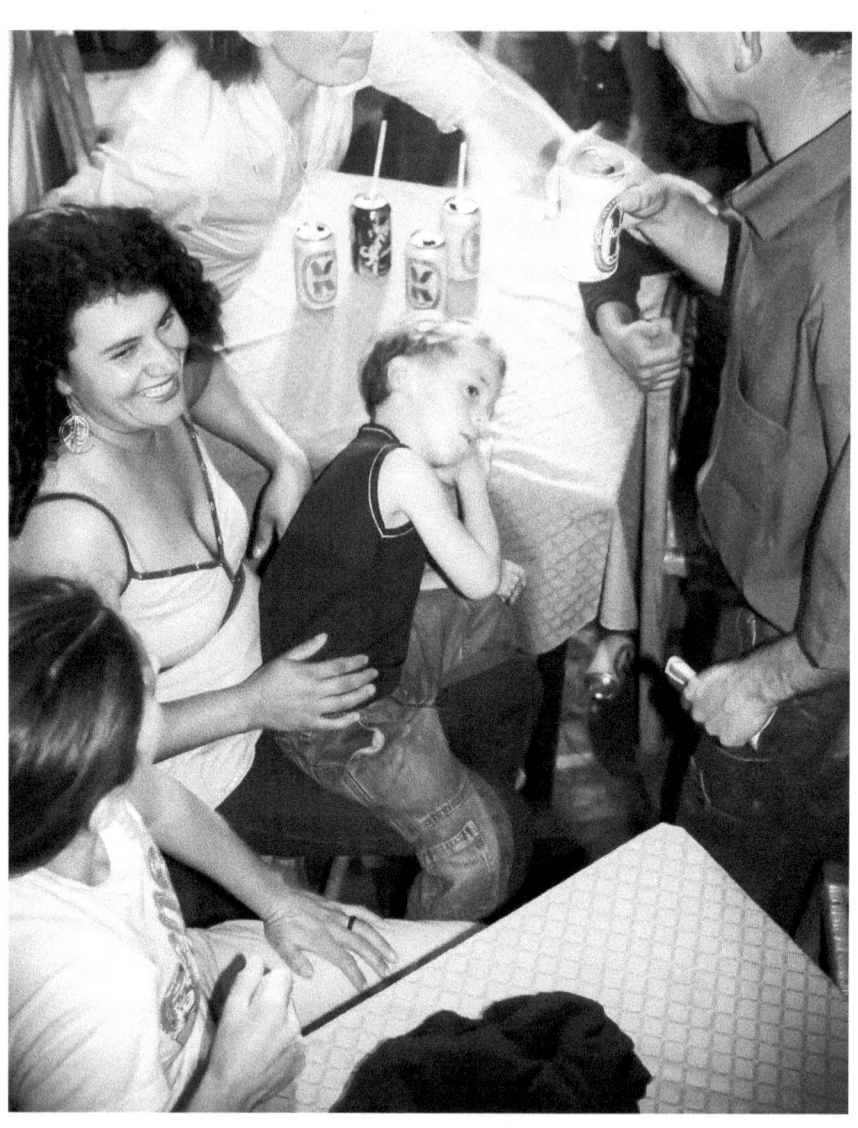

13

Community, Small Spaces

Never trust the enemy, never allow yourself any amount of trust. They are there to destroy you, capitalism is there to destroy you.

INVITED SPEAKER, A PROFESSOR, AT THE 2008
SANTA CATARINA MST STATE MEETING

When I first met Vera and André, they both were deeply committed to the movement. André was constantly traveling and leading occupations or protests. Vera was active on the settlement but also beyond it, creating relations with people in Bom Jardim and the wider Planalto Norte. Vera was a passionate believer in the MST and spoke with conviction. One of our early conversations addressed her identification with the movement and her pride in being a part of it. In early 2008, I asked her if she remembered when she joined the movement.

"I joined the movement in 1996, 15 June 1996," she replied. "It's a very important date for me, this date, because it was the start of understanding a new reality, and this new reality transformed my life and my political understanding, my understanding of life. I was always poor, and when we went to encamp it was really difficult. We camped up there for eight years, and the first forty days there was so much rain. There was a huge flood, like the one in Blumenau just past."

I asked her whether she missed that time or whether, like others I had spoken to, she preferred not to recall it too much. She answered, "I miss it. You know why I miss it? It's because that time inspired me, to imagine, to wake up. I woke up to a new reality, one where we had the ability to transform things. I was held back, but I managed to gain a freedom—in quotes, of course, because none of us are free."

We spoke about the movement clothing that she almost always wore. I asked her if, when she wore the red T-shirt of the movement, she felt pride while walking around the streets of the city. I asked her what the T-shirt represented for her.

"The T-shirt represents the struggle, no?" she said. I asked whether she was frightened to use it sometimes in the city. "Not a bit," she answered quick as a flash.

"But there are people who are afraid."

"It's good to take care of yourself," she replied. "In this respect, the well-known leaders, for example." She paused. "But me, I'm not frightened, I don't take the trouble to hide. You know, if they come to take me and put me in prison, I'll go to prison."

Both Vera's and Lúcia's houses had MST flags flying from the roof as well as pinned above the door. I asked about them.

"There are two. And always on the children's backpacks and on André's bags as well."

I asked her why she used these flags. "It's identification, no? In fact, the flag is always inside you. I want to identify myself as a sem terra. Some people don't talk to me around here, and perhaps it's because of that."

I remember I asked Vera what being free meant to her. "You mentioned none of us are free, right?" I commented.

"It's like with my mother," Vera said. "I don't know whether it's her background, but she doesn't speak to many people. She goes to meetings, but she doesn't really participate. So, she instilled this mentality in us, her children. Another question is to do with husbands. My father, he beat my mother. He beat her, he beat her so much. But she stayed with him, she never left him."

Vera's father lived on the settlement with Vera's brother, José. I saw him from time to time in the community space, next to the soccer pitch, sitting silently behind the settlement bar. Lúcia told me that their father had been a landowner with a thousand hectares and a herd of cattle. Dona Neusa, who lived with Lúcia, never once spoke about him. The importance of Vera's comment about the history of her father and mother didn't strike me until much later.

*   *   *

In early 2009, when Vera left home in fear for her life, she had few places to turn. Going back to André was out of the question. As Lúcia had told me, it was not the first time that André had been violent, and Vera had had to seek refuge with her before. Although Vera had siblings living on the settlement,

André was close at hand, and Vera worried about the authority that, despite everything, he still exerted in movement spaces. She took refuge with Lúcia and was living in a small wooden shack in the back garden. When I traveled with Lúcia to speak face-to-face with the state leadership about the standoff, all we encountered was Bianchini's intransigence: at the end of our conversation, having denied that André was in any way dangerous and affirmed that he saw the situation as "calm," he promised to reach out to Vera to make sure she was OK. He never did.

Vera had limited access to the state leaders, as is common for most MST members in Santa Catarina, and she had few allies. Somewhat surprisingly, Kleber was one of them. He thought that what the leadership was doing was wrong and told Vera that she could always count on him for help. Another point of contact was Dona Franciele, who was in the state leadership and, importantly, was a member of the frente de massa sector, the sector that seemed to exert the most influence. Despite their advocacy, however, it seemed there was no institutional will to address Vera's situation and provide a resolution. The leadership knew that André was causing a problem by getting involved with a young encamped woman. They sought to solve this by expelling this woman from the movement, an action in which Grimaldi was particularly involved. However, when André subsequently installed the woman in a flat in nearby Bom Jardim, there was widespread disapproval, but no action was taken. It was commonly assumed that André was using the money entrusted to him by the movement for frente de massa duties to pay the apartment's rent, and while up for renewal at the state meeting, André's reappointment as regional frente de massa lead was met with a variety of reactions. Lúcia fell into despair. Alvise, Gaetano's son, spoke directly.

"Can I say something very short and curt?" he commented. "The leaders did nothing because André has something on them."

The state leadership's reluctance to intercede sparked comment for a variety of reasons, but Vera's treatment seemed particularly strange given that she was such a committed MST activist. In the northern settlement people found it hard to rationalize the way in which Vera was being treated. In many ways, Vera was the ideal militante, and our early conversations were shaped by her absolute faith in the MST. Her advocacy was so unwavering that after a few months, Vera's sister Lúcia advised me to go and speak to Gaetano and Silvia, saying it would be good for my work. "They criticize," she commented. "They're not like us, they have other views." Vera's passion for the struggle didn't encompass such views, and she often spoke with pursed lips about Gaetano's opinions, describing them as "strong" or "direct."

In those early years, Vera took it on herself to show me every aspect of the life she lived through the movement. Her family started to make a joke out of it, asking me in the mornings what kind of *rolê*, what kind of itinerary, Vera was taking me on that day. I was grateful, of course, to be introduced to so many different facets of movement life, but sometimes my energy would flag whereas Vera's never did. I would go and lie down somewhere for a rest, and Vera would shake me awake and inform me where we were going next.

One of the first things we did together in 2008 was take part in a *carreata*, a type of political procession in support of the local Workers' Party (PT) candidate, Hildebrando Dunkel. Dunkel was running for the position of vereador, or town councillor. After two hours driving around Bom Jardim, waving the PT flag and honking the horn, we went to vote. Vera and Dunkel were good friends, and their friendship deepened over time. When Dunkel ran for the position of state deputy in 2018, Vera was just as active in her support for him, mobilizing and canvassing in the city. Local politics was key for Vera, and she recognized that the MST needed to cultivate strong relations with the politicians who represented progressive parties. Santa Catarina was traditionally one of the most conservative states in Brazil, and Vera's work in making these connections was all the more important in that respect. In Bom Jardim, the PT's main political opposition was the PP, the Partido Progressista, a right-wing party that emerged as a successor to the Aliança Renovadora Nacional (ARENA), the ruling party of the Brazilian military dictatorship. Several local large landowners were power brokers on the town council, and Vera understood that having good road access to the settlement and having adequate funding for the municipal agricultural school that was situated on the settlement were in the gift of the local politicians.

Another time, Vera took me to a large workshop in Bom Jardim that had been established by the disability community to offer employment specifically for people with disabilities. The manager of the space, Willian, showed us the different products that were being manufactured using off-cuts of wood and recycled plastic and spoke about the support the group had received from Vera's settlement and the close links that many people working in the space had with the MST. Over a communal lunch, Vera told me how 14 percent of Bom Jardim's population was claiming disability benefits, and we spoke about the workshop's longer-term plans to set up a community radio station in partnership with the assentamento. Vera's energy in these moments was unflagging, and while André was organizing occupations and protests, she was in the city forging relations between the MST and civil society in autonomous and horizontal networks of solidarity. Another space in which Vera made these connections was through the EJA program, Edu-cativo de Jovens Adultos, a night school for adults who had not been able to complete formal schooling. Vera studied three nights a week in Bom Jardim and mentioned that she got along well with all the other students, even those with different political views.

She seemed to know everyone in the community, and another favorite space was the local radio station. Alvise, who worked at the station, never wanted to work on the land and got his first job washing the school buses that belonged to the municipality. Over time he shifted from one role to an-other before finally landing on what he wanted to do, which was be a DJ. His show on the local radio station was popular, and Vera and I went one time to see him at work. Walking around Bom Jardim like this, we often passed the city's community college, and one time Vera asked me to come and meet a history professor she had bumped into at an event. Standing in front of the faculty buildings waiting for the professor to arrive, I understood that although she hadn't communicated anything, it was Vera's dream to gain a university degree, and this was one of the main motivations for her to con-tinue with her night schooling.

While Vera's work took place in the local community, creating relations and building bridges, André was just as busy in his role as a regional leader of the frente de massa. Beyond organizing encampments, scouting out new tracts of land to occupy, and maintaining discipline in the region, André also organized protests in the city. These interventions included squatting offices of INCRA, putting together roadblocks on important highways, and carrying out symbolic occupations of high-profile targets. Such acts were designed to bring about pressure on the federal and state governments and keep the MST in the headlines, speeding up the processes of expropriation pending on MST encampments. Taking part in these actions, which were designed to make a political statement, could be dangerous.

In November 2007, the MST decided to occupy a research facility in Paraná owned by Syngenta AG, a multinational company focused on seeds and pesticides. The rationale for the occupation was that Syngenta was car-rying out experiments with genetically modified seeds in Iguaçu National Park, where such genetically modified organisms were prohibited. The in-tention was to raise awareness, and in this action, Valmir Mota de Oliveira, known as Keno, a friend of André and Vera's, was killed. Keno was a frente de massa leader participating in the occupation when thirty gunmen, em-ployed by NF Security, a company contracted by Syngenta, arrived in a black van and opened fire on the MST members. In the ensuing confronta-tion, Keno and a gunman were killed, and eight others were injured, three of them movement members. Syngenta absolved itself of responsibility for the incident, claiming that the action amounted to a lawful repossession of property, but a judge disagreed, describing the incident as a massacre. The judgment of unlawful killing in favor of Keno's family, placing ultimate responsibility with Syngenta, was made only in 2015 and finally confirmed in 2018, a delay of eleven years.

André had been involved in a similar type of occupation only a few months earlier, in April 2007 in Papanduva, Santa Catarina. Although no one was harmed on this occasion, the occupation was particularly contentious. The land belonged to the Brazilian army and was used for military exercises, but the MST's occupation was based on the fact that forty-one families had been expelled from the area in the 1960s and never compensated. The action mobilized five hundred families who occupied the land on Sunday morning, April 15, 2007. Supposedly the movement was demanding the land be expropriated, but in reality the occupation was done to raise awareness and gain publicity. The state leadership, who had organized the occupation, were seeking to antagonize the army and were counting on a disproportionate use of force. When word reached military commanders that their exercise fields were being occupied, the army reacted predictably and surrounded the encampment with tanks, armored personal carriers, and soldiers armed with live ammunition. Throughout the day, M60 tanks from the cavalry barracks in Rio Negro performed military exercises in the area adjoining the families' encampment, threatening to destroy the acampamento through force. Threats were made through bullhorns and amplified speakers, and a sense of panic descended on the families and particularly their young children. Meanwhile, negotiations with the army command were ongoing, and the MST agreed to vacate the area the following morning. The land was never going to be subject to expropriation, but the attention that the occupation garnered allowed a senator of the PT to request a hearing with the minister of defense. Feeling that their point had been made, the MST's state leadership authorized a sem terra withdrawal.

The contrast between Vera's and André's *militância*, their activist practice, was stark. And yet they both were equally committed to the movement. The contrast was made forcefully to me when I asked Vera about the other students at the night school. She casually mentioned that one of her friends happened to be a military policeman. I told Vera I was surprised, and she laughed, telling me how at the occupation in Papanduva, her friend had been one of the policemen tasked with patrolling the perimeter. Vera told me she had seen him there and said hello. Knowing the context, and how André had been involved on the front lines of the occupation, I was amazed

Vera maintained her friendship with the night school policeman, but she explained that the policeman was just doing his job and offered to introduce him to me. During this conversation about Papanduva, Vera told me that being part of the movement was also about defending wider social causes—for example, if people spoke badly about the unhoused community, it was necessary to step in.

"You don't have to be a leader in the institutional structure," she told me. "You can be a leader *em paralelo*, in a complementary sense."

In the period from 2007 to 2009, Vera's position on the movement began to change. When we first met, she was a committed and dedicated supporter. But as the situation with her husband deteriorated, Vera began to question things in a way that was previous unthinkable. In a conversation we had in early 2009, while she was living with Lúcia, she told me that the lack of dialogue with the state leadership was frustrating: "You know, with the question of psychological problems, human questions. It's important to discuss them here in small spaces before you can bring them to a bigger debate. It's always a question of trying to understand these things."

I agreed. She continued, "We can't do these things like capitalism does. Capitalism is at the very brink of the edge. I think that there has to be more room to allow us to create these discussions in smaller spaces."

I understood that she was speaking very cautiously about André, but also the intransigence she had encountered among the state leadership in trying to resolve their domestic situation. The lack of willingness to act expressed by a majority of the state leadership could be ascribed to many different factors: the transcendent moral force of the family as a unit of occupation; a relation between normative understandings of gender and productivity; and a decision to allow a naturalized justice to take its own path. In part, however, the lack of support for Vera also speaks to the differentiation between institutional and community dimensions of militância, of what it means to be an activist. Vera was active on many different fronts in Bom Jardim and, particularly through her friendship with Dunkel, the local PT politician, had managed to bring about substantial improvements for the settlement in the form of better access, better schooling, and job opportunities. This kind of work was invisible to the state leadership, whereas André's risky frente de massa work was fully legible to his male peers, who had shared similarly intense bonding experiences in dangerous environments, in some cases alongside André.

As Maple Razsa points out in *Bastards of Utopia*, a special bond is formed between activists when the instruments of state violence are unleashed; in the case of Papanduva, the instruments included live ammunition, infantry, and a full detachment of tanks. Razsa (2015, 25) writes how in such moments "protesters felt the state on their own skin" and argues that "these experiences, which generate profound subjective transformation, may have been one of the most overlooked and significant consequences of participating in such collective struggles." The affective dimension of being members of the frente de massa, the revolutionary vanguard of the MST, cannot be underestimated. And the manner in which Vera had sought to bring about agrarian reform in "small spaces" as opposed to mounting spectacular acts of confrontation did not count in her favor. The only woman on the state leadership with any heft was Dona Franciele because of her trajectory on the front lines. But Dona Franciele's advocacy was not enough. These were long years of struggle. From 2009 to 2015, Vera lived on the margins, struggling to make ends meet while André moved his girlfriend from the encampment into the family home on the settlement. This relationship lasted until he threw this young woman from a moving car. Another woman moved in. And another. The state leadership were satisfied that a family was occupying the plot, and things would have continued ever thus. But Vera would not be denied.

14

Victory, in a Heartbeat

> The MST, as a name, needs to exist so that people have a
> reason to occupy land, to continue the struggle, to have a
> flag, but at the end of the day the movement is the people.
>
> CLARICE

Vera and André first encamped in 1996. They were formally settled by INCRA on December 10, 2003, and it took a further three years before they managed to build a house on their plot and begin a full life together with their family. The house was provisory, built simply with wooden boards on a frame made of roughly hewn branches. At night, the wind whistled through the gaps, and the toilet was an outdoor shack over a pit. When I first met Vera and André on the assentamento in 2008, they were building something more permanent, and the shape of this structure slowly came into being over the next few months. From a concrete foundation, brick walls emerged, reaching up to timber joists and smart red roof tiles. The house had three bedrooms, a bathroom, a space for the family to relax, and a patio overlooking their fields of maize. By the end of 2008, the outer structure was nearing completion, and Vera spoke excitedly of living in a degree of comfort for the first time in her life. Then, in January 2009, everything changed. Vera fled the family home to take refuge with her sister, Lúcia, and her mother, Dona Neusa.

I traveled to Florianópolis with Lúcia shortly after this occurred to speak about Vera's situation with Bianchini, one of the state leaders. He told us that hopefully Vera and André would reconcile but that fundamentally, there was nothing untoward about the situation. When we pressed Bianchini and told him that André was dangerous, he became defensive, and the meeting was over. From this point on, Vera was on her own. For Bianchini and his fellow leaders, Vera's only path back into the movement, and back to her home and livelihood, was reconciliation with André, a man who caused her to she fear for her life. As Lúcia and I were ushered toward the door of the MST's office in Florianópolis, we felt a deep sense of powerlessness, and a few weeks later, in March 2009, I left Brazil with great unease. I had concluded a period that had started in October 2007, and I had no real means of staying in touch with Vera and Lúcia. No one had home access to the internet, no one had a cell phone, and our communication was limited to brief messages on Orkut, a social media platform of the time, which they would pick up on occasional visits to the LAN House, or cybercafé. I was worried about Vera because I had no idea what would happen. I left them both in a terrible situation: Lúcia was continuing her treatment but could fall gravely ill at any moment; Vera was holding out against unimaginable odds just trying to scrape enough money together to survive day to day. In many senses I felt like I had abandoned them when they had taken such good care of me over the last two years.

In 2010, Vera was still living in Bom Jardim. She worked at a nearby motel doing the laundry, a stigmatized role given the connotations that motels in Brazil have with sex workers. In this period, she worked hard to take care of her children. They were living all together in the garden shed, the casinha. The children felt uncomfortable at the family house because of André's girlfriend. The woman who had been encamped had now moved into the settlement. Despite these challenges however, Vera had many friends, and among them was a man named Irineu. Gradually they become close.

Vera was unsure of how to continue her struggle. She had been physically distanced from the settlement and therefore the movement. She thought about giving in. But toward the end of the year, something happened. Vera was driving with Irineu when they saw André's car coming toward them. André, with his new partner in the front seat, caught up with them and forced them off the road. Looking back, Vera recounted what happened that day: "It was in the first days that we got to know each other, and André tried to kill Irineu. I was in the car with Irineu that day, and because of what happened we went to the police. They interviewed me, they interviewed Irineu. It was a mess. And it was at that moment that I realized, I really have to report this guy, stand up for my rights, for my children's rights, the rights of my marriage. This guy, it's over. I mean, he has another family, and even though he has another family, he has absolutely zero respect for me. So that's why I sought justice in 2010."

When Vera first told me this, I was so shocked I didn't really understand what had happened, so I asked her to explain. "He tried to run Irineu's car off the road. And then, I don't know if it was for real or not, but once we were stopped, he began looking for a gun in his car. He approached us and smashed his hand on the windshield shouting, 'I'll kill you.' We managed to get out of there, and that's when I called the police. He followed us in his car for two miles, and that's when the police came."

Even though many years had passed since that day, Vera found it difficult to revisit what had happened. Normally so composed and cheerful, her voice cracked slightly when describing this confrontation, and I could tell she was close to tears.

"It was after this attempt that I really woke up once and for all," she continued. "Enough of this. I ran out patience entirely. And it was because of this that I decided, I want my rights, I want to live my life and I will report this guy, it's over. So in this way, it became an official matter, like the courts and such. Not because of the house and the land but because of this confrontation, in which André made this attempt on Irineu's life."

When Vera told me about this episode, I thought of how she had described André in the past. He was someone who knew violence, had been beaten with a belt buckle by his father, had been shot in the hand in a hail of *pistoleiro* bullets. He was someone who had hit her repeatedly, someone from whom she had fled. I found it hard to imagine what it must have meant to find the beginnings of her new life being crushed like this, while everything she had worked for and built lay in the hands of that very same person. Vera knew that the MST didn't want her to involve external actors. She knew that she was taking a risk just telling me what had happened. Perhaps the only reason I even knew about the situation with André was because that night, when everyone else had gone to church, I happened to pass by the casinha to offer support for a friend who looked like she was struggling. Thinking back to Bianchini and the way he very firmly told Lúcia and me that the situation between Vera and André was "calm," I asked her what the leadership thought about the involvement of the police.

"In the MST, and principally in Santa Catarina, they say that we don't divide the plots of land, like between husband and wife, or parents and children. It's to promote a collectivist mentality on the settlements. There was a lot of resistance from Grimaldi, Bianchini, and the others. They didn't want to involve the courts, INCRA, or the police. They wanted to silence the whole matter." Despite everything, Vera spoke matter-of-factly: "Maybe one day one of them will say to me, you shouldn't have spoken about all this. And I'll say, I can, and I will. Because if we censure ourselves, we end up in a bad place. Kleber was different. He didn't tell me to go to the courts, but when I had to leave my home, he came to my mother's house and he told me, 'Hold your head high, look to what's best for you, take care of your children, and continue your studies. And as regards André and the future, he will bring himself down by his own actions. One day you will return to your land.' Kleber didn't explain how he thought this might happen though. Maybe because he didn't want to call attention to problems that were already happening in the leadership."

Vera had mentioned to me previously that although she did have some support in the state leadership, they had been outvoted by a larger block. The transcendent moral force of the family came into play here as André duly replaced Vera with another woman, and for the leaders the situation was resolved. Vera commented on how not all the state leadership had agreed: "Franciele and Osni were always on my side. When they heard about what was happening, I think it was difficult for them to take. And I didn't know about this, but one day a guy from INCRA got in touch with me and asked, 'Why has Osni requested that André be removed from the settlement?' So I explained the situation to him. But Osni didn't ask me if I wanted this kind of support, like for things to be documented. But he did it all the same. He even went to Florianópolis, to the main INCRA office to speak to them about it. I believe that Franciele and Osni were in conversation the whole time. They understood André was violent and they knew it was a problem, not just for me but for others as well, him being on the settlement."

I asked Vera why Osni took action when no one else did, and she told me she never understood. In the end, however, Vera got her house back through her own force of will, resilience, and conviction in what was right. After seven years, she won. Just as she faced Roberto on his tractor, with his machete in his hand, in defense of her friend Davi and his rights, she had decided that enough was enough. Just as Tais had uttered *vou quebrar isso*, I will break this, Vera too stood firm. "André received an order to leave the house on 12 May 2015," she told me. "It was a judicial decision. The divorce was finalized in 2013, but it took two more years for things to be carried out."

André's removal from the newly built brick house was a complex process with three state entities involved: INCRA, the courts, and the police. I asked about the details of the judgment. Vera said, "The decision was as a result of André's threats to Irineu and that police incident in 2010. When that case was resolved and the judgment made, INCRA were notified of the judge's decision and instructed by the judge to remove André from the plot. They gave him twenty-four hours' notice to vacate the house, and I had twenty-four hours to occupy it. It was wild, if I didn't move in and take possession, I would lose all rights to the property. André had to leave and also a woman, who was the third one after me. The first one, the encampment one, was no longer with him after he threw her out of his car. He beat her a lot, here in this house. And she had him arrested for this in 2012 or 2013, he was behind bars for a couple of nights. And after that, she left him."

I asked Vera how she felt when she retook possession of the house, perhaps expecting a response reflecting on her triumph. She told me it was great, that she was really happy in that moment, but that her thoughts had immediately turned toward her children and how things would be. "Straightaway my two boys decided to get married, and they said they wouldn't be moving back in. But Clarice became pregnant shortly after, and it was wonderful because when the order came through in May, Clarice's baby could be born here, and we could take care of her in our own house."

I had been staying with them when Clarice found out she was pregnant, and the sense of that house being their home was so strong even then. Vera's moment of triumph was exactly this: thinking about others and reflecting on what had led people to act the way they did.

"There's always violence," she said. "There's the discourse, but sometimes reality is very different. In this question of the MST's struggle, for instance, sexism, this machismo has deep roots, and it can take flower in someone at any moment. I don't condemn the movement in relation to this because the movement reflects society, and society is like this. So, for us to free ourselves from these roots, it's not easy." She continued after a pause: "Like André, I don't condemn André, because he came from a place of tremendous violence: hunger, physical hurt, a brutality in speech, working as a child from the age of eight doing agricultural labor. These things impacted him as a child, they took away the space into which he could grow, but at the age he had reached, he should have been able to reflect and think, no, I can't continue this violence. And we can't continue. At the time when all of this was happening, I told people that you were going to write about it, and they told me that we had to talk about things, because if we continued to be silent, the violence wouldn't stop. Just yesterday a friend dropped by the house, and I said that you were here, and we had been talking about questions of gender within the movement. And she said to me, don't hide anything. We need to talk about these things. She told me that she couldn't bear to lie anymore, that it was no longer like that, and that she will no longer be like that."

Clarice, who had been listening, joined us and commented, "It's happened to practically all the women here. But some leave, because of the pressure of marriage and so on. But it's common because of the history of the countryside. My father is a very clear example of where these men came from. Sometimes I wonder why this happened in our house, even after having taken part so much in the movement, having discussed various gender issues, read many things. And even though these men have participated so much and thought about what the struggle is in a theoretical way, I don't understand why this has continued."

Sensing it was a difficult discussion for Vera, I tried to change the subject. But she brought us back to the question of silence: "When I saw violence in my parents' house, I saw that my mother couldn't argue. She couldn't express herself. I see so much silence in women, even though they understand that they suffer violence, like, I'll cry to myself, I'll keep myself to myself, I'll hide way, and that's not right. Even me sometimes, I'm like, enough of this, I'll just get on with my life. *Mas se nos não falar, não se libertamos,* but if we don't talk, we can't free ourselves."

One of my favorite photos of Vera is from her graduation, smiling under a black mortarboard, wearing a blue and black robe. I asked her about this difficult time from 2008 to 2015. She said, "Kleber told me, hold your head high, do something with your life. The first thing he said was for me to continue with my studies. And those were the words he used, *vai estudar,* and don't get stuck where you are. He said, you've done many things, and you have many things yet to do. And ever since I arrived here, every time I passed in front of the university, I dreamed about doing a degree. I still dream of doing a master's or a PhD. But I didn't know what course to do. And I was talking to Dunkel, and he said I should do a sociology degree because of my trajectory and profile."

Vera started to laugh. "So I was like, what the hell is this sociology thing you're talking about? I was working in the town hall in 2012, and I don't know how it happened, but a newspaper appeared on my counter, and there was a notice for the university: 'final scholarships available for sociology degree.' You can't imagine my face; I was shouting, and no one knew what I was on about. There were five spots available, so I went around asking who wanted to do sociology, because we had to do it quickly. So there was someone else who wanted to apply as well but the deadline was that day, we only had that day to do our applications. So in his office, he had a printer and everything, and we put together all our documentation to make the application in a huge rush because the degree was due to start that week. I didn't ask anyone, not even Irineu, I just did it. And we managed: we started the degree 2013, went through it, managed to finish, and that's that. I guess there are some things that just work out, and I graduated in 2017."

When Vera led the families in the occupation for Davi's land, she was breaking with a series of established conventions that constituted a social order. Her action called into question how and where the female bodies could be seen and act, how the hierarchy of the MST could be called into question, and, fundamentally, what constituted a productive assentado by what metric would a person's right to hold land be judged? In insisting on Davi's right to land, she challenged the MST's linear teleology by undermining and disaggregating the link between time and space; she put forward a counter-utopian practice, one that was embedded in community. Davi was not awarded land on the basis of space granted for an amount of time served; rather, he was settled on a piece of land for being a good human being, being a hard worker, and contributing to the social cohesion of the assentamento. As regards winning her own land, Vera had to win it *twice*. She was encamped for eight years before she was formally settled by INCRA; she was left landless once again and then had to enter into legal proceedings to win what was hers by right. In insisting on her rights, again Vera had to break with a series of movement conventions. She was subjected to the idea that involving external actors was unwise and unwelcome. In this discourse there was a continuing thread that the situation would somehow resolve itself, even though eight years after leaving in fear of her life, the movement had taken no active steps against André, and he was still living on the settlement. Vera was also acting in contravention of expectations regarding becoming "a woman without a man." Leaders offered her a position in an encampment school some sixty miles away from her home, effectively placing her in the same position that she had been in 1996. Rejecting this proposal, Vera refused to be silent, continuing to advocate for herself before André's actions eventually became so reckless that they drew the attention of the police.[1]

The precise details pertaining to André's eviction from the house are confidential. And because of this it is impossible to know whether Osni's actions in writing to INCRA impacted the case or whether this intervention was inconsequential, and André's fate was sealed by the police action in 2010 and its judicial consequences. In many senses, however, such detail is not relevant. What occurred highlights how Vera's counter-utopian positionality found resonance with elements of the state leadership and emboldened them to act. Osni, Kleber, and Franciele's alignment with Vera demonstrate the tensions that are at play within the MST and how Vera's pushback against normalized sem terra values gave rise to a split among the state leadership. In the years following what happened in Bom Jardim, there was reflection on the part of the Santa Catarina state leadership. Vera's stance provoked a shift, one that would not have taken place without such contestation from within, one that impelled the movement in new and unexpected directions.

It's hard to say what occurred for Vera herself in the moment when she stood up for Davi. Was her conviction in doing what she thought to be the right thing, her moral compass, always there within her? Where did the gesture that would bring about transformation for Davi's family and their life come from? How did this gesture and those moments come to impact her own life and the struggle she would have to endure? The connection between these events spread across time is not linear; it's not that one decision led to another and then on to another in turn. And yet there is a something that binds them, and it's doubtless that Vera's gesture echoed across the period of intervening years, both for herself and for the wider movement.

In 2019, a decade after Vera was forced from her home, Aline da Silva, a young trans woman and MST militante, was murdered in Pernambuco. The case attracted a huge amount of attention and became emblematic of the MST's struggle against agrarian violence. Such a representation of landlessness and the diversity of MST members was simply not present when I began my fieldwork in 2007. As de Melo (2023, 2) notes, "Discussing the persistence of patriarchal structures inside the MST consequently paved the way for also discussing sexuality," and much has changed since Bianchini's days in the Santa Catarina state leadership. A new generation of leaders has brought about a meaningful shift in the movement's politics with regard to gender and sexuality, and the MST of today has taken great strides. Lucineia Freitas of the national gender sector, for example, has commented on understanding agroecology as a space for discussing human relationships as opposed to simply implementing a different kind of production. In this view, leaders like Freitas acknowledge that production has traditionally been based on violence and argue that part of the movement's work is to put forward a different relationship with the land and social space.

Such a stance resonates with the MST members we have met in this book. From Davi and Jurema's insistence on "human values" to the actions pertaining to culture, production, and sem terra identity taken by Tais, Maíra, and Vera, women in the MST have led the way in the movement remaining relevant and vital for twenty-first-century politics. Vera's determination in particular stands out. Her belief that she was doing the right thing pushed the movement in an unexpected direction, breaking an impasse rooted in decades of entrenchment. Her conviction in those moments simultaneously drew on her actions to fight for Davi and put forward the kind of movement she wanted to be a part of. In a linear understanding of time, Bergson argues, it is the real that makes itself possible and not the possible that becomes real—that is, most theories of transformation focus solely on what has been selected, neglecting the process by which these results come into being. But Vera's actions strayed from that narrow, unbending pathway. Instead, she stepped into the unknown to bring about change. Importantly, she did not reach back or project forward; these moments did not occur in a linear progression. They were, and are, interpenetrating and contiguous to her life, and the life of the movement. In the flux of duration, we can already perceive the presence of things that are as-yet-to-be, and we can grasp what will shortly become. In this way of seeing the world, Vera's actions signaled a transformation already in process, and her possible was fully real, and from our standpoint today, we can see it as a vital and living element of our world.

Alex: Momentos ponto

Momentos engraçados e inesquecíveis
* Também momentos de reflexões do
cotidiano Brasileiro
* Momentos de saúdades juntos
        Saúdades...   29/03/2003

22nd March 2009

Thought I wouldn't make any more
notes but here am I all the
same. I don't want to work
I want to go to sleep but
having talked to   I can't

Conclusion

"You know one time in court in 2013, André's lawyer, she asked me right at the end of a hearing to go outside with her."

Vera was talking to me about the process that resulted in her finally winning back her land. "I think her idea was for us to come to some kind of settlement. She said to me, 'Honey, what do you want to go back there for, what are you going to do with that land? Why do you want to go back there and suffer? Think about the great life you have here in the city.' She couldn't even imagine the struggle I had gone through to call that land my own. I told her, I've worked the land since I was a child. This is a safe place, where I can be with my children. And it's a space where they will have their own homes as well."

Vera and I laughed. There was something defiant in her tone. "That's what this lawyer didn't understand in that moment," she continued. "You have to have security, not just for yourself but for your children as well. And she offered nothing in return. And you know André has recently entered a plea to be awarded 50 percent of everything, under the notion of *divisão de bens*. Half the land, half the house, everything. And it's that same lawyer. But I will fight. Because the land, it's a feeling of peace. Security. I'm not on the street, I have somewhere to live. Eight years under those black tarps [*debaixo da lona preta*] from 1996 to 2004." She paused. "10 December 2003, the day we were formally settled. And by 2006 we had managed to build our little house. It's a kind of paradise. I look out the back of my house and I see the two little ones, my grandchildren, smiling back. My family, my boys building their own houses. They come by for a coffee, they're full of fun. So, it's security for them, it's a feeling of safety for me."

* * *

Vera's struggle goes on. When she recounted the process of winning back her land, she didn't attach particular importance to the moment when André was ordered to leave the house. I expected her to dwell on this moment, to savor it somehow. This is how narrative works, we are told. There is a crisis and a moment of resolution. There is a moment where we "cut the wire." But Vera knows this isn't the case. Moments cannot be separated, and there is no clear delineation of time; there is only ongoing struggle and dignity through perseverance. Winning back her land against all the odds was a victory. But Vera faces an ongoing legal battle to remain on the settlement with her family and children. Victories are fleeting, but based within an understanding of time as duration, it is the struggle that is transformational. Struggle is a longitudinal lived experience replete with subjective expression—the power to evoke mística, the power to articulate a force of gesture that cannot be contained. Vera always believed she would prevail. I don't know where her conviction came from, but she never lost faith that things would change for the better. As time enveloped us both and I came to understand her better as a person, I learned that I would never lose faith in her.

Vera was set aside by the movement from 2008 to 2015, a period of seven years. She won justice, and just as she fought for Davi, she showed that change is possible. But beyond her resilience and determination, Vera's story, and the stories of Tais, Maíra, and Davi, point to the very nature of what is visible and invisible and how we have come to understand change. Put simply, we confront the notion that it is our very understanding of transformation that precludes us from perceiving it, even when it occurs in front of our very eyes. Our preoccupation with size, scale, and measurable impact has led to an imprecision with regard to the discernible beginnings of what will become the salient forces that determine people's everyday lives. These are not imperceptible by any means; rather, such elements do not fit into regimes of seeing and quantification that determine significance and meaning. When I left Brazil in 2009, I was beset by such a foreboding of what was yet to unfold. And yet, I heard Tais tell me about her intervention in front of the leaders, I saw Maíra assert herself in the coastal settlement, and I knew Vera and the families had stood up to Roberto to insist that Davi be settled. But I was unable to see how those actions would go on to subvert my linear and predetermined notions of the inevitable. It is not debatable that these actions exist; rather, it is a question of how to ascribe legibility to them and by which register we choose to assign importance. This has particular importance for our understanding of social movements, community-based projects, artistic interventions, and other forms of sociality that seek change. If we continue to pay attention only to events of size and scale, we risk overlooking that which instigates transformation in our very midst. And with this approach, we will only ever be able to understand what events have already occurred instead of building an understanding of what will arise.

What I have written about in this book are moments that might otherwise be overlooked or dismissed as of minor importance. After all, why would a dancing female body matter in a muscle-bound social movement? But these interventions—for that is what they are—are based within duration; and characterized by a commitment to social justice as struggle, they articulate counter-utopian practices that impel sociality in unexpected directions: nonhierarchical, bound by relations, and premised on diversity. These are the smallest of actions shaping the largest of social movements, and in their powerful connection to subjective and creative expression, they rework the forms through which the MST seeks to change the world. To observe these interventions and the way they reconstitute the movement, only to dismiss their importance from a perspective that seeks to pinpoint, measure, or enumerate transformations that are considered significant, is akin to seeking to comprehend time by simply following the minute hand as it moves around the face of a watch.

Like many progressive movements, the MST was obliged to retreat in the past years. MST national leader João Paulo Rodrigues estimates that under the poisonous government of Jair Bolsonaro from 2019 to 2022, the movement lost 15 percent of its base in encampments across Brazil.[1] Bolsonaro liberalized gun control laws and asserted landowners' rights to defend territory with lethal force. The MST has endured, however, and since Lula's return to the presidency in 2023, the movement has articulated the landless struggle with new vigor, building particularly on long-standing connections with urban movements such as the Movement of Homeless Workers (Movimento dos Trabalhadores Sem-Teto—MTST) to strengthen its presence in major cities. One of the most successful initiatives in this sense has been a network of stores in state capitals that sell MST produce direct to consumers. Named Armazém do Campo, the network sells groceries produced by MST settlements and co-ops and offers a home delivery service as well as an urban hub to bring people together via events and gatherings. The first store opened in São Paulo's downtown in 2016, and there are now more than thirty across the country in similarly urban locations (Flynn 2024). Supported by a strong Instagram presence, the strategic choice to make the movement visible and sell organic produce in urban centers marks a departure from the politics of earlier generations of leaders and reflects how the movement is changing, ready to better position itself for the challenges to come.

Without doubt, as a mass movement, the MST has made incomparable gains for marginalized rural peoples and is still one of the main rallying points for international networks of solidarity. As a movement, its success is premised on complex forces held in tension, a utopian terrain from which counter-utopian practices are articulated. Vera told me that despite everything that happened, she still believed in the MST: "It's not that I've taken a step back because I don't like the MST or that it's all wrong. I needed time to return to myself. Listen, there are a lot of truths. I'm an assentada, and it was through the movement's struggle that I got this land. It's not just the movement that has to change, it's Brazil. I worry a lot about that, there are these questions, but I never forget what the MST has done, nor my own struggle as part of the movement. I value this a lot."

Vera articulates the complex and multifaceted relationships that many assentados have with the movement. There is an acknowledgment of the MST's limitations, but there is also deep gratitude and loyalty, and this tension speaks eloquently of the movement's power to endure. In part, the movement's resilience and organizational capacity have provided people like Vera with opportunities to work the land alongside other families as part of a sustained and committed struggle. Wouldn't such longevity be far more difficult, if not impossible, without the movement's emphasis on organization? It is undeniable that the durability of the MST resides to a certain extent in its central strategic planning and programmatic rollout.

And yet, while such connections are important to MST members and how they configure their sense of belonging to a larger entity, at a local level, what makes a settlement endure over a period of decades is the daily work of relationship building between neighbors and a strong sense of social cohesion. MST settlements are largely autonomous spaces, and this facilitates the emergence of minoritarian, community-based perspectives that sit in tension with more normalized sem terra values. Sometimes, assentados delve into their MST tool kit, refashioning modes of protest they know well for use in their particular situations. Tais employed a reworked form of mística to assert the independence of her body and her desire to change labor relations in her settlement while in Davi's case, settlement families chose to occupy the cooperative's land in a retooled form of occupation. For Vera, insisting on justice was achieved only through her persistence and her belief in the movement, not as an institutionalized entity but as the purest expression of struggle. Importantly, her actions highlighted a difference of opinion in the state leadership, provoking a shift in attitudes that continues to this day.

Vera's recognition of the MST's central role in her life demonstrates that the movement offers a a complex array of pathways and possibilities. And as the MST celebrates its fortieth anniversary in 2024, it is certain that transformative counter-utopian practices articulated from within by people like Vera are paramount to its continuing resilience. This is the contribution of a durational activism contextualized by broader organizational structures. Social movements the world over are subject to forces that at times cohere and at other times conflict, inducing new and unexpected directions, a rejuvenating sting of the new, a sense of transformation brought about from within. This is the foundation of the MST's durability: the encounter of the normative and minoritarian in contraposition under duress, the generation of a febrile elasticity and tensile strength that ensures the movement's continuing relevance and underlines its role as a cornerstone of international activist politics.

In 2011 Naomi Klein was not alone when she drew positive comparisons between the nascent Occupy Wall Street (OWS) encampment and the anti-globalization protests of a decade earlier. She placed emphasis on the taking of urban space and the need for a "fixed target" (Klein 2011), noting how OWS would have "time to put down roots, which makes it a lot harder to sweep them away, even if they get kicked out of one physical space" (Klein 2011). Klein was aware of the power of occupation and sought to contrast this with the episodic and transnational nature of the anti-globalization movement's appearances at major summits. But fifty-nine days later the OWS encampment was over, and other Occupy encampments around the world were dismantled as they lost momentum and faded from the public consciousness. Noting that the OWS camp was relatively short lived is of course not meant to downplay its significance; the intangible legacy of Occupy has been hugely influential (Milkman 2017; Reed 2019). But in 2021, I asked a class of undergraduates studying arts activism for their reflections on the Occupy movement only to be met with a collection of blank faces and furrowed brows, followed by furtive search engine inquiries.

This is why forty years of the Landless Workers Movement is a triumph to be celebrated, as are the contradictions that underpin its constant unfolding. Held in tension, the actions of Vera, Clarice, Tais, Maíra, and Davi point to the kind of movement members of the MST want to lead Brazil in the quest for social justice. Through lives lived as struggle, they contest social order, they disaggregate time and space, and they refuse a linear progression toward victory, seeking instead to articulate an agrarian reform in the small spaces at a community level. From within a wider structure, such actions are life changing and immediate, but they are not individual: in their resonance and recognition of the complex relations that bind people, they articulate a fundamental transformation of the kind of movement the MST is in this moment—and will continue to be for years to come. Through aesthetics and sociality hinged together, creative expression reaches to envelop, spark, and provoke, to move spirits and mountains. Such interventions will shake the earth. Nothing is foreclosed, and nothing is predetermined as we walk our own pathways to utopia.

GLOSSARY

À vista: money up-front
Abertura: opening, especially of a ceremony
Acampado: one who is encamped, one living in an acampamento
Acampamento: encampment
Agronegócio: agribusiness
Agrovila: an area of an assentamento where assentados live, their houses close to one another
Alimentação: food
Alqueire: a measure of land area, equivalent to 2.42 hectares, or 5.98 acres
Apoiador: supporter
Aprendizagem: apprenticeship
Arroz: rice
Articulação de Mulheres Trabalhadoras Rurais do Sul (AMTRS): Articulation of Rural Working Women of the South
Assembléia: assembly
Assentado: an MST member who has won land, living on a settlement with a plot and a house
Assentamento: settlement
Assistência técnica: technical assistance
Baile funk: funk carioca, a genre of music from Rio de Janeiro
Barraca: a temporary shelter constructed in an acampamento
Bobo: silly, ingenuous
Bóias frias: poorly paid day laborers
Bolsa Família: a state payment, part of the welfare state mechanism
Bom dia: hello
Bomba: straw
Boné: baseball cap
Borrachudo: blackfly
Brigada: brigade
Burguesia: the bourgeois
Burro: stupid
Cachaça: strong alcoholic spirit
Cadastramento: registration
Casinha: small house, shed
Castanheira: chestnut tree

Cesta básica: basic food basket

Chamar atenção: to call attention to yourself, to distinguish yourself

Chefão: big boss

Chimarrão: a tea made with erva maté commonly drunk in South Brazil and Argentina

Cidade: city

Coletivo do gênero: gender collective

Coletivo Nacional de Mulheres (CNM): National Women's Collective

Comissão Nacional de Mulheres (CNM): National Commission of Women

Comissão Pastoral da Terra (CPT): Pastoral Land Commission

Comunidades Eclesias de Base (CEBs): Ecclesiastical Base Communities

Coordenação: coordination, leadership

Crise: crisis

Cuia: vessel from which chimarrão is drunk

Deputados: members of Brazilian congress

Desemprego: unemployed

Desviado: lit. deviated, fig. corrupt

Direção: leadership

Direção estadual: state leadership

Direção national: national leadership

Divergência: lit. divergence, fig. argument

Educação: education

Encontro: meeting

Encontro estadual: state meeting

Erva maté: the herb from which chimarrão is brewed

Escola itinerante: encampment school

Expulso: expulsion

Favela: marginalized community, typically urban

Fazendeiro: landowner

Feijão: black beans

Firme na cabeça: lit. firm in the head

Foice: long-handled scythe

Formação: education, formation, training

Formação política: political education, formation, training

Frente de massa: MST sector responsible for recruitment, assembling acampamentos, and, more generally, movement mobilizations

Futsal: a type of indoor soccer

Gauchesca: a type of folk music from the state of Rio Grande do Sul, a partner dance

Gaúcho: adj. relating to, pertaining to Rio Grande do Sul

Gerontocracia: gerontocracy

Grito: a type of MST ritual where an individual makes a call and the group makes a known response

Guarita: lookout post

Ilha da Magia: Island of Magic, the island of Santa Catarina

Instancias: centers of leadership

Invadir: to invade

La Via Campesina: The International Peasant Movement

Ladrão (pl. ladrões): thief

Latifúndio: property covering vast areas, the system of concentrated landholdings

Lindo: beautiful

Litoral: coast

Lixo: rubbish

Lona (debaixo da lona preta): plastic sheeting, under the black plastic sheeting that characterizes an MST acampamento

Lote: tract of land, property lot

Lutar: to fight, to struggle

Machismo: sexism, chauvinism

Maconha: marijuana

Mal-educado: ill-educated, impolite

Massa: the masses

Mata: forest

Militantes: activists

Mística: MST ritual, a principal element of MST cultural life and expression

Morro: lit. hill, fig. favela

Movimento de Mulheres Camponesas (MMC): The Movement of Peasant Women

Movimento de Mulheres Trabalhadoras Rurais (MMTR-NE): Rural Workers' Women's Movement of the Northeast

Movimento dos Atingidos por Barragens (MAB): The Movement of People Affected by Dams

Movimento dos Pequenos Agricultores (MPA): The Movement of Small Farmers

Movimento dos Trabalhadores Sem-Teto (MTST): The Movement of Homeless Workers

Município: township, county

(Tele)Novela: soap opera

Núcleo: unit of people working together

Ocupar: to occupy

Pagode: a style of music that originated in Salvador, a subgenre of samba

Partido dos Trabalhadores (PT): The Workers' Party

Passe Livre: movement that agitates for fairer public transport prices

Peonagem: feudal servitude

Periferia: the fringes of a city, characterized by insecure housing and marginalization

Perigoso: dangerous

Planalto: a northern region of Santa Catarina

Por justiça social e soberania popular: for social justice and the people's sovereignty

Povo: the people

Prefeitura: municipal government and town hall

Problemas conjugais: marital problems

Reforma agrária: agrarian reform

Roça: the countryside

Sector: sector

Sem oportunidades: without opportunities

Sem terra: lit. without land, fig. the MST identity

Sem terrinha: lit. without small land, fig. the unofficial youth movement of the MST

Sertaneja: Brazilian country music

Serviço: unofficial day labor

Sonhando: dreaming

Sorteio: lit. the draw

Terra: land

Tranquilo: calm

União federal: a type of public land
Uso fruto: full rights of use without ownership
Vagabundo: tramp, delinquent
Veneno: lit. poison, fig. pesticide
Vereador: town councillor

NOTES

Introduction

1. Author's own translation.

2. Brazil is a union of twenty-seven Unidades Federativas, or federative units: twenty-six states and one *distrito federal*, or federal district, in which the capital, Brasília, is located.

3. https://viacampesina.org/en/brazil-since-the-return-to-democracy-there-have-been -nearly-2-000-political-assassinations-in-rural-areas.

4. Wolford mentions how a colleague referred to her fine-grained analysis as the airing of "dirty laundry," and I received a similar comment at a conference in 2009 on agrarian issues in Latin America. Before presenting my paper, I was told that my presentation of MST members voicing concerns about the wider movement was "not ethical" as it could impair the wider struggle. This argument is not new; all manner of minoritarian positions in diverse walks of life have been silenced by a supposed necessity to maintain unity at any cost. The ethical stance of MST members and their notions of solidarity with the movement and social justice more widely are far more complex than such binary perspectives, contextualized as they are by the notion of a lived struggle.

Scene I—Promise

1. This quotation comes from Fernando Birri when he was asked about what utopia is for. His response is cited in "Gleaning the Current Conjuncture: Notes from the 3rd *Antipode* Institute for the Geographies of Justice," available here: https://onlinelibrary.wiley.com /doi/10.1111/anti.12019.

1. Landlessness

1. Bakhtin (1981).

2. There is a tax, the Rural Territorial Tax (ITR), but even in more recent periods its levy has been minimal—for example, accounting for 0.05 percent of the total tax revenue in 2015 according to OECD data, available at https://stats.oecd.org/Index .aspx?DataSetCode=REVBRA.

3. See *O livro branco da grilagem de terras*, 2, published by INCRA. Available at http:// www.incra.gov.br/media/servicos/publicacao/livros_revistas_e_cartilhas/Livro%20 Branco%20da%20Grilagem%20de%20Terras.pdf.

4. Report "On Dangerous Ground" published June 20, 2016, available online at https:// www.globalwitness.org/en/campaigns/environmental-activists/dangerous-ground, accessed August 18, 2017.

5. The southern states had been the setting for a separatist uprising from 1835 to 1845, which came to be known as the Revolução Farroupilha. At the conclusion of this war, the Riograndense Republic, a de facto state that seceded from the Empire of Brazil and roughly coincided with the present state of Rio Grande do Sul, was constitutionally reintegrated.

4. Human Values

1. Author's own translation.
2. INCRA (Instituto Nacional de Colonização e Reforma Agrária) devolved ninety-five hectares to the MST for the Garuva assentamento knowing that eighty hectares could not be farmed, as they were protected Mata Atlântica—the Atlantic rainforest.

5. Time

1. As Delitz states, "The essence of any 'mechanical explanation, in fact, is to regard the future and the past as calculable functions of the present, and thus to claim that all is given' (Bergson 1944, 43)" (Delitz 2014, 87).

Scene III—Expression, Creative Gesture

1. Flynn (2024).

9. The Culture Sector

1. Author's own translation of an interview of Bogo: https://nucleopiratininga.org.br /ademar-bogo-mst-e-cultura-ideologia-tradicao-pensar-fazer-e-sentir-fazem-parte-da -politica-cultural-do-movimento.

11. Occupy, Hold Firm

1. Bardi (1994).

12. Remaking the Movement from Within

1. The term *vaga* means a vacancy to be filled, as in a space to dwell, as well as an employment opportunity, as in a job vacancy. Rangel Loera (2014, 49) discusses the importance of this dual meaning in the context of finding a space in MST encampments.
2. At the time the Bolsa Família was capped at 182 reais per month, 40 percent of the minimum monthly wage.

14. Victory, in a Heartbeat

1. It is significant that the chain of events that led to the judicial decision ordering André to leave the house was sparked by his threats to kill Irineu. That is, although Vera suffered violence and domestic abuse at the hands of André, as did the woman who was formerly encamped who moved into Vera's house, the process to remove André, whether from within the MST or executed by a state entity, was initiated only when André addressed a violent act to another man.

Conclusion

1. See https://deolhonosruralistas.com.br/2019/04/11/efeito-bolsonaro-fez-mst-perder -15-de-sua-base-em-acampamentos.

BIBLIOGRAPHY

Ali, Tariq. 2006. *Pirates of the Caribbean: Axis of Hope*. London: Verso.

Aliaga, Luciana, and Fernanda Maranho. 2021. "O MST e a agroecologia: entre autonomia e subalternidade." *Revista Katálysis* 24 (3): 576–84.

Alvarez, Sónia, Elisabeth Jay Friedman, Ericka Beckman, Maylei Blackwell, Norma Stoltz Chinchilla, Nathalie Lebon, Marysa Navarro, and Marcela Ríos Tobar. 2003. "Encontrando os feminismos latino-americanos e caribenhos." *Revista Estudos Feministas* 11 (2): 541–75.

Anderson, Benedict. 1983. *Imagined Communities: Reflections on the Origin and Spread of Nationalism*. London: Verso.

Ansell Pearson, Keith. 2019. "Deleuze's Bergsonism." Notre Dame Philosophical Reviews. Last modified March 21, 2019. https://ndpr.nd.edu/news/deleuzes-bergsonism.

Bakhtin, Mikhail. 1981. *The Dialogic Imagination: Four Essays by M. M. Bakhtin*. Translated by Caryl Emerson and Michael Holquist. Austin: University of Texas Press.

Bardi, Lina Bo. 1994. *Tempos de grossura: o design no impasse*. São Paulo: Instituto Lina Bo e P.M. Bardi.

Barmeyer, Niels. 2009. *Developing Zapatista Autonomy: Conflict and NGO Involvement in Rebel Chiapas*. Albuquerque: University of New Mexico Press.

Barrett, William. 1968. "The Flow of Time." In *The Philosophy of Time*, edited by Richard Gale, 355–77. Atlantic Highlands, NJ: Humanities Press.

Bastos, Pablo Nabarrete. 2016. "Rap da roça: Diálogos políticos entre a juventude do campo e da cidade." *Comunicação & Educação* 21 (2): 39–47.

Beasley, Vanessa. B. 2020. "The Trouble with Marching: Ableism, Visibility, and Exclusion of People with Disabilities." *Rhetoric Society Quarterly* 50 (3): 166–74.

Bell, Lucy, Alex Ungprateeb Flynn, and Patrick O'Hare. 2022. *Taking Form, Making Worlds: Cartonera Publishers in Latin America*. Austin: University of Texas Press.

Benhabib, Selya. 1995. "Subjectivity, Historiography and Politics." In *Feminist Contentions: A Philosophical Exchange*, edited by Selya Benhabib, Judith Butler, Drucilla Cornell, and Nancy Fraser. , 107–25. London: Routledge.

Bergson, Henri. 1910. *Time and Free Will: An Essay on the Immediate Data of Consciousness*. Translated by F. L. Pogson. London: George Allen and Unwin.

———. 1920. *Mind-Energy: Lectures and Essays*. Translated by H. Wildon Carr. London: Macmillan.

———. 1944. *Creative Evolution*. Translated by A. Mitchell. New York: Random House.

————. 1991. *Matter and Memory*. Translated by N. M. Paul and W. S. Palmer. New York: Zone.

————. 2002. *Key Writings*. Edited by Keith Ansell-Pearson and John Mullarkey. New York: Continuum International.

Bethell, Leslie, ed. 1991. *Mexico since Independence*. Cambridge: Cambridge University Press.

————. 2018. *Brazil: Essays on History and Politics*. London: Institute of Latin American Studies.

Biancalana, Gisela Reis. 2014. "Danças Tradicionalistas Riograndenses, Gênero e Memória." *Conceição/Conception* 3 (2): 23–33.

Blanes, Ruy, and Bjørn Enge Bertelsen. 2021. "Utopian Confluences: Anthropological Mappings of Generative Politics." *Social Anthropology* 29 (1): 5–17.

Blanes, Ruy, Alex Ungprateeb Flynn, Maïté Maskens, and Jonas Tinius. 2016. "Micro-utopias: Anthropological Perspectives on Art, Relationality and Creativity." *Cadernos de Arte e Antropologia* 5 (1): 5–20.

Boal, Augusto. (1974) 2000. *Theater of the Oppressed*. London: Pluto.

Boaventura Leite, Ilke. 2015. "The Brazilian Quilombo: 'Race,' Community and Land in Space and Time." *Journal of Peasant Studies* 42 (6): 1225–40.

Bogad, Larry M. 2010. "Carnivals against Capital." *Social Identities* 16 (4): 537–57.

Boggs, Carl. 1977. "Marxism, Prefigurative Communism and the Problem of Workers' Control." *Radical America* 6:99–122.

Borges, Barsanufo Gomides. 1997. "Silva, Lígia Osório. Terras devolutas e latifúndio." *História Revista* 2 (2): 177–82.

Boundas, Constantin. 1992. "Gilles Deleuze: The Ethics of the Event." In *Joyful Wisdom*, edited by D. Goicoechea and M. Zlomislic, 169–99. St. Catharines: Thought House.

Bourdieu, Pierre. 1979. *La distinction: Critique sociale du jugement*. Paris: Minuit.

Bourriaud, Nicolas. 2002. *Relational Aesthetics*. Dijon: Presses du Réel.

Branford, Sue, and Jan Rocha. 2002. *Cutting the Wire: The Story of the Landless Movement in Brazil*. London: Latin American Bureau.

Burdick, John. 1995. "Uniting Theory and Practice in the Ethnography of Social Movements: Notes toward a Hopeful Realism." *Dialectical Anthropology* 20 (3–4): 361–85.

Burns, E. Bradford. 1970. *A History of Brazil*. New York: Columbia University Press.

Butler, Judith. 1990. *Gender Trouble: Feminism and the Subversion of Identity*. New York: Routledge.

————. 1993. *Bodies That Matter: On the Discursive Limits of Sex*. London: Psychology Press.

————. 2016a. "Performativity." In *In Terms of Performance Anthology*, edited by Shannon Jackson and Paula Marincola. Berkeley: Arts Research Center at University of California and Philadelphia: Pew Center for Arts & Heritage. Last modified March 17, 2022. http://intermsofperformance.site.

————. 2016b. "Performativity. In Terms of Performance." http://intermsofperformance.site/keywords/performativity/judith-butler.

Cabet, Étienne. 1840. *Voyage et aventures de Lord William Carisdall en Icarie*. Paris: H. Souverain.

Caldeira, Rute. 2008. "My Land, Your Social Transformation: Conflicts within the Landless People Movement (MST), Rio de Janeiro, Brazil." *Journal of Rural Studies* 24:150–60.

————. 2009. "The Failed Marriage between Women and the Landless People's Movement (MST) in Brazil." *Journal of International Women's Studies* 10 (4): 237–58.

Calderón, F., A. Piscitelli, and J. Reyna. 1992. "Social Movements: Actors, Theories, Expectations." In *The Making of Social Movements in Latin America: Identity, Strategy, and Democracy*, edited by A. Escobar and S. Alvarez, 19–36. Boulder, CO: Westview.

Calvo Gonzalez, Elena. 2004. "Power, Mediation and the Construction of Community: A Case Study of a Landless Movement Settlement in Brazil and an Indigenous Agrarian Community in Mexico." Unpublished doctoral dissertation, University of Manchester.

Campanella, Tommaso. 2010. *The City of the Sun*. London: Merchant Books.

Campbell, Emahunn Raheem Ali. 2011. "A Critique of the Occupy Movement from a Black Occupier." *The Black Scholar* 41 (4): 42–51.

Campos Martins, Leonardo. 2022. "A mística Do MST Como Organizador Coletivo." *Mangút* 2 (1): 22–34.

Carter, Miguel. 2010. "The Landless Rural Workers Movement and Democracy in Brazil." *Latin American Research Review* 45:186–217.

Chaves, Christine. 2000. *A Marcha Nacional dos Sem-terra: Um Estudo Sobre a Fabricação do Social*. Rio de Janeiro: Relume Dumará.

———. 2021. "Rituais da Mística: Fronteiras borradas entre política e religião." *Mana* 27 (2): 1–33.

———. 2022. "Rituais da Mística. A mística do MST e as aporias da ação coletiva." *Revista de Antropologia* 65 (3): 1–33.Chaves, Miguel Sobrado, and Richard Stoller. 2002. "Organizational Empowerment Versus Clientelism." *Latin American Perspectives* 29 (5): 7–19.

Chinchilla, N. 1977. "Mobilizing Women: Revolution in the Revolution." *Latin American Perspectives* 4 (4): 82–102.

———. 1991. "Marxism, Feminism, and the Struggle for Democracy in Latin America." *Gender and Society* 5 (3): 291–310.

Coelho, Fabiano. 2010. "A Prática da Mística e a Luta pela Terra no MST." Unpublished master's thesis, Universidade Federal da Grande Dourados.

Comerlatto, Giovani Vilmar. 2010. "A dimensão educativa da mística na construção do MST como sujeito coletivo." Unpublished doctoral thesis, Universidade Federal do Rio Grande do Sul.

CONCRAB. 1997. *Método de Trabalho Popular*. Caderno de Formação, n. 24. São Paulo: Confederação das Cooperativas de Reforma Agrária do Brasil.

———. 1999. *A Evolução da Concepção de Cooperação Agrícola do MST (1989 A 1999)*. Cadernos de Cooperação Agrícola, no. 8. São Paulo: Confederação das Cooperativas de Reforma Agrária do Brasil.

Conquergood, Dwight. 1989. "Poetics, Play, Process, and Power: The Performative Turn in Anthropology." *Text and Performance Quarterly* 1:82–95.

Cooper, Davina. 2014. *Everyday Utopias: The Conceptual Life of Promising Spaces*. Durham, NC: Duke University Press.

Cristina de Souza, Danieli, and Dimas de Oliveira Estevam. 2021. "Panorama Dos Assentamentos Rurais Em Santa Catarina." *Revista Grifos* 30 (54): 267–91.

D'Araújo, Maria Celina. 2003. "Estado, classe trabalhadora e políticas sociais." In *O Brasil Republicano: O tempo do liberalismo excludente*, edited by Jorge Ferreira and Lucília Delgado, 115–77. Rio de Janeiro: Civilização Brasileira.

Darwin, Charles. 1864. *On the Origin of Species by Means of Natural Selection; or, The Preservation of Favored Races in the Struggle of Life*. 5th ed. New York: Appleton.

De Almeida, Lúcio Flávio, and Félix Ruiz Sánchez. 2000. "The Landless Workers' Movement and Social Struggles against Neoliberalism." *Latin American Perspectives* 27 (5): 11–32.

Dean, Warren. 1971. "Latifundia and Land Policy in Nineteenth-Century Brazil." *Hispanic American Historical Review* 51 (4): 606–25.

Debiasi, Rose Elke. 2022. "A criação de um método de formação de militantes no MST." In *Os sem terra e o MST: Memórias de lutas e experiências transformadoras*, edited by Davi Félix Schreiner, 181–98. Uberlândia: Navegando Publicações.

De Carvalho, Benjamin. 2015. "The Modern Roots of Feudal Empires: The Donatary Captaincies and the Legacies of the Portuguese Empire in Brazil." In *Legacies of Empire: Imperial Roots of the Contemporary Global Order*, edited by S. Halperin and R. Palan, 128–48. Cambridge: Cambridge University Press.

Deere, Carmen, and Magdalena León. 2001. *Empowering Women: Land and Property Rights in Latin America*. Pittsburgh: University of Pittsburgh Press.

Deleuze, Gilles. 1994. *Difference and Repetition*. New York: Columbia University Press.

Delitz, Heike. 2014. "'True' and 'False' Evolutionism: Bergson's Critique of Spencer, Darwin & Co and Its Relevance for Plessner (and Us)." In *Plessner's Philosophical Anthropology*, edited by J. De Mul, 79–98. Amsterdam: Amsterdam University Press.

Della Porta, Donatella. 2006. *Social Movements, Political Violence, and the State: A Comparative Analysis of Italy and Germany*. Cambridge: Cambridge University Press.

Delphy, Christine. 1977. *The Main Enemy: A Materialist Analysis of Women's Oppression*. London: Women's Research and Resources Centre.

de Melo, José G. 2023. "The Rise of LGBT Representation in the Landless Workers' Movement in Brazil." *Gender, Place & Culture*. https://doi.org/10.1080/0966369X.2023.2201399.

DeNardo, James. 1985. *Power in Numbers: The Political Strategy of Protest and Rebellion*. Princeton, NJ: Princeton University Press.

Deutschmann, David, ed. 2005. *Che Guevara Reader: Writings on Politics and Revolution*. Melbourne: Ocean Press.

De Vries, Hugo. 1909–10. *The Mutation Theory: Experiments and Observations on the Origin of Species in the Vegetable Kingdom*. 2 vols. Chicago: Open Court.

Dutra, Francis A. 1973. "Duarte Coelho Pereira, First Lord-Proprietor of Pernambuco: The Beginning of a Dynasty." *Americas* 29 (4): 415–41.

Ernst, Germana, and Jean-Paul De Lucca. 2021. "Tommaso Campanella." In *The Stanford Encyclopedia of Philosophy*, Summer 2021 ed., edited by Edward N. Zalta. https://plato.stanford.edu/archives/sum2021/entries/campanella/.

Eschle, Catherine, and Bice Maiguashca. 2018. "Theorising Feminist Organising in and against Neoliberalism: Beyond Co-optation and Resistance?" *European Journal of Politics and Gender* 1 (1–2): 223–39.

Escobar A., and S. Alvarez. 1992. "Introduction: Theory and Protest in Latin America Today." In *The Making of Social Movements in Latin America: Identity, Strategy, and Democracy*, edited by A. Escobar and S. Alvarez, 1–15. Boulder, CO: Westview.

Escobar, Arturo. 1992. "Imagining a Post-development Era? Critical Thought, Development and Social Movements." *Social Text* (31/32): 20–56.

———. 2004. "Beyond the Third World: Imperial Globality, Global Coloniality and Anti-Globalisation Social Movements." *Third World Quarterly* 25 (1): 207–30.

Eyerman, Ron. 2006. "Performing Opposition or, How Social Movements Move." In *Social Performance*, edited by Jeffrey C. Alexander, Bernhard Giesen, and Jason L. Mast, 193–217. Cambridge: Cambridge University Press.

Fernandes, Bernardo. 1999. *MST, Movimento dos Trabalhadores Rurais Sem-Terra: Formação e Territorialização*. São Paulo: Editora Hucitec.

———. 2000. *A Formação do MST no Brasil*. Petrópolis: Vozes.

Fernandes, Bernardo Mançano. 1996. *MST: Formação e territorialização em São Paulo*. São Paulo: Editora Hucitec.

Fischer-Lichte, Erika. 2008. *The Transformative Power of Performance: A New Aesthetics*. London: Routledge.

Flynn, Alex Ungprateeb. 2013. "Mística, Myself and I: Beyond Cultural Politics in Brazil's Landless Workers' Movement." *Critique of Anthropology* 33 (2): 168–92.

———. 2015a. "Re-imagining Political Subjectivities: Relationality, Reflexivity, and Performance in Rural Brazil." In *Anthropology, Theatre, and Development: The Transformative Potential of Performance*, edited by Alex Ungprateeb Flynn and Jonas Tinius, 33–52. London: Palgrave.

———. 2015b. "Transformation and 'Human Values' in the Landless Workers' Movement of Brazil." *Ethnos* 80 (1): 45–70.

———. 2018. "Aesthetic Gestures, Moral Frameworks: Performing Landlessness in Brazil." *Critique of Anthropology* 38 (2): 172–87.

———. 2024a. "Art in Movement—A Conversation between Alan Leite and Luciana Melo of the MST Theater Collective Banzeiros and the Visual Artists Bárbara Wagner and Benjamin de Burca." In *Forty years of Sem Terra: Landless Perspectives*, edited by Alex Ungprateeb Flynn, 175–97. London: Routledge.

———. 2024b. "From Demonization to Canonization: The Landless Workers Movement's Shifting Relationship to the City." In *Forty Years of the Landless Workers Movement: Landless Perspectives*, edited by Alex Ungprateeb, 198–226. London: Routledge.

Flynn, Alex Ungprateeb, and Jonas Tinius, eds. 2015. *Anthropology, Theatre, and Development: The Transformative Potential of Performance*. London: Palgrave.

Friends of the MST. n.d. "Culture Collective." Accesses February 6, 2025. https://www.mstbrazil.org/content/culture-collective.

Foster, Susan. L. 2003. "Choreographies of Protest." *Theatre Journal* 55 (3): 395–412.

Fourier, Charles. 1971. *Design for Utopia: Selected Writings. Studies in the Libertarian and Utopian Tradition*. New York: Schocken.

Freire, Paulo. 1975. *Pedagogy of the Oppressed*. London: Penguin Education.

Galeano, Eduardo. 2003. *Notes from Nowhere, We Are Everywhere: The Irresistible Rise of Global Anticapitalism*. London: Verso.

García Canclini, Néstor. 2014. *Art beyond Itself: Anthropology for a Society without a Story Line*. Durham, NC: Duke University Press.

Gell, Alfred. 1992. *The Anthropology of Time: Cultural Constructions of Temporal Maps and Images*. Oxford: Berg.

Gott, Richard. 2011. *Hugo Chávez and the Bolivarian Revolution*. London: Verso.

Graeber, David. 2002. "The New Anarchists." *New Left Review* 13:61–73.

———. 2009. *Direct Action: An Ethnography*. Oakland, CA: AK Press.

Grosz, Elizabeth. 2005. "Bergson, Deleuze and the Becoming of Unbecoming." *Parallax* 11 (2): 4–13.

Guevara, Ernesto. 2005. "Socialism and the New Man in Cuba." In *Che Guevara Reader*, edited by David Deutschmann, 212–30. Melbourne: Ocean.

Guivant, Julia. 2003. *Agrarian Change, Gender and Land Rights: A Brazilian Case Study*. Geneva: United Nations Research Institute for Social Development.

Gurr, Melinda. 2017. "Limits of Liberation: Youth and Politics in Brazil's Landless Rural Workers' Movement." Unpublished doctoral thesis, Syracuse University.

———. 2019. "Celebratory Socialism: Subcultural Politics of Dancing, Drinking, and Hooking Up among Youth of Brazil's MST." *Journal of Latin American and Caribbean Anthropology* 24 (3): 690–708.

Hale, Charles. 2002. "Does Multiculturalism Menace? Governance, Cultural Rights and the Politics of Identity in Guatemala." *Journal of Latin American Studies* 34 (3): 485–524.

Hammond, John. 1999. "Law and Disorder: The Brazilian Landless Farmworkers' Movement." *Bulletin of Latin American Research* 18 (4): 469–89.

———. 2004. "The MST and the Media: Competing Images of the Brazilian Landless Farmworkers' Movement." *Latin American Politics and Society* 46 (4): 61–90.

Harnecker, Marta. 2003. *Landless People: Building a Social Movement*. São Paulo: Expressão Popular.

———. 2007. *Rebuilding the Left*. London: Zed.

Hartmann, H. 1979. "The Unhappy Marriage of Marxism and Feminism: Towards a More Progressive Union." *Capital and Class* 8 (2): 1–33.

Haugerud, Angelique. 2010. "Neoliberalism, Satirical Protest, and the 2004 U.S. Presidential Campaign." In *Ethnographies of Neoliberalism*, edited by Carol Greenhouse, 112–27. Philadelphia: University of Pennsylvania Press.

Hetland, G., and J. Goodwin. 2013. "The Strange Disappearance of Capitalism from Social Movement Studies." In *Marxism and Social Movements*, edited by C. Barker, Cox Laurence, J. Krinsky, and A. Gunvald Nilsen, 83–102. Boston: Brill.

Hodges, Matt. 2008. "Rethinking Time's Arrow: Bergson, Deleuze and the Anthropology of Time." *Anthropological Theory* 8 (4): 399–429.

Hohle, Randolphe. 2009. "The Body and Citizenship in Social Movement Research." *The Sociological Quarterly* 50: 283–307.

Horst, Heather A., and Daniel Miller, eds. 2012. *Digital Anthropology*. London: Bloomsbury Academic.

INCRA. 2015. "Na Luta Pela Reforma Agrária: INCRA 45 anos." Last modified January 29, 2025. https://www.gov.br/incra/pt-br/centrais-de-conteudos/publicacoes/incra-45-anos.pdf.

Issa, Daniela. 2007. "Praxis of Empowerment: Mistica and Mobilization in Brazil's Landless Rural Workers' Movement." *Latin American Perspectives* 34 (2): 124–38.

Jackson, Shannon. 2011. *Social Works: Performing Art, Supporting Publics*. Abingdon: Routledge.

Jasper, James. 2011. "Emotions and Social Movements: Twenty Years of Theory and Research." *Annual Review of Sociology* 37: 285–303.

JST Editorial. 1990. *Fazer uma ofensiva passiva e radical*. São Paulo: Associação Nacional de Cooperação Agrícola.

Juris, Jeffrey S. 2008. *Networking Futures: The Movements against Corporate Globalization*. Durham, NC: Duke University Press.

———. 2012. "Reflections on #Occupy Everywhere: Social Media, Public Space, and Emerging Logics of Aggregation." *American Ethnologist* 39: 259–79.

———. 2015. "Embodying Protest: Culture and Performance within Social Movements." In: *Anthropology, Theatre, and Development: The Transformative Potential of Performance*, edited by A. Flynn and J. Tinius, 82–104. London: Palgrave Macmillan.

Kane, Liam. 2000. "Popular Education and the Landless Peoples Movement in Brazil (MST)." *Studies in the Education of Adults* 32 (1): 36–50.

Kasmir, Sharryn. 1996. *The Myth of Mondragon: Cooperatives, Politics, and Working-Class Life in a Basque Town*. Albany: State University of New York Press.

———. 1999. "The Mondragon Model as Post-Fordist Discourse: Considerations on the Production of Post-Fordism." *Critique of Anthropology* 19 (4): 379–400.

———. 2016. "The Mondragon Cooperatives and Global Capitalism." *Forum* 25:52–59.

Kay, Cristóbal. 1988. "Economic Reforms and Collectivization in Cuban Agriculture." *Third World Quarterly* 10 (3): 1239–66.

Klein, Naomi. 2011. "Occupy Wall St. Learns from Globalization Protests." *New York Times*, October 6, 2011. Last modified January 31, 2025. https://www.nytimes.com/roomforde bate/2011/10/06/can-occupy-wall-street-spark-a-revolution/occupy-wall-st-learns -from-globalization-protests.

Langfur, Hal. 2006. *The Forbidden Lands: Colonial Identity, Frontier Violence, and the Persistence of Brazil's Eastern Indians, 1750–1830*. Stanford, CA: University of Stanford Press.

Lara Junior, Nadir. 2005. *A Mística no Cotidiano do MST: A Interface Entre a Religiosidade Popular e a Política*. São Paulo: Master's thesis at the Pontifícia Universidade Católica de São Paulo.

Lazar, Sian. 2014. "Historical Narrative, Mundane Political Time, and Revolutionary Moments: Coexisting Temporalities in the Lived Experience of Social Movements." *Journal of the Royal Anthropological Institute* 20 (1): 91–108.

Lebner, Ashley. 2019. "On Secularity: Marxism, Reality, and the Messiah in Brazil." *Journal of the Royal Anthropological Institute* 25 (1): 123–47.

Lefebvre, Henri. 2004. *Rhythmanalysis: Space, Time and Everyday Life*. Translated by Stuart Eldon and Gerald Moore. London: Continuum.

Leite, Sérgio, Beatriz Heredia, Leonilde Medeiros, Mocair Palmeira, and Rosângela Cintrão, eds. 2004. *Impactos dos assentamentos: um estudo sobre o meio rural brasileiro*. Brasília: Núcleo de Estudos Agrários e Desenvolvimento Rural (NEAD), UNESP.

Lenin, Vladimir Ilyich. (1906) 1965. "Party Discipline and the Fight against the Pro-Cadet Social-Democrats." In *Lenin Collected Works*, 11, edited by David J. Romagnolo, 320–23. Moscow: Progress Publishers.

Léon, Marisol. 2006. "Learning to Fight: The MST's Escola Nacional and Its Pedagogy of Resistance." Last modified January 29, 2025. http://digitalcollections.sit.edu/cgi/view content.cgi?article=1376&context=isp_collection.

Levitas, Ruth. 1979. "Sociology and Utopia." *Sociology* 13 (1): 19–33.

Levy, Maria Stella Ferreira. 1974. "O papel da migração internacional na evolução da população brasileira (1872 a 1972)." *Revista de Saúde Pública* 8:49–90.

Locke, John. (1690) 2016. *Second Treatise of Government and a Letter Concerning Toleration*. Oxford: Oxford University Press.

Löwy, Michael. 2001. "The Socio-religious Origins of Brazil's Landless Rural Workers Movement." *Monthly Review* 53 (2): 32–40.

Lundy, Craig. 2018. *Deleuze's Bergsonism*. Edinburgh: Edinburgh University Press.

Maeckelbergh, Marianne. 2009. *The Will of the Many: How the Alterglobalisation Movement Is Changing the Face of Democracy*. London: Pluto.

Mannheim, Karl. 2001. *Sociology as Political Education*. Edited by David Kettler and Colin Loader. New Brunswick, NJ: Transaction.

Mansur, Douglas. 1989. *A Respeito do Método*. São Paulo: Associação Nacional de Cooperação Agrícola.

Martins, José de Souza. 1994. *O Poder do Atraso: Ensaios de Sociologia da História Lenta*. São Paulo: Editora Hucitec.

———. 1999. "Reforma agrária: O impossível diálogo sobre a História possível." *Tempo Social Revista de Sociologia da USP* 11 (2): 97–128.

———. 2000. *Reforma Agrária: O Impossível Diálogo*. São Paulo: Editora da Universidade de São Paulo.

———. 2002. "Representing the Peasantry? Struggles for/about Land in Brazil." *Journal of Peasant Studies* 29 (3): 300–335.

Marx, Karl, and Friedrich Engels. 2012. *The Communist Manifesto: A Modern Edition*. London: Verso.

Massey, Doreen. 1994. *Space, Place, and Gender*. Minneapolis: University of Minnesota Press.

McGarry, Aidan, Hande Eslen-Ziya, Itir Erhart, Olu Jenzen, and Umut Korkut, eds. 2020. *The Aesthetics of Global Protest: Visual Culture and Communication*. Amsterdam: Amsterdam University Press.

McKee, Yates. 2016. *Strike Art: Contemporary Art and the Post-Occupy Condition*. London: Verso.

McNee, Malcolm. 2005. "A Diasporic, Post-traditional Peasantry: The Movimento Sem Terra (MST) and the Writing of Landless Identity." *Journal of Latin American Cultural Studies* 14 (3): 335–53.

Meszaros, George. 2000a. "No Ordinary Revolution: Brazil's Landless Workers' Movement." *Race & Class* 42 (2): 1–18.

———. 2000b. "Taking the Land into Their Hands: The Landless Workers' Movement and the Brazilian State." *Journal of Law and Society* 27 (4): 517–41.

———. 2007. "The MST and the Rule of Law in Brazil." *Law, Social Justice and Global Development* 1 (1): 1–24.

Metcalf, Alida C. 2005. *Go-betweens and the Colonization and Brazil, 1500–1600*. Austin: University of Texas Press.

Milkman, Ruth. 2017. "A New Political Generation: Millennials and the Post-2008 Wave of Protest." *American Sociological Review* 82 (1): 1–31.

Monteiro, John. 2018. *Blacks of the Land: Indian Slavery, Settler Society, and the Portuguese Colonial Enterprise in South America*. Cambridge: Cambridge University Press.

Moore, Henrietta. 1990. "Visions of the Good Life: Anthropology and the Study of Utopia." *Cambridge Anthropology* 14 (3): 13–33.

Morais, Clodomir de Santos. 1986. *Elementos sobre a teoria da organização no campo. Caderno de Formação 11*. São Paulo: MST.

Morris, William. (1890) 1897. *News from Nowhere, or, An Epoch of Rest*. London: Longmans, Green.

Moscal, Janaina dos Santos. 2017. "Sentimentos da Luta: Música e mística no Movimento dos Trabalhadores Rurais Sem Terra." Unpublished doctoral thesis, Universidade Federal de Santa Catarina.

Munarim, Antônio, and Evandro Costa de Medeiros. 2002. *A dimensão educativa da mística sem terra: A experiência da Escola Nacional Florestan Fernandes*. Florianópolis: Universidade Federal de Santa Catarina.

Munn, Nancy D. 1992. "The Cultural Anthropology of Time: A Critical Essay." *Annual Review of Anthropology* 21:93–123.

Nascimento, Claudemiro Godoy do, and Leila Chalub Martins. 2008. "Pedagogia da mística: as experiências do MST." *Emancipação* 8:109–20.

Navarro, Zander. 2002. "Mobilização sem emancipação: As lutas sociais dos Sem-Terra no Brasil." In *Produzir para viver: os caminhos da produção não capitalista*, edited by Boaventura de Sousa Santos, 189–232. Rio de Janeiro: Civilização Brasileira.

Nealon, Jeffrey T. 1994. "Theory That Matters. Review of Judith Butler's 'Bodies That Matter: On the discursive limits of "sex."'" *Postmodern Culture* 5 (1). https://doi.org/10.1353/pmc.1994.0055.

Netto, José Paulo. 2014. *Pequena história da ditadura brasileira (1964–1985)*. São Paulo: Cortez.

Novaes, Henrique, Angelo Mazin, and Lais Santos, eds. 2016. *Questão Agrária, cooperação e agroecologia*. 2nd ed. São Paulo: Outras Expressões.

Oiticica, Hélio. 1992. "Appearance of the Supra-Sensorial (1967)." In *Hélio Oiticica*, edited by Mat Verberkt, translated by Stephen Berg et al., 127–30. Rotterdam: Witte de With/Galerie Nationale du Jeu de Paume.

Ondetti, Gabriel. 2008. *Land, Protest, and Politics: The Landless Movement and the Struggle for Agrarian Reform in Brazil*. University Park: Pennsylvania State University Press.

O'Shea, Janet. 2022. "A Beautiful Disruption: Extinction Rebellion's Red Brigade and a Theory of Emotional Representation in Protest." In *Politics as Public Art: The Aesthetics of Political Organizing and Social Movements*, edited by Z. Zane MacNeill, and Martin Zebracki, pp. 26–41. London: Routledge.

Osório Silva, Lígia. 1996. *Terras devolutas e latifúndio: Efeitos da lei de 1850*. Campinas: Editora da Unicamp.

Owen, Robert. 1991. *A New View of Society and Other Writings*. Edited by G. Claeys. London: Penguin.

Pahnke, Anthony. 2018. *Brazil's Long Revolution: Radical Achievements of the Landless Workers Movement*. Tucson: University of Arizona Press.

Parker, Andrew, and Eve Kosofsky Sedgwick, eds. 1995. *Performativity and Performance*. Routledge: New York.

Pedersen, Morten Axel. 2012. "A Day in the Cadillac: The Work of Hope in Urban Mongolia." *Social Analysis: The International Journal of Social and Cultural Practice* 56 (2): 136–51.

Pereira, Anthony. 2009. "Brazil's Agrarian Reform: Democratic Innovation or Oligarchic Exclusion Redux." In *Latin American Democratic Transformations: Institutions, Actors, Processes*, edited by W. Smith W, 251–70. Oxford: John Wiley.

Petras, James, and Henry Veltmeyer. 2001. "Are Latin American Peasant Movements Still a Force for Change? Some New Paradigms Revisited." *Journal of Peasant Studies* 28 (2): 83–118.

———. 2002. "Age of Reverse Aid: Neo-liberalism as Catalyst of Regression." *Development and Change* 33 (2): 281–93.

Pleyers, Geoffrey. 2013. *Alter-Globalization: Becoming Actors in a Global Age*. Cambridge: Polity Press.

Prieto, Gustavo Francisco Teixeira. 2017. "A aliança entre terra e capital na ditadura brasileira." *Mercator Revista de Geografia da UFC* 16 (1): 1–14.

Rancière, Jacques. 1999. Dis-agreement: Politics and Philosophy, trans. Julie Rose. Minneapolis: University of Minnesota Press.

———. 2004. *The Politics of Aesthetics: The Distribution of the Sensible*. London: Bloomsbury

———. 2009. *Aesthetics and its Discontents*. Translated by Steven Corcoran. Malden, MA: Polity Press.

Rangel Loera, Nashieli. 2006. *A Espiral das Ocupações de Terra*. Belo Horizonte: Editora Polis.

———. 2010. "'Encampment Time': An Anthropological Analysis of the Land Occupations in Brazil." *Journal of Peasant Studies* 37 (2): 285–318.

———. 2014. *Tempo de acampamento*. São Paulo: Editora UNESP.

Razsa, Maple. 2015. *Bastards of Utopia: Living Radical Politics after Socialism*. Bloomington: Indiana University Press.

Reed, Thomas V. 2005. *The Art of Protest: Culture and Activism from the Civil Rights Movement to the Present*. Minneapolis: University of Minnesota Press.

———. 2019. "#Occupy All the Arts: Challenging Wall Street and Economic Inequality Worldwide." In *The Art of Protest: Culture and Activism from the Civil Rights Movement to the Present*, 2nd ed., 325–70. Minneapolis: University of Minnesota Press.

Ribeiro, Vanderlei. 2010. "Fazendas e Quartéis. A Questão Agrária sob Ótica Militar no Brasil e no Peru: (1961–1988)." *Passagens. Revista Internacional de História Política e Cultura Jurídica* 2 (4): 94–128.

Robles, Wilder. 2018. "Revisiting Agrarian Reform in Brazil, 1985–2016." *Journal of Developing Societies* 34 (1): 1–34.

Rockefeller, Stuart. 2011. "Flow." *Current Anthropology* 52 (4): 557–78.

Rua, Maria das Gracas, and Miriam Abramovay. 2000. *Companheiras de luta ou coordenadoras de panelas? As relacoes de genero nos assentamentos rurais*. Brasília: UNESCO.

Ryan, Holly Eva. 2017. *Political Street Art: Communication, Culture and Resistance in Latin America*. London: Routledge.

Safa, Helen. 1990. "Women's Social Movements in Latin America." *Gender and Society* 4 (3): 354–69.

Sanjek, Roger, and Susan W. Tratner, eds. 2015. *eFieldnotes: The Makings of Anthropology in the Digital World*. Philadelphia: University of Pennsylvania Press.

Sargent, Lyman Tower. 2016. "Five Hundred Years of Thomas More's Utopia and Utopianism." *Utopian Studies* 27 (2): 184–92.

Sauer, Sérgio. 2019. "Rural Brazil during the Lula Administrations: Agreements with Agribusiness and Disputes in Agrarian Policies." *Latin American Perspectives* 46 (4): 103–21.

Sauer, Sérgio, and Sérgio Perreira Leite. 2012. "Agrarian Structure, Foreign Investment in Land, and Land Prices in Brazil." *Journal of Peasant Studies* 39 (3/4): 873–98.

Sayers, Sean. 2006. "Review of Jacques Rancière's 'The Politics of Aesthetics: The Distribution of the Sensible.'" *Culture Machine* 8 (1). https://culturemachine.net/reviews /ranciere-the-politics-of-aesthetics-sayers/.

Schwartz, Stuart B. 1978. "Indian Labor and New World Plantations: European Demands and Indian Responses in Northeastern Brazil." *American Historical Review* 83 (1): 43–79.

Serafini, Paula. 2018. *Performance Action: The Politics of Art Activism*. London: Routledge.

Sholette, Gregory. 2017. *Delirium and Resistance Activist Art and the Crisis of Capitalism*. London: Pluto.

Shtyrkov, Sergei. 2022. "Ressentiment, War, and the Anthropologist's Silence." Society for Cultural Anthropology. Last modified March 28, 2022. https://culanth.org/fieldsights /ressentiment-war-and-the-anthropologists-silence.

Shukaitis, Stevphen. 2004. "An Ethnography of Nowhere: Notes toward a Re-envisioning of Utopian Thinking." *Social Anarchism* 35:5–13.

Shukaitis, Stevphen, David Graeber, and Erika Biddle, eds. 2007. *Constituent Imagination: Militant Investigations, Collective Theorization*. Chico, CA: AK Press.

Sigaud, Lygia. 2000. "A forma acampamento: notas a partir da versão pernambucana." *Novos Estudos CEBRAP* 58:73–92.

———. 2005. "As Condições de Possibilidade das Ocupações de Terra." *Tempo Social* 17:255–80.

Silva, Cristiani Bereta da. 2004. "Relações de Gênero e Subjetividades no Devir MST." *Revista Estudos Feministas* 12 (1): 269–287.

Skidmore, Thomas E. 2010. *Brazil: Five Centuries of Change*. Oxford: Oxford University Press.

Snow, David, Burke Rochford, Steven Worden, and Robert Benford. 1986. "Frame Alignment Processes, Micromobilization, and Movement Participation." *American Sociological Review* 51 (4): 464–81.

Spencer, Herbert. 1867. *Illustrations of Universal Progress: A Series of Discussions*. New York: Appleton.

Srnicek, Nick, and Alex Williams. 2015. *Inventing the Future: Postcapitalism and a World without Work*. New York: Verso.

Stédile, João Pedro, and Bernardo Fernandes. 1999. *Brava Gente: A Trajetória do MST e a Luta Pela Terra no Brasil*. São Paulo: Editora Fundação Perseu Abramo.

Stephen, Lynn. 2001. "Gender, Citizenship, and the Politics of Identity." *Latin American Perspectives* 28 (6): 54–69.

Swain, Dan. 2017. "Not Not but Not Yet: Present and Future in Prefigurative Politics." *Political Studies* 67 (1): 47–62.

Tarlau, Rebecca. 2019. *Occupying Schools, Occupying Land: How the Landless Workers Movement Transformed Brazilian Education*. Oxford: Oxford University Press.

Taylor, Diana. 2003. *The Archive and the Repertoire: Performing Cultural Memory in the Americas*. Durham, NC: Duke University Press.

Taylor, Verta. 1989. "Social Movement Continuity: The Women's Movement in Abeyance." *American Sociological Review* 54 (5): 761–75.

Teubal, Miguel. 2009. "Agrarian Reform and Social Movements in the Age of Globalization: Latin America at the Dawn of the Twenty-first Century." *Latin American Perspectives* 36 (4): 9–20.

Thompson, Nato. 2012. *Living as Form: Socially Engaged Art from 1991–2011.* Cambridge, MA: MIT Press.

Turner, Ralph H., and Lewis M. Killian. 1957. *Collective Behavior.* Englewood Cliffs, NJ: Prentice-Hall.

Turner, Victor. 1977. "Variations on a Theme of Liminality." In *Secular Ritual*, edited by S. Moore and B. Myerhoff, 36–52. Amsterdam: Van Gorcum.

———. 1995. "Liminality and Communitas." In *The Ritual Process: Structure and Anti-Structure*, edited by Victor Turner, 94–115. Chicago: Aldine Publishing.

Valdes, Constanza. 2022. *Brazil's Momentum as a Global Agricultural Supplier Faces Headwinds.*Washington, DC: USDA-ERS. https://www.ers.usda.gov/amber-waves/2022/september/brazil-s-momentum-as-a-global-agricultural-supplier-faces-headwinds/.

Van de Sande, Mathijs. 2013. "The Prefigurative Politics of Tahrir Square." *Res Publica* 19 (3): 223–39.

van der Watt, Liese. 2004. "Do Bodies Matter? Performance versus Performativity." *De Arte* 39 (70): 3–10.

van Gennep, Arnold. (1909) 2019. *The Rites of Passage.* Chicago: Chicago University Press.

Veltmeyer, Henry. 1997. "New Social Movements in Latin America: The Dynamics of Class and Identity." *Journal of Peasant Studies* 25 (1): 139–69.

Vergara-Camus, Leandro. 2014. *Land and Freedom: The MST, the Zapatistas and Peasant Alternatives to Neoliberalism.* London: Zed.

Weibel, Peter. 2014. *Global Activism: Art and Conflict in the 21st Century.* Cambridge, MA: MIT Press.

Welch, Cliff. 2006. "Movement Histories: A Preliminary Historiography of the Brazil's Landless Laborers' Movement (MST)." *Latin American Research Review* 41 (1): 198–210.

Welch, Cliff, and Bernardo Fernandes. 2009. "Peasant Movements in Latin America: Looking Back, Moving Ahead." *Latin American Perspectives* 36 (4): 3–8.

Werbner, Pnina, Martin Webb, and Kathryn Spellman-Poots. 2014. *The Political Aesthetics of Global Protest: The Arab Spring and Beyond.* Edinburgh: Edinburgh University Press

Williams, Raymond. 1978. "Utopia and Science Fiction." *Science Fiction Studies* 5 (3): 203–14.

Wolford, Wendy. 2003. "Producing Community: The MST and Land Reform Settlements in Brazil." *Journal of Agrarian Change* 3 (4): 500–520.

———. 2010. *This Land Is Ours Now: Social Mobilization and the Meanings of Land in Brazil.* Durham, NC: Duke University Press.

Wordsworth, William. 1985. *The Fourteen-Book "Prelude."* Edited by W. J. B. Owen. Ithaca, NY: Cornell University Press.

Wright, Angus, and Wendy Wolford. 2003. *To Inherit the Earth: The Landless Movement and the Struggle for a New Brazil.* Oakland, CA: Food First.

INDEX

ALEX UNGPRATEEB FLYNN is Associate Professor of Art
and Anthropology at the University of California, Los Angeles.

For Indiana University Press

Sabrina Black, *Editorial Assistant*

Tony Brewer, *Artist and Book Designer*

Anna Garnai, *Production Coordinator*

Sophia Hebert, *Assistant Acquisitions Editor*

Samantha Heffner, *Marketing and Publicity Manager*

Katie Huggins, *Production Manager*

Gigi Lamm, *Director of Sales and Marketing*

Nancy Lightfoot, *Project Manager/Editor*

Annie L. Martin, *Editorial Director*

Bethany Mowry, *Acquisitions Editor*

Dan Pyle, *Online Publishing Manager*

Michael Regoli, *Director of Publishing Operations*

Leyla Salamova, *Artist and Book Designer*

www.ingramcontent.com/pod-product-compliance
Ingram Content Group UK Ltd.
Pitfield, Milton Keynes, MK11 3LW, UK
UKHW041932140725
460780UK00002B/50